W9-BKA-669

CHOICE
an introduction
to economics

CHOICE

an introduction to economics

SECOND EDITION

Augustus J. Rogers III
University of Wisconsin–Milwaukee

PRENTICE-HALL, INC., Englewood Cliffs, New Jersey

Library of Congress Cataloging in Publication Data

Rogers, Augustus James
Choice; an introduction to economics.

1. Economics. I. Title.
HB171.5.R7 1974 330 73-20028
ISBN 0-13-133223-6

Printed in the United States of America

10 9 8 7 6 5 4

PRENTICE-HALL INTERNATIONAL, Inc., *London*
PRENTICE-HALL OF AUSTRALIA, Pty. Ltd., *Sydney*
PRENTICE-HALL OF CANADA, Ltd., *Toronto*
PRENTICE-HALL OF INDIA Private Limited, *New Delhi*
PRENTICE-HALL OF JAPAN, Inc., *Tokyo*

To my Econ 100 students,

past, present, and future—

Bless 'em!

Contents

Preface to Second Edition

In the three years since the publication of *CHOICE*, a good many students and professors have had a chance to use and criticize the book. This considerably expanded edition meets some of the most important of these critiques. A look at the table of contents shows that some chapters have been shortened, and that more chapters have been added. This improves the organization of the book considerably.

It is still intended primarily for a one-semester survey course, but with careful supplementing, it can also provide a two-semester base.

As in the first edition, marginalism is only implied through the use of changing totals. The theory of the firm is still skimpy because I feel that there are simpler and more interesting ways of presenting the core of microeconomics than the usual memorization of different cost and revenue functions. The Keynesian Cross has crept into the book because I have found it useful in demonstrating the similarities of various macroeconomic models and the importance of the underlying assumptions in such models.

I wish to give particular thanks to the reviewers of this edition whose comments and suggestions have helped me immeasurably. Professors Donald Kline, James Hiss, and Douglas Madigan provided this assistance. I accept full responsibility for any remaining errors.

As with the first edition, I invite your comments and suggestions for future printings or editions. Improvement can only come from communication between writer and teachers.

Augustus J. Rogers III
University of Wisconsin–Milwaukee

Preface to First Edition

This book is dedicated to the proposition that an introductory economics course does not have to be as bloody dull as such courses often are. Basically, we're trying to get you to realize the fantastic number of choices available to you and to mankind. Economics is the study of these choices made among scarce alternatives.

You will first be exposed to one of the most basic reasons for any economic interaction—comparative advantages. Chapter 2 is used to develop that very important tool—good old supply and demand. Almost no math is used, although simple geometry is pushed hard. Some of the examples in Chapter 3 (for example, the draft) may go beyond the point that many instructors will wish to reach. Fair enough. You can choose examples of whatever level of difficulty seems most appropriate. The most important thing is that *you, the student,* practice using the analytic concepts presented here to discuss current problems that affect your own lives. Chapter 4 gives a skeleton of decision making without *explicitly* using the marginal approach.

Chapters 5 and 6 present "macroeconomics" in a manner quite different from the usual Keynesian Cross on which so many students have been crucified. The analysis is admittedly sketchy, owing to the scarcity of time and intended level of difficulty of the course. What is presented is correct, useful, and follows from the micro analysis developed in the earlier chapters. The last chapter discusses some of the issues of poverty and development.

Any book is really a joint effort and this one is no exception. Several people must receive specific mention. Dr. John M. Hunter and

Dr. Laughlin Currie influenced my decision to enter the academic world. At this stage at least, I thank them both immensely.

All my colleagues in the Department of Economics, University of Wisconsin—Milwaukee, have contributed in some way. Particularly helpful in this enterprise were my teaching assistants, Messrs. Becker, Brugger, Geiger, Hansen, Hegji, Lephardt, Massino, Salomone, and Seeling. Miss Chris Brown joins this august group as well. Dr. Boris Pesek, Dr. John Makin, and Dr. Tom Crocker were most patient in catching some of the worst errors in the several trial editions. As always, Mrs. Lois Grebe and Miss Annelie Zimmer, the poor gals who had to type the different manuscripts, deserve medals in addition to their meager pay. For any goofs still in the product, I accept and admit full responsibility.

A. J. Rogers III

CHOICE
an introduction to economics

1

Alternatives, Scarcity, and Choice

OBJECTIVES

Economics concerns itself with the study of that phenomenon called scarcity. *Even though man has succeeded in increasing available material goods and services, he has not substantially reduced the difference between what he* wants *and what he is able to acquire. Ultimately,* time *itself is scarce, so that even in a world of abundance, usable time would still be limited. Things can be categorized into goods versus non-goods, positive versus negative goods, and free versus economic goods. When goods are transferred from one person or entity to another, it is really* property rights *that change hands.*

SCARCITY

There's one great thing about taking a course in economics. At least everyone knows what it will be all about. It will include all those crazy graphs and curves which, if understood, will make it possible for everyone to go out and earn a fortune in the material world. All you have to do is memorize a bunch of curves and information, and bingo, you're all instant businessmen who can go out and rip off the public for some gadget the public probably doesn't need in the first place. Obviously, the whole process including the course itself is an exercise in dehumanizing yourself and everyone around you. After all, economics has nothing to do with man, except what concerns his worst nature—his material welfare.

Well, folks, if this is the idea you have about economics, either you're in the wrong course or your instructor chose the wrong book. Economics is *not* a cookbook course in how to make a buck, nor is it a course in how to rip off your neighbor. Economics concerns itself with the very basic fact that most of the time man is plagued by a thing called *scarcity*. Even this word, scarcity, is probably not being used in quite the way you may be accustomed to. For example, who today, in an urban environment, would dare to suggest that the automobile is scarce? Obviously, there are too many of them around. But, by the definition of the economist, the automobile is scarce. Every person who purchased those "overabundant" cars had to give up some alternative purchase to get the car. *That* fact is what makes the things scarce.

George and Clara are lovers. Clara still likes Herman. George says that if Clara continues to see Herman, then he, George, is going to leave her. Assuming that George is not making just an idle threat, then Clara is faced with a scarcity. If she is to continue with George, it will cost her her relationship with Herman. She is going to have to make a *choice* between limited options or alternatives. If there were no constraints placed upon her, then the relationship with either Herman, George, or both would impose no costs. But George has imposed a constraint and her decision is an *economic* one. It may not involve a single penny of monetary cost, but it does involve a cost in terms of her own subjective measure of giving up something else of value *to her*. Her relationships with both George and Herman are *economic goods* because she is willing and able to give up something of value to maintain them.

An economic good, then, is something that is not *free*—in the sense that some *cost* is involved in obtaining it or keeping it. The cost may be reflected in money, lost time, pain and suffering, or some other kind of foregone opportunity.

Fresh air in northern Wisconsin is generally a free good. This assumes, of course, that the wind is not blowing from the smokestack of a pulp digester at the local papermill. But fresh air in Milwaukee is *not* a free good. If you want that good northern fresh air quality, you will have to pay to remove the pollution. At this point, "fresh air" is no longer a free good but rather an economic good. Something must be given up in order to obtain it.

When we get into economic goods such as our clean air example, there are many questions that have to be answered. For example, who is going to pay to clean the air? Should it be cleaned at all? Should the factories or the stockholders of the companies that are spewing forth the wastes be made to cease and desist? If so, who really pays for the resulting cleanup, the owners or the customers of the products manufactured in the offending plants? Should the taxpayers of the city subsidize clean air or should only those persons who are affected by dirty air be made to pay?

Like other economic decisions, many of these questions can be answered only after somebody or some group makes up its mind as to what is "right" or "just" or "equitable" or "fair" or some other value judgment. The economist holds value judgments just like anyone else. But his primary job, *as an economist* is to figure out the ramifications of alternative courses of action, given some particular set of values and/or goals. As an economist, it is not his job to pass on his own ideas but rather to find the implications in each case. As an individual and as a citizen, he should *have* and *preach* his beliefs just like anyone else; however, these can be separated from his analytical efforts and pronouncements. A large part of this course will be an attempt to get each student to separate biases, beliefs, prejudices, and creeds from that most precious of all man's talents—his ability to think. If nothing more is accomplished than the reexamination of some closely held preconceptions, the course will have succeeded. Much of the success of this venture will depend on how each one uses his *time*, another basic scarcity.

TIME

There is much talk today about the affluence of not only our own society but many others as well and that a materialistic utopia is close upon us. Some of this talk indicates that if we could redistribute what we now have, man's "needs" would be taken care of and we would not have to worry about economics any more. We pick up this idea of needs again in a few paragraphs, but a point to be made at this juncture concerns the future relevance of economics itself—of the study of alternatives, given constrained choices. Even if we grant the possibility of a materialistic utopia, there is still one aspect of man's life that will probably remain scarce as long as man exists as the being we perceive. We may be able to accumulate all of the cars, all of the chrome plated gadgets, even all of the food, shelter, and clothing that we might want, but something will still remain scarce. That something is *time*. As long as man is born into this world and departs upon physiological death, time will be something that constrains him.

At any given moment, man has three possible uses for his time. First of all, he may be able to *work*. By work we mean some kind of effort that has as its goal the increase of income, either material or psychological. Generally, but not always, work is something that people would prefer not doing. Normally, they would prefer using their time either for *maintaining* themselves (like sleeping or eating) or for something called *leisure*. Actually, it could be argued that one who prefers work to leisure is actually enjoying a form of leisure in his work. But, particularly today, when many industrial jobs are creating a new complaint, job boredom, the distinction between work and leisure is becoming more clear-cut. People are faced with one kind of choice involving the category of use of any given moment or period of time. They can use it for *work,* for *maintenance*, or for *leisure*.

But even within each category of time usage, there are myriads of decisions to be made. Even if work time were to become unnecessary, there would still be the problem of how to use the increased leisure time. As a matter of fact, this is an increasing problem of our affluence. Many people are finding it very difficult to use increased leisure time in a way that is satisfying to them. Often, the choices available with increased leisure *increase* the economic problem. When someone is existing in a life that requires most of the waking hours to be spent just staying alive, the *range* of choice sets is small. The number and complexity of the decisions between alternatives is relatively small. But as affluence increases, the number of alternatives available increases. This means that the number of choices required also increases.

The more affluence we attain, the greater also is the time required to obtain satisfaction from our increased material goods. You can buy a new sailboat, but what good is it if you have no time to use it? A new set of skis would be an exciting purchase for many people, but how about the time it takes to use them? What we are facing is a series of paradoxes. The more our choice sets expand, then, by definition, the more complex decision-making becomes. The more time we spend trying to obtain consumption goods, the more time we require to gain satisfaction or pleasure from such goods.

Another decision about time involves choices between present and future activities. How does one split up use of time today versus tomorrow versus ten or fifty years from now? When we talk about decisions *over* time, then a whole new range of preferences must be faced. Many of these involve the uncertainty of the future and the many risks that the future implies. Of course, much of the formal discipline of economics is concerned with such *intertemporal* choices. Again, affluence by itself will not eliminate the need to make such choices among time alternatives.

THINGS

Because much of the concern that follows in these pages involves *things*—material or otherwise—it is useful to set up a framework for the upcoming analysis. As in grade school arithmetic, a "universe" of all things is divided into sets and subsets based on several criteria. We are interested in whether a thing yields services, disservices, or offers nothing of any importance to man. This last category (yielding nothing good or bad to man) we will call *nongoods* and disregard. We must ignore with caution, however, because history has shown us that many things that man ignored as not impinging on his existence turned out to be very important indeed. The North Star meant nothing to the caveman but became a navigational bench mark for early sailors. In more recent times, the same North Star has become a critical focus for space navigation. However, we will assume that there are things that do not affect man at the moment and leave them in the corner of the Venn diagram in Figure 1-1.

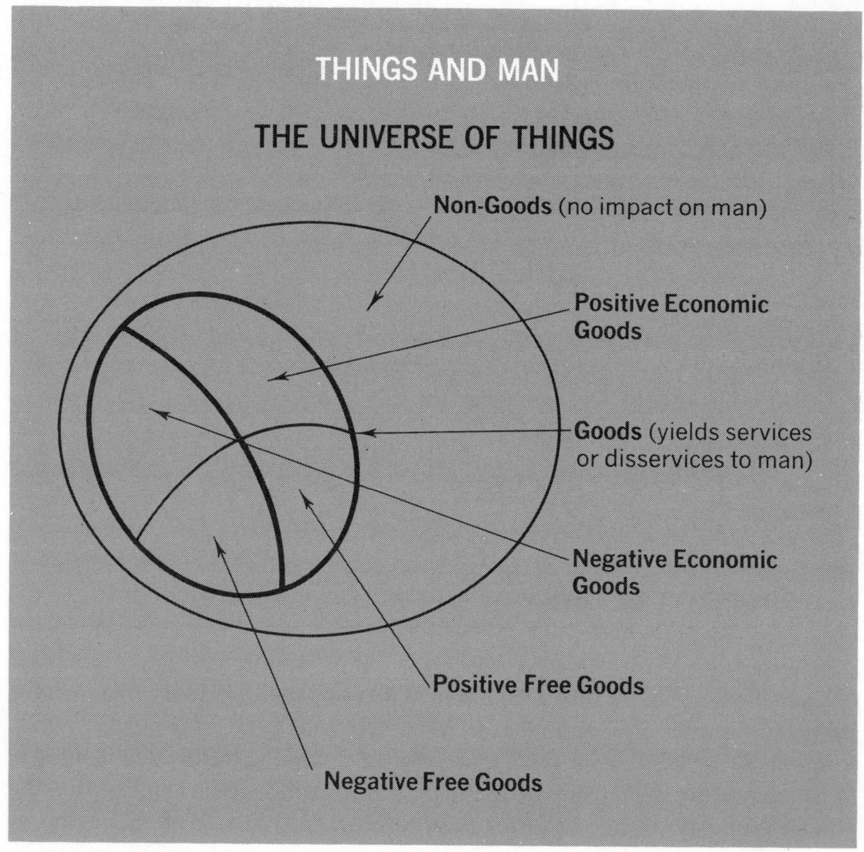

Figure 1-1

The other broad category of things consists of those that yield some service or disservice. These are things that affect the life of at least one person somewhere or can be expected to do so sometime in the future. We will call these things *goods*. We might call things that yield disservices *bads* instead of *goods*. But we can make it sound much more impressive without complicating the idea by saying that things yielding services are *positive goods* and those yielding disservices are *negative goods*.

One more breakdown is required to make the overall picture interesting to the economist. We are interested in knowing whether obtaining the good (or the service flowing from the good) involves a cost. In the case of positive goods, this is determined by whether something else of value has to be given up to obtain that good or service. If so, if it *costs*, then we have a positive *economic* good. If it does not cost (like our "free" fresh air) but yields a service, then the thing is a positive *free* good. By analogy, negative goods can also be split into economic and free components. A thing may be yielding a disservice, but the disservice may not be bothersome enough to make anyone *pay* to get rid of it. By *pay*, of course, we mean giving up anything of value to the person—not just money. The person sitting next to you may be polluting the air you are breathing with the echoes of his luncheon salami sandwich. If you grin and bear it, you are living with a *negative free good*. His breath is yielding a disservice but it is not bad enough to make you (or him) pay to get rid of it. On the other hand, if it gets unbearable, you may be prepared to "give up" his friendship by telling him to breathe the other way. If it is really bad, you might even give him sixty-nine cents and tell him to get some mouthwash at the corner drugstore. At this stage, you are confronted with a negative *economic* good. Someone is willing and able to pay to get rid of it or at least reduce its disservices. We will be talking about both negative and positive goods throughout the course. The definitions and descriptions above will, we hope, take on considerably more meaning as things progress.

PROPERTY RIGHTS

What do you buy when you buy a car? "Simple enough," you say, "When we *buy* a car it means just that. The good *belongs* to us. We *own* the thing. It is ours." Fair enough, but let us see what ownership really means. Somebody never really *buys* a thing. Rather, what is purchased is a *set of rights* over a good that allows one to obtain some flow of services from that good. Property rights often are forgotten, particularly in a beginning economics course. It is vital that property rights and their implications be fully understood.

Under English common law, when a person buys something without specific restrictions, it is called a purchase in *fee simple*. Such a purchase means that the purchaser buys the rights that are recapped in Figure 1-2. First of all, the person buys the right to *use* the good. This does not mean that he can use it without restriction. On the contrary, it only means that he

FEE SIMPLE PROPERTY RIGHTS

THE FEE SIMPLE PURCHASE of a good IMPLIES the rights to:

1. **USE the good**
2. **Prevent Others from Using the Good**
3. **DESTROY the Good**
4. **TRANSFER RIGHTS to the Good to Others**

Figure 1-2

can use the item as long as such use does not interfere with someone else or someone else's property rights. In the car example, you can use the vehicle for transportation purposes as long as you stay on roads and not other persons' front lawns. You can also use it to impress your neighbor. You can even use it to "store value," although the value of a car will clearly go down over time and with usage. But you will be in trouble if you try to use "your" automobile to kill someone. The *law*, those rules and regulations set up by the community, will limit this right because it clearly imposes substantial costs on someone else.

A second right that purchase implies is the right to keep other people from using the good in question. If someone tries to use your car without your permission, the rules and regulations can again be called on to prevent such action. Even this right has its limits, however. For example, if you own a house on a piece of land on which the community has decided to build a freeway, your rights to that land can be taken away upon reimbursement and court review. Similarly, confiscation by government is usually possible under emergency conditions of one sort or another.

The third piece of the set of rights is the right to destroy the item concerned. Here again, there are limits that such destruction must follow. Leaving your stripped down car downtown in the middle of the street will probably produce a summons from the local magistrate.

Finally, property rights normally include the right to transfer your rights to someone else. This generally means that you could give such rights away or sell them to someone else—to trade for something else you feel is of equal value. But, society may impose limits as to whom you may transfer these rights or even set specific conditions for such a transfer. Federal gun laws today prohibit the sale of handguns to ex-felons. When rationing takes place in an economy where shortages exist, some kind of coupon is required from the purchaser in addition to any money that might be involved.

Property rights are *always* maintained by force of some kind. The force may be as unostentatious as moral conscience or as overt as an automatic rifle in the hands of secret police. It may be imposed by whomever happens to be the strongest person or group around, by an elected body, by a hereditary elite, or by any other combination of forces. Another important point is that property rights and private property rights are not the same thing. Property rights can be held by the state or by other groups. Private property rights are held only by individuals or nongovernmental groups. *Who* holds property rights is one question, but *having* property rights that are enforced is quite another.

Continuing with your car as an example, assume that tomorrow morning Congress passes a law stating that property rights over automobiles no longer exist. Because property rights, along with something called money, seem to be at the base of all evil in the world, property rights—at least for the automobile—are hereby eliminated. You go out to get in your brand-new car only to find that your neighbor is in the process of claiming it. You punch your neighbor and phone the police, but when they arrive, you are the one who gets arrested. It is still illegal for you to hit your neighbor but it is not illegal for him to take "your" automobile. It just is not yours any more. When you realize that two can play at this game, you try to find another car that you can "steal." But it is not stealing any more, it is just using it as if it were a *free good*. This works for a while except that it becomes harder to find a car that is still in running order. Obviously, no one is going to bother to do anything more than is absolutely necessary to get the car to move from point A to point B on a one-trip-only basis. Equally obviously, no one is going to bother making cars because no one will buy one. If you are foolish enough to buy a car, there is no way that you can keep the use of it beyond the first time you pick it up. If property rights are illegal, then it is even illegal to lock your car and thus restrict others from using it.

Cars *are* scarce. Their manufacture requires the use of resources that have alternative uses and, therefore, are in themselves scarce. This means that there are *not* enough cars to go around at a zero price or at zero cost. As a free good, people will want to have more cars than are available. *No allocation can take place without property rights being assigned and enforced.* This does not mean that individuals must necessarily hold these property rights, but *someone* must and they must be able to enforce such rights.

You have just been exposed to a rather usual sort of problem to which economics addresses itself. The existence of enforced property rights is a necessary condition for any organized allocation process involving scarce goods. The economist can point out and even describe some of the consequences of poorly defined or enforced rights. But the question of who should hold those rights and under what conditions gets into the value judgment area in which the economist has less to say *as an economist.*

These introductory remarks are the basis for the main body of economics. As you read and study the upcoming material there will probably be times when you will wonder just what any of it has to do with the scarcity and choice that were stated to be the essence of this course. It will all come together and with luck and a good bit of effort, it will make sense. It should make sense not only for any materialistic ventures that you might get involved in, but also the much broader and more interesting aspects of living in a world in which constraints exist.

QUESTIONS

1. List six things that are completely free, i.e., no one has to give up anything to get them. Be sure to carry out the process beyond the impact on only one person or group.
2. What sorts of changes would you expect in the allocation of a person's time as he gets older?
3. Putting aside your personal religious beliefs, how and why do you think an upsurge in the belief in life after physical death would affect the economy?
4. Positive economic goods are often expended to eliminate negative economic goods. Discuss.
5. Take any good that you own and discuss the implications of removing each property-right characteristic from that good.

6. When a labor union wants more "non-economic benefits," what does it really mean? Are costs involved to anyone when such things as better working conditions and greater fringe benefits are gained?

2

Specialization, Productivity, and Exchange

OBJECTIVES

In an attempt to increase the production of economic goods, man has found that specialization *is absolutely essential. But specialization means that some kind of exchange must take place so that people can get goods that they themselves are not making. The* trade *and* exchange *that results can improve total welfare rather than just the well-being of a single, most efficient partner. The principle of* comparative advantage *shows how one partner can be the least efficient in the production of* all *items and yet the more efficient partner can still benefit from trade. In the analysis contained in the chapter, the principles of* constrained choice *and* relative prices *are also developed, along with the idea of constant and increasing costs.*

INTRODUCTION

What a simple life the cavemen had! No worries about a timeclock, no anxiety about sullen repairmen, no concern about shoddy merchandise from the local department store. But, what he did have was the need to find enough food, clothing, and shelter to stay alive, and this was a real problem. With only his bare hands, a few crudely shaped rocks, and an assortment of sticks, our prehistoric heroes did not have much going for them. But at an almost imperceptible rate, man began to accumulate knowledge. Part of this knowledge involved ways and means of creating things that could assist him in the several tasks he needed to accomplish. These creations served as extensions of his own raw abilities. The pointed stick became an arm that could extend into a running animal. The sharpened rock improved the scraping abilities of the fingers and nails or the cutting ability of the teeth. These were the earliest forms of *capital* or *capital goods*—goods that are not primarily meant for immediate consumption but rather to assist in the production of other goods that *are* for immediate consumption.

What an incredible thing man started way back then. Little did these early forebears realize where the use of capital would carry man in his material pursuits in just a few years on the timeclock of the universe. The use of capital grew, from crude stones that extended the power of the arm to computer complexes capable of extending the human brain in magnitudes that themselves stagger human comprehension. Capital has become vitally important in virtually every production operation conducted by man. Even primitive peoples away from the mainstream of industrial life use some level of capital in their production processes.

SPECIALIZATION

As early man created capital, he learned something else about the nature of his abilities. Although he could muddle through on his own abilities, these abilities were not equally good in all endeavours. He learned that other persons were also in the world, and that they too had abilities, though not necessarily the same as his own. Even without capital, it became obvious that *specialization* into occupations that people were *best* at performing could improve the total output of any group of people. The best hunters could hunt while the best fishermen could fish and stonecutters could improve the community's caves and shape their knives and spears. But one thing had to take place if this specialization was going to work. If the hunter did nothing but hunt, then he had to find some way to get his fish and cave. The same sort of problem arose for the fisherman and the stonecutter. The answer to the problem was obvious, but once it happened, man was never again the same. Obviously, one who is very good at something can produce it in quantities exceeding his own wants and then exchange that excess. Lo and behold, it worked! People did just that and the output of the total community rose.

But this process also lost for people something that very few would ever recapture—complete autonomy from others. It would no longer be possible for a person to live in complete isolation. True, there have been rare examples of hermits, but, for the most part, people have remained committed to economic interdependence. Of course, the reason for this commitment is very strong. The whole process of specialization has made possible the complex and incredibly productive material output that we have today. Although there is a great deal of talk about going back to the simple life, most people do not mean it, at least to the extreme of subsistence do-it-yourself. Given the population level of the world today, this is probably fortunate. If all of us were to return to the simple life, using only our hands and the simplest of homemade tools, our output would be well under the minimum needed to sustain human life. Somehow, the population level of the earth would have to be decreased before such a scheme would have a chance. Actually, reducing the population would not be difficult because the familiar plague, pestilence, and famine would eventually do the job with a minimum of preplanning on our part.

Specialization and the use of capital are at the base of all modern economies. But specialization is a two-edged sword. Along with the great potential productivity comes a curse of inflexibility. A recent example will illustrate the point. A few years ago, the Administration and Congress cut back the aerospace program drastically. Of all of our industries, this one probably utilizes the most highly specialized resources. The participants in the program also have specialized talents that have virtually no alternative use. As a result, when the cutback came, it brought severe unemployment —unemployment not only of people, but also unemployment of the capital equipment that was part of the aerospace production system.

At the national level, people demanded a reordering of national priorities. Both the voting public and many of their elected representatives were saying that all we needed to do to attack problems like poverty and pollution was to stop spending dollars on programs like aerospace and the Vietnam war, and spend those dollars on the "good" uses. But what they forgot was that dollars do not make programs. *Resources* make programs, and the resources released from employment in the aerospace cutback were not immediately transferable into cleaning up an inner city or a major river. Part of the problem was the fact that the resources were so specialized that they could not make the transition without major modification in the physical capital and retraining of the human capital. This whole subject of inflexibility will come up again when we discuss national policy.

COMPARATIVE ADVANTAGE

One technique that will be put to heavy use is *abstraction*. This involves taking a recognizable situation, with all of its complexities and multiple problems, and drawing from this only those items that bear on the problem we wish to study. Using this method, it is possible to make a large, incomprehensible problem into a series of small and understandable ones.

It means that we can get insight into basic principles and concepts that influence the world we live in. Abstraction, then, is a process of simplification.

We have already talked about the cave society, and one way to abstract from today's world is to set up a hypothetical example from the relatively simple world of that period. So, we go back in time. Our first character, Charlie, has been managing on his own, doing all of the things that he needed to stay alive. He was able to exist in isolation and life was truly simple. Then along came Clyde. When the two met it became obvious that although they were very similar in many respects, their natural talents and experiences were such that their productive abilities in different fields were not the same. One was better at producing one thing and the other was better at producing something else. They found that by specializing in the task for which they either absolutely or *relatively* better qualified, and then *trading* goods, they could *both* increase their available goods. Here are some simple examples to show what we mean and how the arithmetic works out.

Assume that we have a society made up of just Charlie and Clyde. Assume further that the only two goods that they care to produce are skunkskin coats and brontosaurus carcasses. The only *input* into getting either product is their own labor. The assumption is that no other *factor of production* is required—no tools or other capital. Both are working 100-hour weeks and in one week of 100 hours they can produce the following, *if* each one devotes *all* his work time to either coat production or carcass production.

	Skunkskin Coats		*Brontosaurus Carcasses*
Charlie	5 Coats	OR	10 Carcasses
Clyde	8 Coats	OR	6 Carcasses

We will also assume that they could each produce any combination of coats and carcasses between the two extremes with the same "cost." What do we mean by cost? Take a look at Figure 2-1. Here we have taken Charlie's *Production Possibilities* and presented them in graphic form. In one week of 100 hours, Charlie can produce *either* five skunkskin coats *or* ten brontosaurus carcasses *or* any *linear combination* in between. The constraint, however, is that under these conditions, for each coat up to five per week that Charlie produces, he will have to *give up* the production of two carcasses. Conversely, for every carcass that Charlie produces up to ten per week, he will have to *give up* or *forego* the production of half a skunk coat. These ratios of what has to be given up to obtain one unit of an

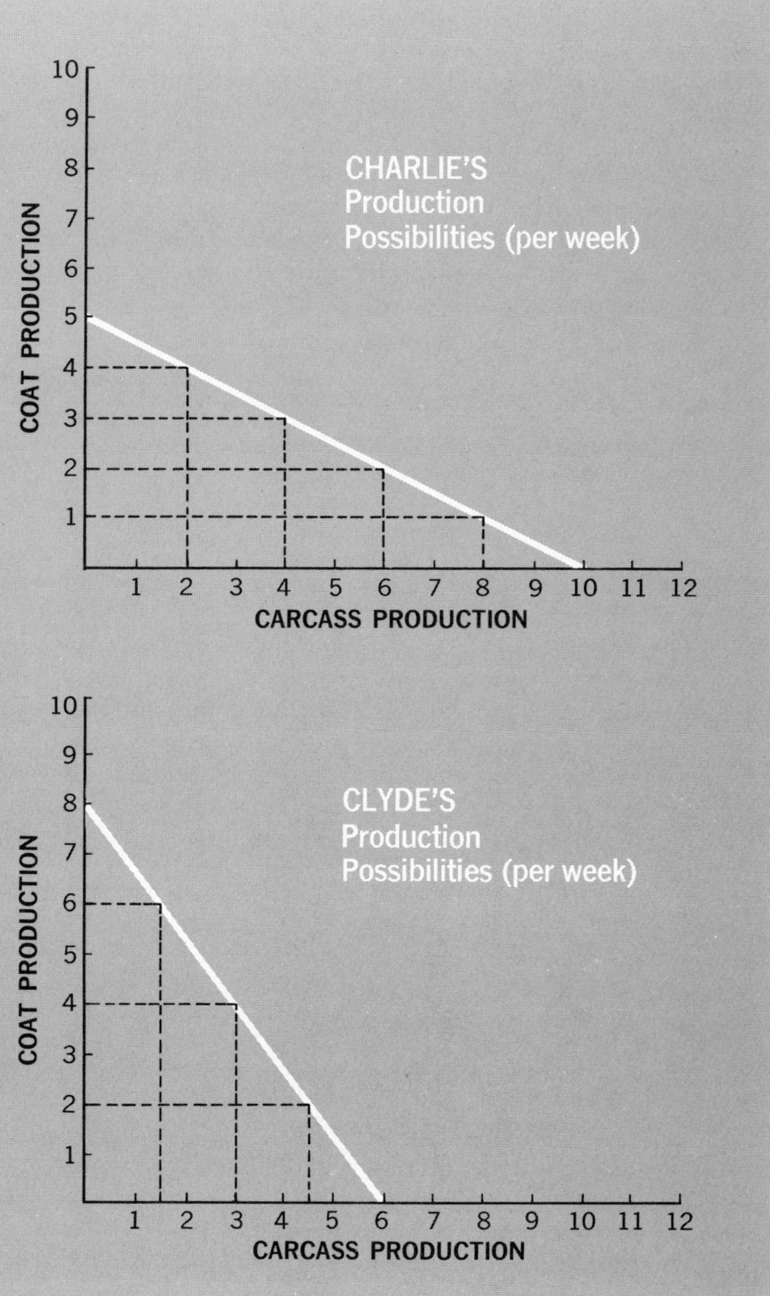
CHARLIE'S
Production
Possibilities (per week)
COAT PRODUCTION
CARCASS PRODUCTION
10
9
8
7
6
5
4
3
2
1
1 2 3 4 5 6 7 8 9 10 11 12
CLYDE'S
Production
Possibilities (per week)
COAT PRODUCTION
CARCASS PRODUCTION
10
9
8
7
6
5
4
3
2
1
1 2 3 4 5 6 7 8 9 10 11 12

Figure 2-1

alternate good are the *prices* of the goods, or, in other words, their *per unit cost.* This is an important matter of definition. Cost and price are not the same thing. If I buy one hundred cups of coffee, the cost to me will be fifteen dollars. The price of the coffee, however, is fifteen cents—the cost per unit.

Now look at that portion of Figure 2-1 showing Clyde's production possibilities curve. Clyde can produce *either* eight coats *or* six carcasses *or* any linear combination in between the two extremes. For him, the cost of producing one coat (hence, the price of the coat) is *not* producing three-fourths of a carcass; and conversely, the cost of producing one carcass is *not* producing one and a third coats.

The prices of the two goods for the two men, *without trade*, are as follows:

	The cost of producing:	
	one coat is	*one carcass is*
For Charlie	2 carcasses	½ coat
For Clyde	¾ carcass	1⅓ coats

Clearly, the cost of producing a coat for Charlie is much more (two carcasses given up) than is the case for Clyde (three-fourths carcass). On the other side of the coin, the cost of production of carcasses for Charlie is much less (half a coat given up) than it is for Clyde (one and a third coats). In this case, one can also look at total production of carcasses and coats and see that with *given inputs* (100 hours of effort per week), Charlie is *absolutely* better at producing carcasses (ten per week versus six per week for Clyde) and Clyde is absolutely better at producing coats (eight per week versus five per week for Charlie). In this case, then, Charlie has an *absolute advantage* in the production of carcasses and an *absolute disadvantage* in the production of coats. On the other hand, Clyde has an *absolute advantage* in the production of coats and an *absolute disadvantage* in the production of carcasses. In other words, both Charlie and Clyde will be better off if each one sticks to his specialty and trades the excess with the other person. Each would have to give up less of the item that is not his strong point if he specializes and trades. Figure 2-2 illustrates the comparison of talents.

This seems to make sense. But this does not mean that one has to be better than everyone else at some production process in order to gain from trade.

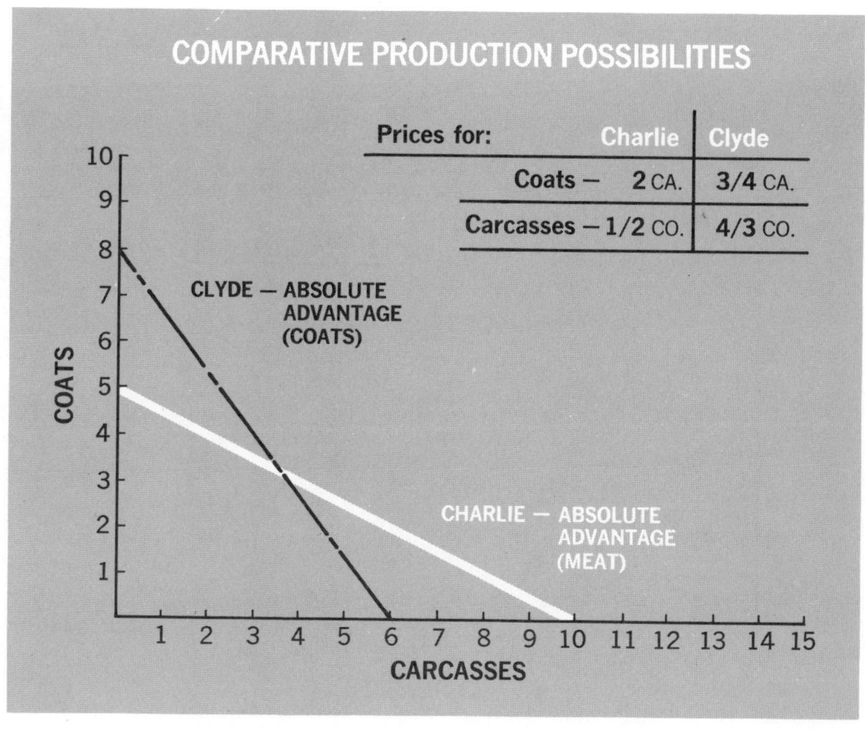

Figure 2-2

Clyde was ambitious and decided to study ways of improving his skills. Clyde expanded his production possibilities curve by improving his abilities to do both jobs, coats and carcasses. This new production possibilities curve is shown in Figure 2-3 along with Charlie's, which had not changed. We now see that Clyde could produce *either* ten coats *or* fifteen carcasses in a week of 100 hours, or, in other words, *more* of either commodity than could Charlie. On the surface, this might seem to indicate that Charlie would lose out. He just is not as efficient as Clyde, so how could specialization and trade help both of them? Remember, if both partners do not benefit at least a little, then *voluntary* trade will not take place. This simple truth is often overlooked. Figure 2-3 holds the answer when we again look at the *relative* prices or costs that each man faces in producing the two goods without trading. For every carcass Charlie produces, he will *not* be able to produce half a coat. For every carcass Clyde produces, he will not be able to produce two-thirds of a coat. In other words, Charlie can still produce carcasses at a lower personal cost than can

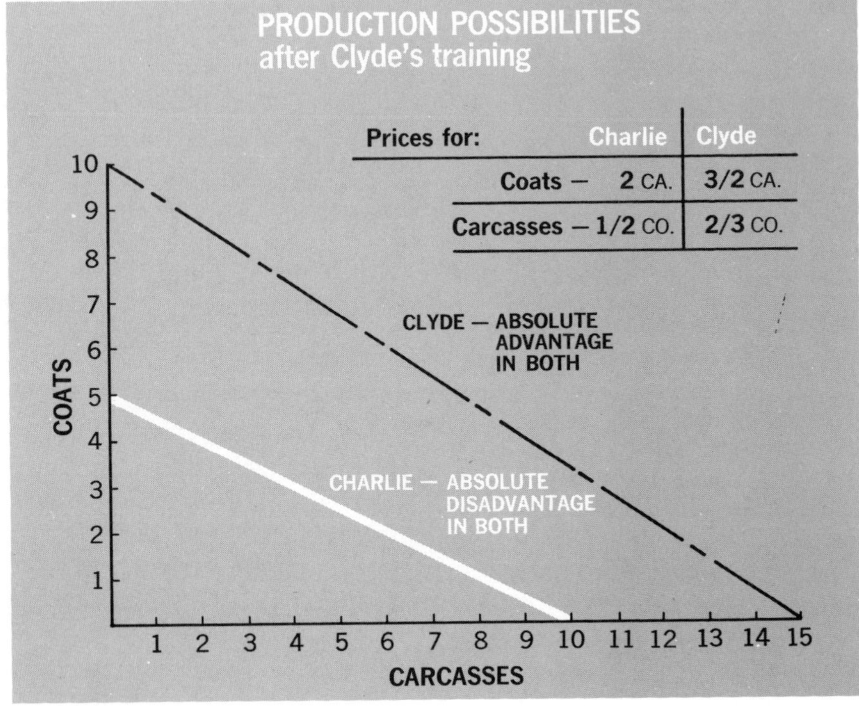

Figure 2-3

Clyde (half coat versus two-thirds of a coat). Charlie has an *absolute disadvantage* in the production of both goods, but he has a *comparative advantage* in the production of carcasses.

Now, look at the production of the other commodity—coats. Charlie must give up the production of two carcasses for every coat he produces but Clyde has to give up one and a half carcasses for every coat he produces. Clyde not only has an absolute advantage in the production of coats, he has a comparative advantage as well. He has to give up less of the alternative good than does Charlie. Again, review the situation. Clyde has an absolute advantage in the production of both goods, and Charlie has an absolute disadvantage in the production of both goods. This is because *per unit of input* Clyde can get more output of both products. However, Charlie still has a comparative advantage in the production of carcasses, which means that Clyde, even with his absolute advantage, has a *comparative disadvantage* in the production of carcasses.

Things are looking a bit brighter for Charlie. Even though he does not do as well in his productive abilities as does his neighbor, he will still be able to gain by specializing in the production of the good that he produces *relatively* better in terms of what each partner has to give up. By trading the excess of his specialized production for coats, he can get coats cheaper than would be the case if he made them himself. Of course, the converse is true for Clyde.

In our simple example, total income is made up of the total production of coats and carcasses by society (Charlie and Clyde). Because Clyde is the more productive, he will probably have the larger income of the two. But nevertheless, even though Charlie's income is lower because of his lower productivity, *Clyde* will still do better by specializing and trading than he will by going it alone.

Another point that is not covered fully as yet is just what price will result if trade opens up between the two partners. The answer to this question must wait until a discussion on the elements of *demand* for the product. Everything talked about so far has dealt with the costs of production, or the supply side of trade. Demand could change the whole picture and will influence the actual trading price. For example, what would happen if skunkskin coats went out of style? In our two-good world, what if neither Charlie nor Clyde wanted any more coats—just carcasses? Clearly, this would mean that both would produce *just* carcasses and Clyde's comparative advantage in producing coats would become a meaningless advantage. The subject of demand will be covered later, but you should realize here that we are assuming it is ''neutral'' and that anything that is produced will be demanded.

Although the exact price of the trade cannot be determined from the information we have now, the limits to trade, as far as prices are concerned, are established by the costs of the trading partners. In our latest example, as long as Charlie can get coats by trading with Clyde for a price of less than his own cost (two carcasses per coat), then he will do so. If Clyde's coats cost more than two carcasses each, then Charlie can make his own more cheaply than he can get them from Clyde. Similarly, as long as Clyde can get carcasses for less than his own cost (two-thirds of a coat per carcass) then he will do so. If Charlie's price to Clyde exceeds two-thirds of a coat per carcass, then Clyde can get his own carcasses more cheaply than trading with Charlie. These extreme prices between which trade can take place are called the *limits of trade*.

One more example may help you understand this most important concept. Let us assume that an economics professor also is a good housepainter. However, that teacher enjoys teaching economics. Referring to Figure 2-4, that teacher can give an economics course with 200 hours of effort and paint a given house with 20 hours of effort. Assume further that a certain housepainter studied so that he could teach the same course with, however, 2,500 hours time and paint a similar house with 50 hours of labor.

MANHOURS REQUIRED TO:	Economics Professor	Painter
Teach 1 Econ Course –	200 hrs	2,500 hrs
Paint 1 House –	20 hrs	50 hrs

ASSUME: Market Exists for Both Services

Look at the RELATIVE PRICES:	To Paint	To Teach
FOR YOUR FEARLESS LEADER:	.1 ECON COURSE PER HOUSE	10 HOUSES PER ECON COURSE
FOR THE PROPER PAINTER :	.02 ECON COURSE PER HOUSE	50 HOUSES PER ECON COURSE

Figure 2-4

Clearly, the professor has an absolute advantage in both occupations; that is, the resources he must expend (time) are less than those that the housepainter must expend in performing either task. Should they specialize, and if so, why?

Again, the relative prices of the two undertakings must be considered. For the professor to paint a house, he would have to give up teaching 1/10 of an economics course. For the painter, only 2/100 of an economics course would have to be given up to paint a house. His cost of painting houses in terms of his foregone alternative is much lower than the teacher's. Conversely, for every economics course the professor teaches, he must give up painting ten houses, but for every economics course taught by the housepainter, he must give up painting fifty houses. Although the housepainter has an *absolute* disadvantage in both tasks, he has a *comparative* advantage in painting houses. Specialization will still "pay." Again, however, this assumes a "neutral" demand for both services. If the people suddenly decide that they do not care about economics courses but do want their houses painted, the professor might find himself on a painting scaffold in order to sustain himself.

What are the fundamental points of the preceding exercises?

1. Given "full employment" of resources, more of one item can be produced *only* if something else is given up. We are *constrained* by scarcity.

2. Given an absolute advantage in the production of an item, the owner of the factor of production will clearly gain by specializing and trading for other products with others who also are specializing.

3. Even if someone does not do as well at *anything* when compared to someone else, he will still increase his potential by specializing and trading *if* he has a comparative advantage.

4. Increasing productivity will increase the *potential* production and consumption for *all* members of society, not merely the factor that has become more productive.

These principles hold not only for individuals, but for other economic units as well, such as businesses, cities, urban-rural relationships, or countries.

There are two implications of these principles that should be kept in mind at all times, not only in this course, but in everyday living.

1. If a person is going to increase his material well-being, he must specialize to some degree rather than attempt to provide all of his own requirements directly from his own labor. For this specialization to be useful, trade with others is an essential corollary. Everything else being equal (although it seldom is), *anything* that restrains or reduces trading potential will also reduce the potential output of a total society. This includes restraints by labor, business, governments, or individuals. Restraints may be necessary for other reasons, but by themselves, they are inefficient.

2. Because an economic unit (individual, business, country, and so on) is not the *best* at some function, it does not follow that the unit is of no value in the economic world. The principle of comparative advantage holds hope for many otherwise disadvantaged persons or peoples.

One other point should be mentioned before leaving the subject of alternative production possibilities. Some students may question the convenience of the straightline production possibilities curves in the illustrations thus far. These indicate that no matter what combination of outputs either Charlie or Clyde produce, their costs in terms of the foregone alternative remains constant. There is nothing wrong with this as long as their *labor* is the sole input. As long as their supply of material remains available and close at hand, their costs will remain the same.

When we start talking about production possibilities between two or more goods that require complex inputs, the straight lines disappear. There is a good chance that many inputs or factors of production are better suited to the production of one product as compared to an alternative. Land provides a good example of this, but it is also true of many other factors or combination of factors.

In the northwestern part of lower Michigan, near Lake Michigan, there is some land with very sandy soil and hilly contours. This combination of characteristics makes it well suited for the production of tree fruits (orchards). One *could* grow wheat on it, but it would be difficult, and the yields would be very low as compared to yields from the Great Plains region. In other words, one could reduce the land employed in orchard production and increase the land used for wheat production, but a wheat-acre added from the fruit farm would yield less than the acres normally used for growing wheat. The reverse is true if wheat land were devoted to orchards. Figure 2-5 illustrates the principle.

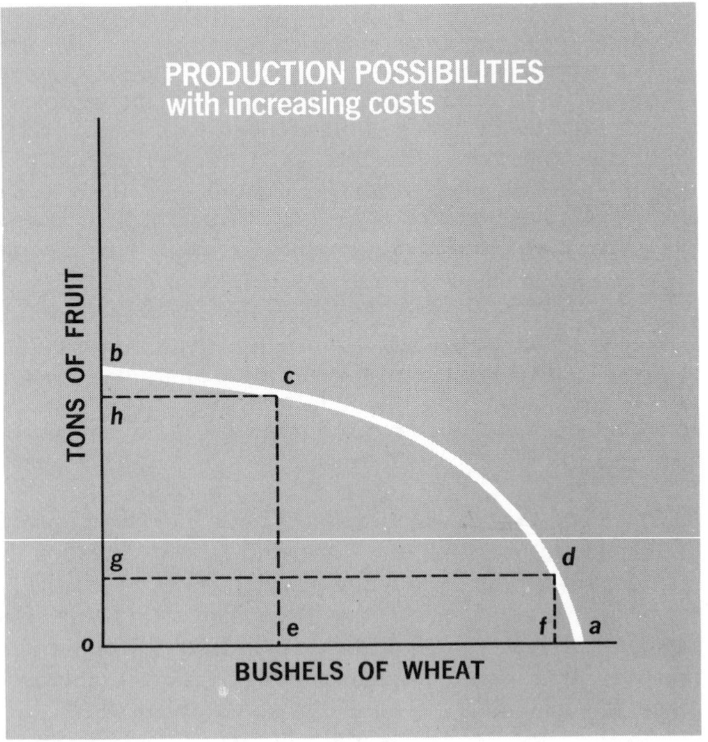

Figure 2-5

If all of the land currently being used for producing wheat and orchard products were devoted exclusively to growing wheat, *OA* bushels of wheat could be produced, but no fruit. If all this land were devoted to orchard products, *OB* tons of fruit could be produced, but no wheat. The curve *BCDA* now represents the production possibilities between these two products (one can assume for this example that all of the other factors required vary as needed). Thus, we could produce *OH* of tree fruit *plus OE* of wheat; *OG* of tree fruit *and OF* of wheat; or any other combination along the curve *BCDA*. Notice, however, that our straight line (constant cost) no longer exists. On the contrary, as we approach specialization in either commodity to the exclusion of the other, then to get a little more of the specialty item requires giving up a lot more of the alternative item. As a point is reached where only fruit is being produced, a great deal of wheat (and hence, wheat land) must be given up in order to increase fruit production even slightly. As specialization occurs, costs of producing the specialty item increase.

It should be clear by this time that this phenomenon tends to *reduce* the tendency toward complete specialization by individuals, firms, or countries. Could complete specialization ever take place under these circumstances? Yes, but it is less likely than in the constant cost case. Even here, if the price of wheat *in terms of fruit given up* becomes high enough, people will tend to produce all wheat and no fruit. *Demand* again will determine the actual quantities of the alternative products actually produced.

QUESTIONS

1. You have probably purchased something within the last week. Why? What would it have cost you to make it yourself rather than buy it?
2. The struggle for economic goods has been the cause of many wars throughout history. What are some ways that specialization and trade might act to inhibit conflicts?
3. Do you have an absolute advantage in anything you do? Do you have a comparative advantage in anything you do? With whom is the comparative advantage? Estimate the relative prices of the activities or goods involved.
4. Give an example of increasing costs in the production of something. Jumping ahead a bit, do you think that the production of most things in a total economy are subject to constant costs or increasing costs? Why?
5. List the alternatives you have foregone by attending the university

this semester. Can money values be estimated for all of these foregone opportunities?

6. Make very sure that you understand and are able to explain precisely the concepts of scarcity, opportunity cost, and comparative advantage *as we are using these terms.*

3

Economic Systems and Their Values

OBJECTIVES

All *economic systems must resolve the questions of* rationing *stocks of goods—deciding what, how, and when production will take place; the level of resource or factor use; and the distribution of the income (product) of the economy. Economies consist of* circular flows *with the services of* factors of production *on one side of the circle and goods for use on the other side. Production is essential to have goods for any use. The "free lunch" just doesn't exist for an economy as a whole, regardless of the system it employs. The essential differences among economies lie in the degree of planning employed in their allocation processes. One form of economic organization uses the so-called* market system *or* price system. *This system allows people to express their willingness and ability to give up resources they possess to get some other good they desire. The* price *of the good becomes the mechanism for expressing the desires of* demanders *of the good in conjunction with the willingness and ability of potential producers or* suppliers *of the good. By the interaction of the separate markets within a system, overall resource allocation takes place.*

INTRODUCTION

We have seen how man has condemned himself to a life of economic interaction with other men. The most fundamental part of this interrelationship involves the trading or exchanging of goods and services. Sooner or later, this is going to involve the establishment of some kind of system through which exchange can be accomplished. *Any* economic system must perform certain functions. Whether in Mao's China or Nixon's U.S., there are certain basic decisions that must be made and the system must provide the framework within which the decisions can be made.

Figure 3-1 lists the required functions, each of which deserves a few words.

AN ECONOMIC SYSTEM MUST:

1. RATION goods & services

2. determine HOW goods & services are produced

3. determine WHAT is to be produced

4. determine LEVEL of factor employment

5. determine DISTRIBUTION of income

Figure 3-1

1. Existing stocks of economic goods are, by definition, scarce; and, therefore, they must be *rationed* among the members of the society. This also applies to goods that will be produced in the future.

2. Somehow the question of *what* is to be produced must be answered. Are resources going to be put into the production of chrome strips on automobiles or day-care centers for working parents? What criteria will be used in making these kinds of decisions?

3. *How* are goods going to be produced? Given the available technology, for example, should cars be produced by gifted workers using a minimum of tools (capital) or by automated factories using a minimum of labor?

4. The *level of factor employment* must be decided, particularly when there are choices involving time. Should redwood trees be cut now for lumber or saved for the future? Should anyone who wants a particular job be able to get that job? What is *full employment* of a factor or factors?

5. How is purchasing power going to be distributed? This is obviously connected to point number one, but the implications in a complex economy are far-reaching and touch the whole area of ethics and values. Later in the book, we will talk about some different approaches to the distribution of income and wealth in different countries and compare some estimates of income distribution in different economies.

Again, it should be emphasized that *any* economic system *must* perform these functions if there is to be any exchange and/or production taking place.

The more one studies economics, the more one begins to realize the tremendous similarities between economic systems. True, huge differences exist too, but the generality of the human problem with scarcity tends to produce likenesses that are underrated. There is a saying that, "There ain't no such thing as a free lunch." Taken literally, it is not true. An individual or group can very well get something for nothing. Making use of that item obtained will usually involve at least some expenditure of time, but the idea of getting greater value than you pay out can certainly exist at a "micro" or individual economic unit level. However, the point of the proverb involves something more generalized. When talking about an economic *system,* specifically an economic system operating without contact with any other economic system, then the saying is absolutely correct.

If a person could lie on his back under a breadfruit tree and have the ripe fruit fall into his mouth without pain or effort, then the following statement is not correct. Otherwise, the following is an axiom without exception. *If something is going to be available for use, it has to be produced.* Does that sound too simplistic? It is, but that fact of life is *still* often ignored. There are other ways of putting the same proposition. If something is going to be *consumed*, it must be produced. If something is going to be *saved* for the future, and that something is scarce, then aside from natural resources, it, too, must have been produced. If the government is going to require some goods, these must be produced, too. Using some illustrations, the point can be made a little clearer and the groundwork can be laid for talking about alternative ways of organizing a system.

In Figure 3-2, a simple economy is broken down into two functions—producers and consumers. Of course, *all* persons are consumers, and most are producers of some sort, too. That production may be nothing more complex than one's own labor, but this is precisely one of the points to be made. Consumers supply producers with the wherewithal to produce goods, that is, the factors of production including labor, capital, and natural resources. Producers, on the other hand, provide consumers with the goods (services are also goods) consumers demand. If we assume no trade with the outside world, then it is a simple system and *closed*, with goods flowing to consumers and factors flowing back to producers. If goods are to be available, *someone or something must produce them.* Further, any production *requires the expenditure of resources.* Here, the "no free lunch" applies exactly.

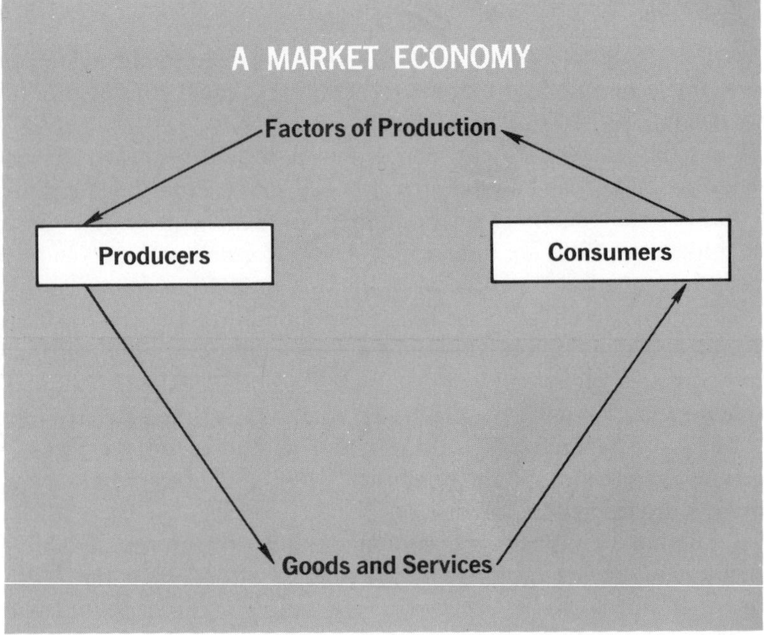

Figure 3-2

This seems obvious; yet, many cling to the idea that this or that system can perform the economic miracle of production without cost, *any* cost. As long as we want something more than the breadfruit-on-the-back example, then work must be done. Resources must be developed and organized into the millions of products that people want and are willing and able to pay for. The organization can and does take many forms, some of which we will take a brief look at now.

Remember the five functions listed in Figure 3-1, and now apply those functions to the circular flow in Figure 3-2. Certainly, the most obvious way to carry out the functions would be for someone or some group to sit down and *plan* just how all of the pieces were going to fit together and end up producing what everyone wanted. In other words, the super planner or planners would first figure out *what* the economy *should* produce. Once that was done, they would then decide just *how* this was going to be made and distributed. After this was done, they would know how much there would be to go around, and they could then decide *who* should get *what* and *how much*.

All economies use some of this planning method, but *no* industrial economy uses it completely. One can see why. Just consider all of the billions and billions of separate decisions that total planners would have to make. Not only would they have to make these decisions, but they would have to *re*make them every time something changed. And things are constantly changing. Of course, if planners are making all the decisions between available alternatives, then, clearly, individuals are not making any. In this extreme case, any individual freedom of action with regard to scarce alternatives is completely removed. The planners do it all.

The real differences among economies can be summed up as the differing degrees to which planning is employed. This difference, plus differences in incentives and sanctions applied to factors of production, covers the major areas that divide people in talking about alternative economic systems. But it is obvious that these areas, individual freedom of action and incentives, involve a tremendous amount of ethical or value judgments.

There is another flow that should be mentioned here, although a whole chapter is devoted to it later on. Regardless of the kind of economy, any society that has developed a degree of specialized effort uses something called *money*. As you will see, money is used to store value and facilitate the exchange of goods. Even if the planners are making all the decisions, most of those decisions will be implemented by using money in some way. As a result, a reverse flow of money goes along with the flow of goods. Consumers provide factors of production for the production sector, which, in turn, pays them in money. The money paid to consumers becomes the purchasing power that consumers use to buy the products of the production sector. Figure 3-3 adds this flow to the picture.

Thus far, everything we have said applies to all economies. But now we are going to talk about *market* economies. It is not to be presumed that there are either planned economies *or* market economies. In fact, all

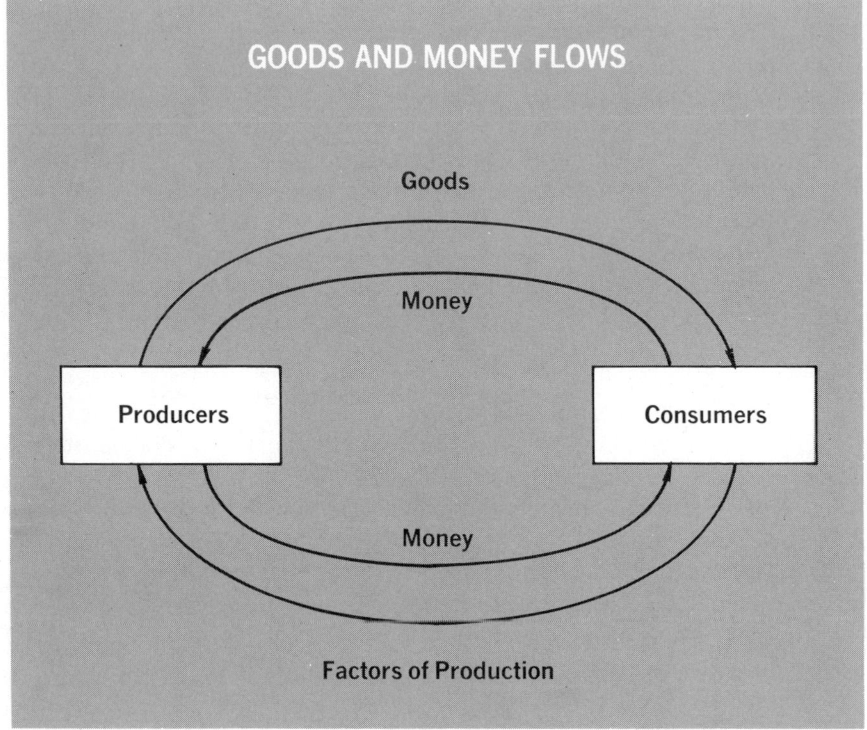

Figure 3-3

economies use some planning *and* some of the market as well. For example, the supposed archetype of all market economies, the U.S.A., uses a large amount of planning in its economy today. Conversely, mainland China still uses the market for many of its allocation processes. In both instances, the actions are against the basic philosophies of the two countries, but pragmatism generally wins out over dogma, and so it has been for the advocates of two extremes of economic operations.

It is sometimes said that a free (meaning uncontrolled) market eliminates the problem of value judgments in the allocation process. The market, operating as a dispassionate mixer and refiner of individual wants and abilities, removes the weight from one person who would have to decide what is right or best for someone else. This may be always, or almost always, true. But using the market in itself rests on the assumption that individuals should have this kind of freedom of action. There are a great many in the world who disagree with that basic position. They feel, on the contrary, that individual choices should be constrained not only by their purchasing power and talents, but also by some social criterion that further limits individual choices. Again, it will not be our job here to talk much about these rights and wrongs, but rather of the analysis that applies no matter what the rights and wrongs turn out to be. One of the purposes of this brief section is to point out how so many of the things that we might feel are *objective* and without personal bias actually rest on biases and judgments. They are difficult to overcome.

THE MARKET SYSTEM—AN OVERVIEW

Charlie and Clyde did not have many problems when it came to trading with each other. Particularly when there were only two goods, the process was elementary. Remember from the limits of trade, as long as both could exchange products more cheaply than they could make the products themselves, then trade would take place.

But this sidesteps an important point. Although the limits of trade were set by the relative prices that faced each partner in the absence of trade, no mention was made about the *actual* price. This price could be set by some authority who was exercising control over Charlie and Clyde's world. This authority would not have to be a dictator. In fact, he could be some neutral person elected by Charlie and Clyde just to perform this pricing function.

But there is another way that the two could organize their trading. The two could get together and bargain. First of all, Charlie might offer Clyde a carcass for one coat. Referring to the prices contained in Figure 2-3, Clyde is just going to laugh at Charlie. He (Clyde) can produce his own carcasses for only two-thirds of a coat so he surely is not about to pay Charlie any price higher than that. Charlie brings down his price to exactly two-thirds of a coat per carcass. Clyde tells Charlie that there still is no percentage in trading. But now we have arrived at the point where trade *might* start. Any price below two-thirds coats and above Charlie's *cost of production* (half a coat) will at least be a possibility. At least one partner can *gain* and the other one *does not lose* anything. At exactly the two-thirds coat price, Clyde would not lose anything by trading with Charlie. Charlie, on the other hand would gain handsomely. He is getting one sixth of a coat *more* than it is costing him to produce the carcasses. As the price falls from the two-thirds coat level, more of the gain will go to Clyde and less to Charlie. Finally, at the half-coat level, all of the gains from trade accrue to Clyde, and Charlie just holds his own.

Getting back to *the* price that is going to evolve, it should be obvious that this price will depend primarily on just how badly each person wants each item. These *relative desires* will be reflected in the *relative price*. If Clyde wants carcasses more than Charlie, the chances are that the price will be bid up, and Charlie will do very well. If, however, Clyde is not very interested in taking carcasses anyway, then the price will fall.

As you will see in the upcoming chapters, the process we are describing involves an idea called a market. In our example above, we had a *seller* (Charlie), a *buyer* (Clyde), a *product* (carcasses), and a *means of payment* (coats). In addition to this, there was *communication* between the two potential trading partners. These are all of the ingredients that are needed for a *market*. A market is a function. It can be a place where buyers and sellers get together, like the stock markets in New York or the farmers' markets in some of our major cities, but it does not have to be. All it takes are buyers and sellers with a chance of interacting with each other to potentially end up exchanging goods for goods. Often, one of these goods is *money*, but money is nothing more than purchasing power over other goods, so introducing money does not really change things much from the *barter* of one consumption good for another consumption good.

A *free market*, as the term is used by economists, does not mean that markets operate without cost. A free market means that there are no restrictions on the buyers or sellers in terms of their rights and abilities to bargain in the buying and selling process. This usually means that we make some assumptions about the general character of a free market. First of all, we assume that there is *competition* between not only buyers and sellers, but also *among* buyers and *among* sellers. Open competition itself implies some most important characteristics. First of all, people must be free to both enter and get out of the picture. A selling firm must be able to enter the market if it wishes and other firms must be able to enter the market if they wish. As you will see when we talk about monopolies, this entry/exit condition is of prime importance.

There must be cheap and easy access to information by all parties in a market. If one seller is offering a bargain price but none of the buyers know it, then the competitive feature of the market cannot operate. Similarly, if sellers do not know about the latest demands of buyers, the market will function with less than perfect efficiency. Finally, a free market must not contain any restrictions that might be caused by power concentration. Again, we will go into this in more detail, but basically, no single buyer or seller can have any appreciable influence on either the *quantity* marketed or the *price* at which some good is marketed.

After that description, you probably are wondering why we even talk about a free market. Obviously, in the world around us, power concentrations are everywhere. Economic units, ranging from General Motors to the steelworkers union to the federal government, exercise considerable influence in many markets within our contemporary economy. This is true, but as we have already discussed, abstraction into a "pure" model is one way of getting insight into the "real" model and this will be explored.

An important distinction in a marketing system is the fact that what is being transferred is not only *goods* but the *property rights* to those goods, as discussed in Chapter 1. It is the right to *use* these goods in certain ways. Even more specifically, the market transfers the rights to gain certain *services* from goods. It is those services that people are looking for. These may be as concrete as the transportation services from your automobile or as ethereal as the joy of seeing a different chrome strip on the side of the car.

In some ways, this specification of a good makes life complicated. It would appear that what we should talk about are markets for the *services* of goods rather than the goods themselves. Perhaps we should talk about the market of the transportation services of the 1973 Plymouth Satellite station wagon with standard equipment and painted blue. Then, we could talk about the market for the esthetic values derived by potential purchasers of 1974 Plymouth Satellite station wagons with standard equipment and painted blue (which blue?). The point of this discussion is that when we talk about a market for anything, for example, cars, we are really talking about an *aggregation* of different markets. Not only are there thousands of combinations of vehicle characteristics that all would qualify as "cars", but the services flowing from these different vehicles are different for different people. The problems that this aggregating process produces will be covered in much greater detail later on. For now, it should be remembered to make distinctions when talking about *the* market for some particular good.

QUESTIONS

1. List some situations in which individuals or groups get "free lunches," that is, situations in which they receive something of value that is not a free good without giving up something in return. In your examples, does anyone pay?
2. Look at the circular flow concept of an economy. Can a country that is exporting part of its product to another country continue to have the same level of material output? What are the implications of this flow?
3. It has been said that money greases the wheels of commerce. Explain and comment.
4. Take an automobile or another major good that you use and consider all the services it provides. Can you place money values on these services? Why or why not?
5. List some costs of carrying out the marketing process for various goods that you purchase.

4

Needs, Wants, and Demand

OBJECTIVES

Human needs *can be defined by individuals for themselves, but such needs are usually impossible to define for others. On the other hand,* wants *can be expressed among people through the operation of prices in a market.* Demand *is defined as the relationship between the quantities of a good that people are willing and able to purchase at various possible prices. The* Law of Demand *states that the price of a good and the* quantity demanded *of the good will be inversely related. This law assumes that all other factors that could also affect the quantity demanded of a good are held constant. Such factors include the prices of substitute and complementary goods, incomes of demanders, peoples' tastes, transactions costs, and expectations about the future. The concept of* elasticity *gives us a way of measuring just how sensitive the change in quantity demanded will be for changes in the price of the good.*

INTRODUCTION

What is a need? More specifically, what is a human need? Most people would start off by talking about air for breathing, food to eat, and some kind of shelter. It is true that without *any* of these categories of things, people die—cease to exist in this world. But just how much of any of these things is a true physiological need in terms of survival, and how much is a *want* in order to live a little better? That is a more difficult question. There have been many studies conducted into the basic nutritional requirements to keep people alive. One of the not-too-amazing conclusions is that different people have very different requirements. It has also been found that we could live on very little compared to what most people in the world today (including very poor people) actually eat.

I can say that I *need* the love of a certain woman to survive. This may or may not be true, but you really can't dispute my assertion until some future time when you see that I *did* survive without her. You say you *need* a room temperature of 70° Fahrenheit to be comfortable. Okay, I'll have to take your word for it because I don't have any accurate method of determining your comfort or discomfort. The point is that the word *needs* is tough to handle. It implies an absolute that is almost impossible to measure in human beings. A car needs an engine to run. That I can understand. But the statement "I need a sailboat to be happy" can only be measured by *me*.

A human *want* is something else and is an emotion that all other humans understand full well. It is the business of human wants that concerns the economist. He is not so concerned about *why* those wants are there. This is a question for the psychologist. The economist is interested in how those wants are expressed and what the impact of *expressed* wants is on the community as well as on economic units within that community.

Want is tied to something defined as *goods*. If something is wanted, it must mean that the desired object will yield some service of value. If something is wanted, and one is willing and able to give up something else to get it, then there is a *demand* for the good. Remember, whatever has to be given up of one good to get another is the *cost* of the second good. The cost *per unit* of the second good is the *price* of that good. When we start talking about the *demand* for a good, we will be talking about the *relationship* between the *price* of that good and the *quantity demanded* of the same good. *Demand* and *quantity demanded* are *not* the same thing.

To analyze the market, one must take note of the various things influencing the quantity of a good that people are willing and able to purchase. The most obvious of these things is the price of the good itself. As the price of a good *rises*, then the *quantity demanded* of that good can be expected to *fall*; as the price of a good *falls*, then the quantity demanded of that good can be expected to *rise*. We say that the price of a good and the quantity demanded of that good are *inversely related*, that is, they move in opposite directions.

This statement, with one more phrase added to it, is *without exception*. The phrase that gets added is *ceteris paribus*—roughly translated, everything else being equal or held the same. The *law of demand* states that the price and quantity demanded of any good are inversely related, *ceteris paribus*. This means that all of the other things that we are about to discuss that can also influence the quantity demanded of a good are conceptually held constant when we talk about the *demand* for a good.

The consumption of some goods is related to the consumption of others. Many goods are consumed or used either *instead of* or *along with* some other good. In other words, there may be *substitutes for* or *complements to* some goods. Examples of substitutes include butter and margarine, automobile transportation and airline transportation, university training and technical school training. Notice, that a substitute does not have to be identical; in fact, *substitute* implies that it may only partially satisfy the functions of the desired good. Nickels and dimes, in the proper proportions, are perfect substitutes in most cases, but they are very imperfect if one only has nickels, the coffee machine takes only dimes, and nobody is around to make change. Complements are found in such items as tires and automobiles, beer and pretzels, sails and sailboats, and so on. As may be guessed, the *prices* of these *related goods* undoubtedly will affect the *quantity demanded* of the good in question. Much as one may dislike margarine, if the price of butter goes much higher (relative to margarine), oleo will become much more acceptable. Notice, as the price of the given good becomes higher relative to its substitute (or the price of the substitute gets lower), the *quantity demanded* of the given good will decrease. The converse is true for complementary goods. If the price of automobiles increases substantially, the demand for automobile tires will *decrease* because there will be fewer automobiles purchased on which to use the tires. Although the example may not be very important for an individual automobile buyer, it is very important if one looks at the total market including all buyers of automobiles and automobile tires.

A third item that can affect the *quantity demanded* of a good is the *incomes* of the demanders. At first, one would think that when there are those with high incomes, more of a good would be demanded than would be the case if demanders had lower incomes. For some goods (economists call them *normal* or *superior* goods), this is true. Rolls Royce automobiles undoubtedly fit this category. But for other goods (*inferior goods*), such as canned pork and beans, the opposite is true. For the latter category, increasing incomes give people the choice of selecting more expensive alternatives, for example, steak and fresh vegetables instead of the canned pork and beans. In this case, increasing incomes actually *reduce* the quantity demanded of Campbell's worst.

Another determinant of demand is sort of a catchall—the tastes of demanders. This includes all of the complex subjective reasons that people have for wanting (or not wanting) a particular good. Such items as style, keeping-up-with-the-Joneses, keeping-down-with-the-proletariat, falling for a new detergent ad on TV—all of these affect the nebulous concept of "tastes." Clearly, if the public's taste for a particular good increases, then the quantity demanded of the good will increase, and vice versa.

The next item that can affect the quantity demanded of a good is something called *transactions costs*. As may have been observed, markets and their operation provide a flow of services to the community. The goods that flow through markets yield services, but the *markets themselves* are economic goods in that they are the vehicle through which other goods are distributed throughout the economy. This means that they are *costing* something in terms of scarce resource use. It takes resources to provide the allocation functions performed by markets. It would be simple to lump all these costs together, but it is useful to separate them into component parts. This is particularly true when we discuss negative goods. The parts will be labeled as follows:

> Information costs
> Contractual costs
> Policing costs

or ICP costs, for short.

Although these terms are fairly self-explanatory, a few words are needed to clarify the exact meaning we will be attaching to them.

Market operations are made up of the choices between alternatives by both buyers and sellers. If these choices are to result in improved well-being for the participants, there must be *information* about alternatives available to both customers and suppliers. The buyer must know not only the price of the product involved, but also the prices of other purchases that he might want to make instead. He must also have at least some information about the services that reasonably can be expected from the potential purchase. As the cost of obtaining such information increases, the quantities demanded of the good can be expected to decrease. Buying the product becomes more expensive. The seller, too, must have information about the market in which he wishes to sell. He also must acquire knowledge of the alternatives to which he might apply the resources under his control. Again, costs will be incurred in obtaining this information, and to the extent that information expenses increase, the seller will be less willing to supply products at a given price. ICP costs for suppliers are covered in detail in the next chapter.

Demanders' *contractual costs* are obvious enough in some major purchases, like houses, but they exist to some extent in virtually all purchase transactions. It may be as simple as the time spent in a checkout line at the local supermarket or as complex as a legal test case when purchasing something for which property rights are poorly defined.

Policing costs usually are not considered as something that would affect the demand for some particular good. Nevertheless, the enforcement of property rights, whatever those rights might be, is crucial if *any* economic system is to work and survive. It is property rights that the market is transferring. It is property rights that make anything a useful good. If the rights are not enforced, it is just as though they did not exist in the first place, and there would be chaos. The revolutionaries of today understand this full well. If the goal is to destroy a particular system, its essentials must be attacked. For an economic system, *any* economic system, these essentials are the particular system of property rights that have been built up to make allocation of goods possible. These rights are generally well defined in all operating economic systems in the world today. If one wishes to destroy any of these systems, breaking down property rights is a good beginning. Human beings being what they are, this procedure of enforcement of property rights will be necessary and will require the use of resources.

As mentioned before, all of these transactions or ICP costs will impinge on both demanders and suppliers. To the extent that they are imposed upon demanders, then the quantity of a good demanded will fall. ICP costs are like a complementary good. To buy the good in question, the market services needed to get the good also must be bought. This is another way of saying that complements also are purchased. This is absolutely correct, but the reason we make ICP costs a separate variable is so that our later analysis can investigate the specific effects of changes in ICP costs in various markets.

The final variable affecting the quantity demanded of any good is *expectations*. The macroeconomic portion of this book will show that people's expectations about future events make up one of the most powerful forces in the economy. And, in individual markets as well, expectations about the future can have a strong influence on the current level of demand for a good. For example, if people feel that the price of a particular commodity is going to fall in the near future, then the chances are that many will try to delay present purchases and wait for the expected price drop. Conversely, if it is felt that the price of a good is going to rise, then purchases will be speeded up in an attempt to beat the price increase. Expectations about future prices are only one influence. Expectations about future income levels, life span, family size, and any other event that might impinge on buying practices will also come into the act.

Figure 4-1 summarizes the determinants of the quantity demanded of any good. It also shows a shorthand method of putting these *variables* or *arguments* down on paper. The use of this notation simplifies discussion and saves a good deal of writing. It says exactly what the verbiage above it says. The *quantity demanded* of a good (q_d) is a function of [$f(\ )$] the price of the good (p), the price of related goods (p_r), demanders' incomes (i), demanders' tastes (t), Information, Contractual, and Policing costs facing demanders (ICP_d), and the expectations of demanders (E_d). Notice, the formula makes no attempt to say *how* these things (arguments) are related. It merely says that some kind of relationship exists between the quantity demanded of a good and each of these variables. One other bit of notation is to put a bar on top of certain arguments at certain times, like this: $\overline{i}$, $\overline{p}_r$, and

The QUANTITY of a good DEMANDED depends upon (is a function of):

1. the PRICE of the good
2. the prices of RELATED GOODS
3. people's INCOME
4. people's TASTES
5. TRANSACTIONS COSTS (ICP_d)
6. EXPECTATIONS

or

$$q_d = f(p, p_r, i, t, ICP_d, E_d)$$

We call this a DEMAND FUNCTION

Figure 4-1

so on. This means that the value of that argument is being held constant for the discussion at hand.

To give an example from the physical sciences, it is known that the pressure exerted by a gas inside a sealed container will depend upon (among other things) the size of the container and the temperature of the gas.

$$P = \text{pressure}$$
$$V = \text{volume of the container}$$
$$T = \text{temperature of the gas}$$
$$P = f(V, T)$$

If it is wished to determine the effect of just temperature, it is necessary to hold the size of the container constant and *just* vary the temperature, or

$$P = f(\bar{V}, T)$$

and study changes in pressure resulting from *just* changes in temperature.

The objection is sometimes raised that a physical scientist can, in fact, establish a controlled experiment in which he is able to hold all variables constant except the one he wishes to analyze, but social scientists cannot accomplish this because their laboratory consists of people interacting in the real world in which *nothing* is constant. The objection is overstated for two reasons. First, the physical scientist *cannot* control his experiment in a perfect fashion. He theorizes about a "perfect vacuum," for example, and yet he has never produced or encountered a perfect vacuum. Second, the social scientist is able to approximate an "everything else being equal" or *ceteris paribus* situation using statistical techniques and real world data. True, he does not attain perfect control over his experiments, but the control is often sufficient to gain insights into the problem at hand. Thus, when we analytically hold constant the prices of related goods ($\bar{p}_r$), incomes ($\bar{i}$), tastes ($\bar{t}$), ICP costs ($\overline{ICP}_d$), and expectations ($\bar{E}_d$) in order to study the *pure* effects of price and quantity demanded, we establish a *ceteris paribus* condition that cannot be found in the real world. Nevertheless, the method is useful in figuring out what happens when just these two variables interact.

In the discussions that follow, you will see that the economist is particularly preoccupied with the "pure" relationship between price and quantity demanded. We are so preoccupied that we even entitle this interaction *demand.* The reason for this interest is that *price* is the basic mechanism by which quantities of scarce goods are allocated between various alternative uses and alternative demanders. For the moment, let us look at the mechanics of demand.

The commodity we will use for illustration purposes is a *gloop*. The gloop is a very useful gadget that was reputedly developed by a resourceful sailor during World War II. This gentleman enlisted as a gloopmaker and managed to sit out most of the war doing nothing, because although no one in the Navy knew what a gloop was, no one wanted to admit his ignorance. Finally, one particularly brash Chief Petty Officer insisted that our hero produce a gloop, and, after several months in the ship's machine shop, the gloop was completed and its function duly demonstrated. The gloop, a highly polished stainless steel ball, was carried to the side of the ship and released into the water below, whereupon it produced a soul-satisfying sound—gloop—as it disappeared into the depths. For some reason, we will assume that the U.S. public develops a passion for gloops. (And if you think that is farfetched, how about frisbees, hula hoops, and the like.) Anyway, we will hypothesize a demand for gloops. Let us assume that we circulate a questionnaire to the entire American public asking each person how many gloops he would be willing and able to purchase at various market prices. We will ask him to answer this question at exactly 12:00 noon on the day after tomorrow. By having this instant in time, we will effectively hold all variables constant for that instant. The question is to be answered *given* the income, prices of related goods, tastes, ICP costs, and expectations as perceived by the demander. From the answers to this questionnaire, we are able to develop a *demand schedule* shown in the table in Figure 4-2.

In a price range of one dollar to five dollars, our potential customers indicate that they would be willing and able to purchase from 6,000 units at the low price to 2,000 units at the high price. Does this relationship make any intuitive sense? Of course. It is merely demonstrating the *law of demand* that was presented earlier. As the price of the good falls, the quantity demanded rises, *ceteris paribus*. The price of a good and the quantity demanded of that good are inversely related, again, *ceteris paribus*.

Also, included in Figure 4-2 is a plot of the prices and quantities demanded that are listed in the demand schedule. It makes a picture out of what has just been said—when prices are high, smaller quantities are demanded than when prices are low. This demand curve happens to be a straight line, but in fact, it could have any form, *as long as* it sloped downward to the right. Otherwise, the law of demand would be violated and people would demand a *larger* quantity at a higher price, *ceteris paribus*. Some people may be bothered by this law of demand and point out such examples as very expensive jewels that may actually be in greater demand when they are expensive. Only then do they have the snob appeal that sells them. This is quite true, but this, too, can be answered under the laws already mentioned. A diamond of about fifty carats and perfect, at a price of one million dollars, will yield a very large number of services. If its cost were only ten cents, the services from it would change considerably. In the one case, it is a fairly stable store of value plus a jewel that can impress everybody. In the other case, it has use only as a pretty stone or, perhaps, as an industrial diamond.

The point is that the law of demand refers to demand *for the same good*. The same good means that essentially the same services are flowing

DEMAND SCHEDULE FOR GLOOPS

Price per Gloop	Quantity Demanded (thousands)
$5.00	2
$4.00	3
$3.00	4
$2.00	5
$1.00	6

HELD CONSTANT:

1. $\overline{i}$
2. $\overline{p}_r$
3. $\overline{t}$
4. $\overline{ICP}_d$
5. $\overline{E}_d$

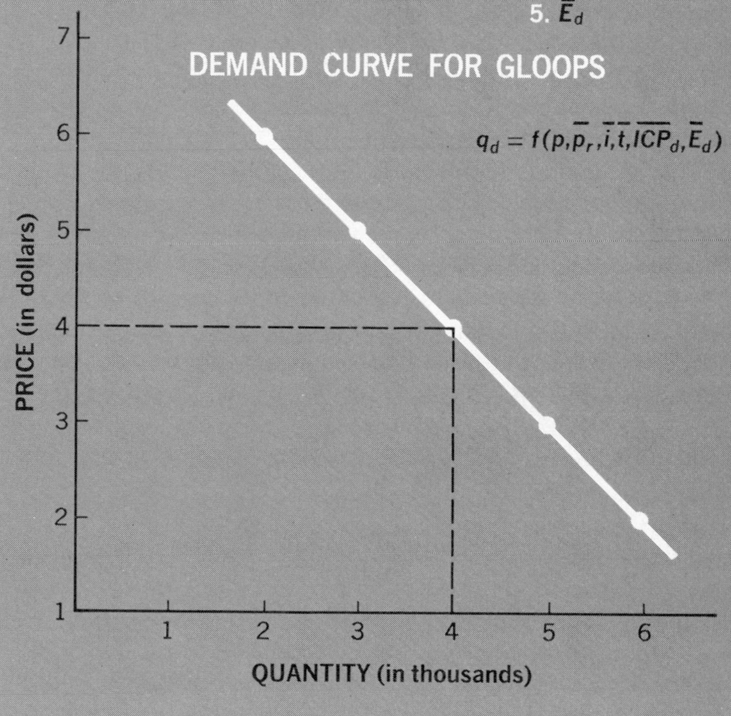

Figure 4-2

from some group of similar commodities. The law of demand says that if one could get the same prestige value from a diamond costing *less* rather than *more* he would do so. The axiom involved holds that rational people prefer paying *less* than *more* for identically the same service. But, in the case of the diamond, the service itself may partially depend upon the price paid, or at least the price people *think* was paid.

Getting back to the example, demand, then, is *not* a single *quantity demanded.* Demand is a series of quantities demanded that people would be willing and able to purchase at different market prices, everything else being equal. A movement along the demand curve, for example, from 4,000 gloops at three dollars to 3,000 gloops at four dollars is *not* a change in demand—it is a change in the quantity demanded with a one dollar price rise at that level. This point is not being belabored, but is very important and has been troubling economics students for many years.

What, then, is a change in demand? Demand changes when there is a change in any of the arguments that have been held constant ($\bar{p}_r, \bar{i}, \bar{t}, \overline{ICP}_d, \bar{E}_d$). Graphically, a change in demand is indicated by a *shift* of the entire demand curve or schedule, and it says that because of a change in the previous constants, the entire series of prices and quantities demanded has changed. Some examples of changes in demand are illustrated in Figures 4-3 through 4-6. In Figure 4-3, we have assumed that gloops are a normal good; that is, an increase in the incomes of gloop demanders will cause an increase in the demand for gloops. In this example, we have assumed that incomes increased, and this increase has shifted the demand curve upward and to the right. This shift implies either one or a combination of two things. At any previous level of price, a larger quantity of gloops will now be demanded, or any previous quantity demanded will now command a higher price. Without empirical data, it is not possible to say how far the income increase will shift the demand curve or whether the shifted curve will maintain the same shape. Even without this exact knowledge, just being able to predict the *direction* of the shift can be extremely useful in many applications.

Figure 4-4 assumes that at least some people drop gloops into swimming pools. Hence, swimming pools are a complementary good to gloops—for some people, the use of a gloop requires the use of a swimming pool. If the *price* (not necessarily *demand*) of swimming pools goes up, people will buy fewer pools and therefore buy fewer gloops to drop into those pools. The cost of consuming the package consisting of gloops and pools has risen. Therefore, at any given price of gloops, fewer will be demanded. The *demand* for gloops has fallen because of an increase in the price of a complementary good. Another way of expressing this reduction in demand is to say that any previous quantity of gloops demanded will now be sold only at a *lower* price.

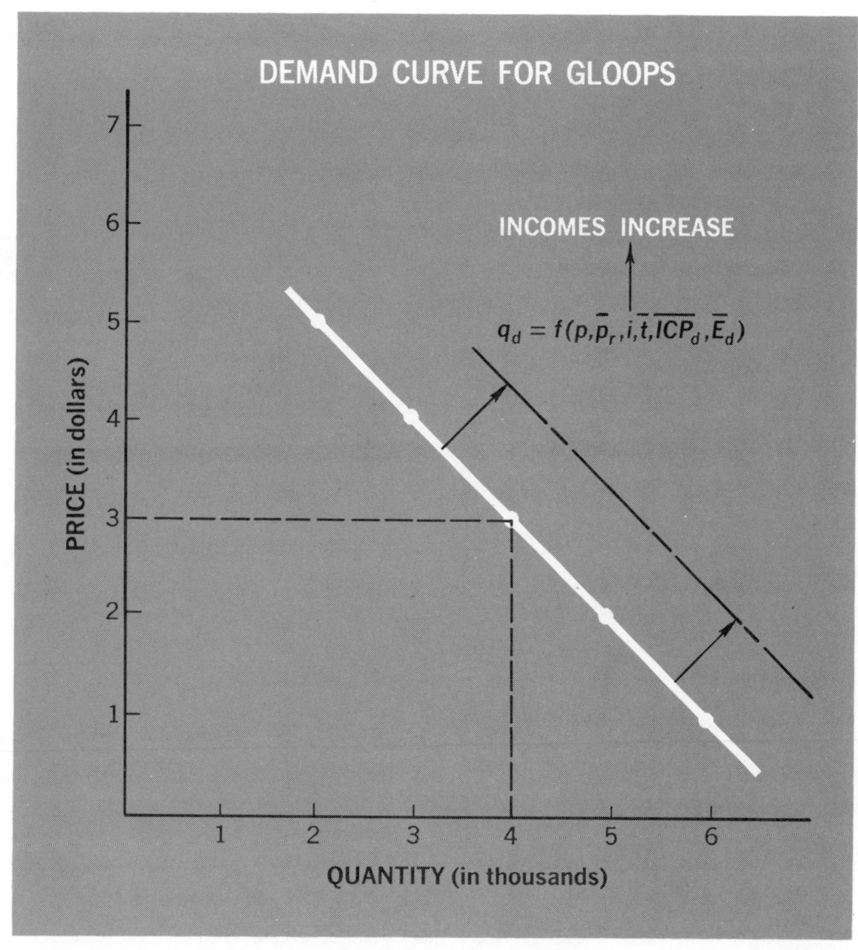

Figure 4-3

In Figure 4-5, we have assumed that someone started making a square gloop and called it a glug. Although true gloop lovers scoffed at the innovation, many people were willing to accept it as a reasonable substitute for a gloop. The glug was cheaper to make, too, and, as a result, its price kept falling. The result was inevitable. A decreasing price of glugs caused a shifting in the demand for gloops. As the *price* of glugs went down, more and more people shifted from gloops to glugs and the *demand* for gloops fell.

Finally, the craze for gloops comes to an end. There are still a few dedicated users, but, for most people, the gloop went the way of the hula

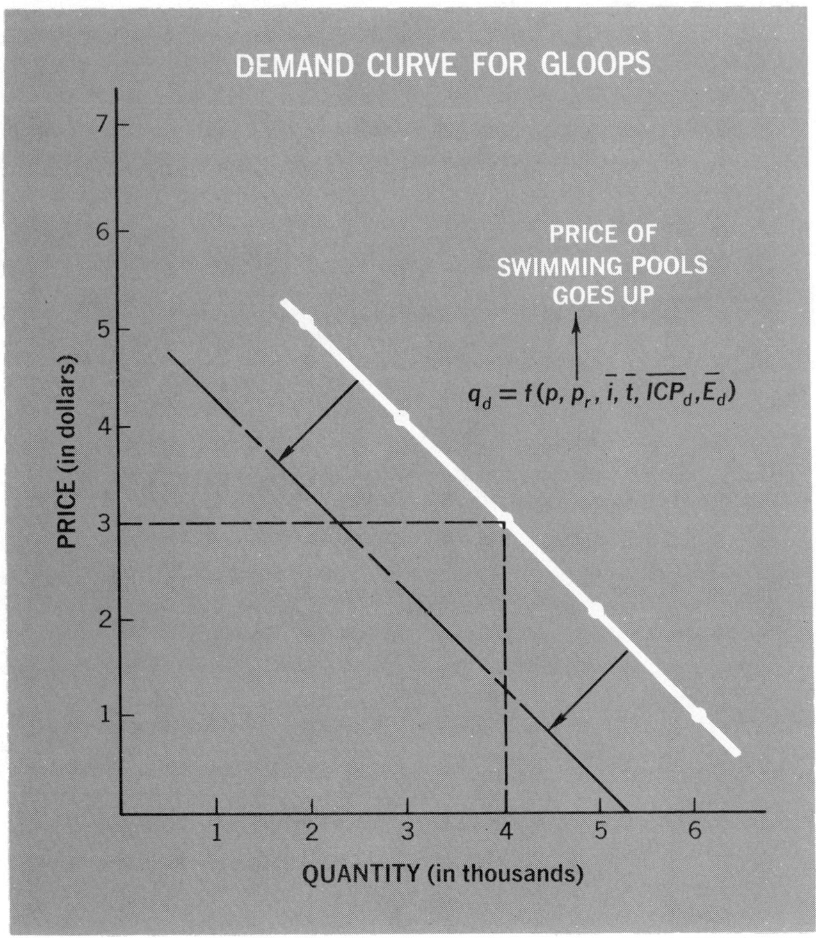

Figure 4-4

hoop. With the reduced *tastes* for the gloop, its demand fell as illustrated in Figure 4-6.

We now have one half of the analytic tools needed to understand the workings of a market. Notice that so far we do not have sufficient information to determine what the price of a good will be. We can only say the relationship between prices and quantities demanded has been established in a given market at a given time with a given set of *ceteris paribus* conditions.

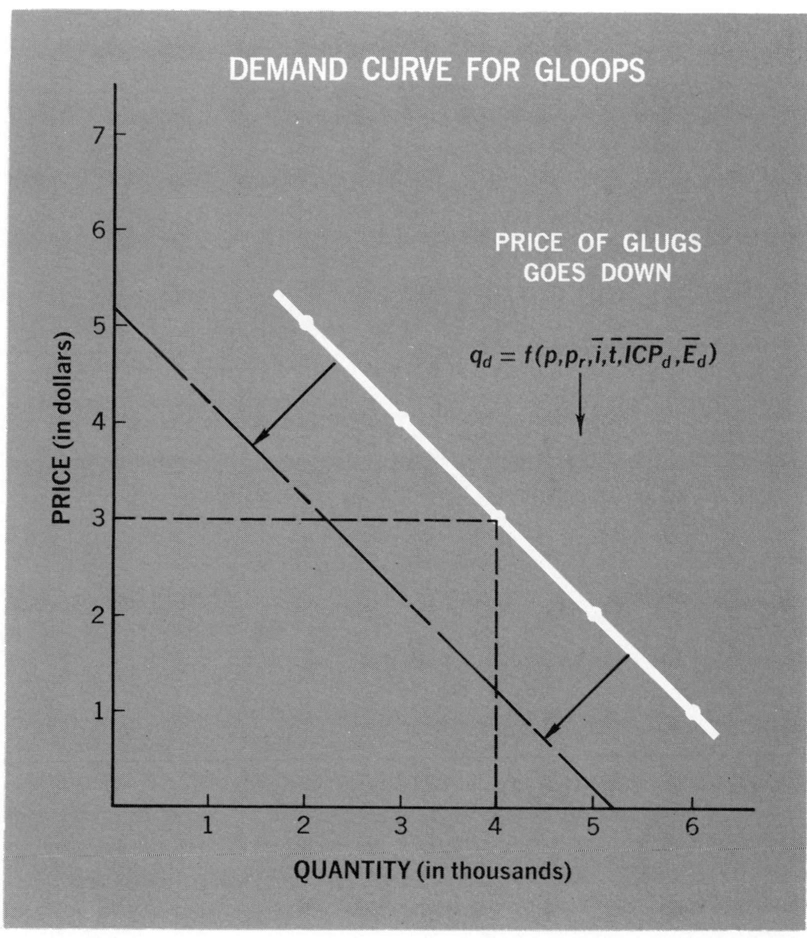

Figure 4-5

ELASTICITY OF DEMAND

Before we go into the other side of the market operation—the supply side—there is one most important concept to master. So far we have said about demand that price and quantity demanded are inversely related—one goes up and the other goes down. But another question is just *how much* quantity demanded changes with a given change in price. There are several good reasons for having some measure of this responsiveness, not only for the demand relationships, but for looking at other variables as well. Just

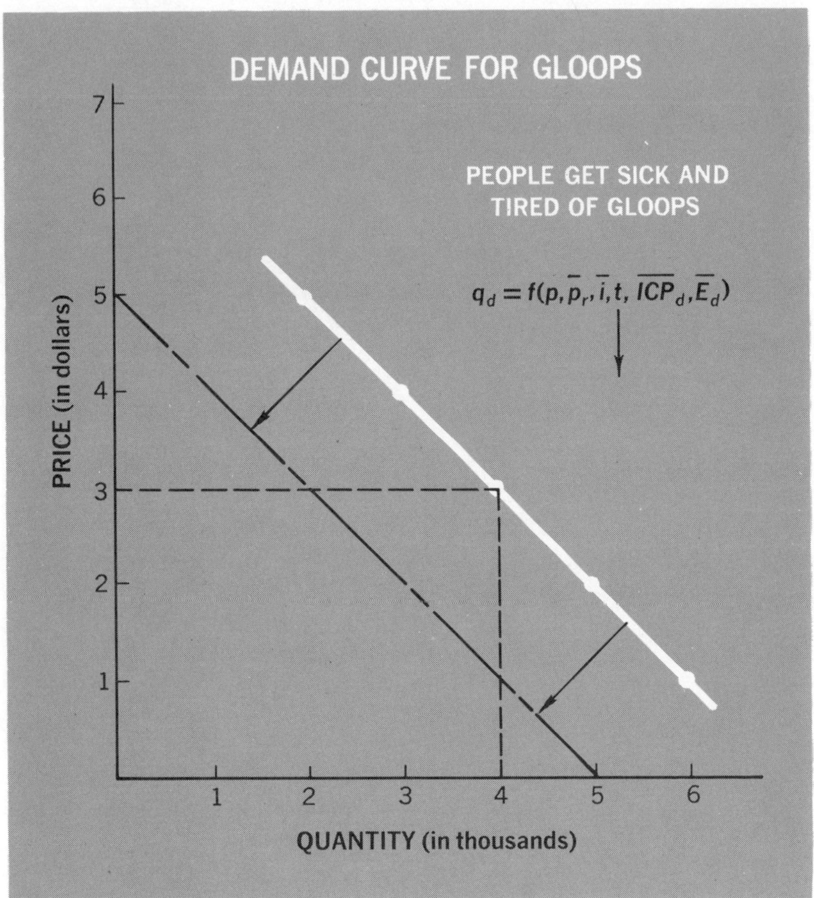

Figure 4-6

saying that the price falling by one dollar will increase the quantity demanded by 1,000 units is not enough. Absolute changes in price and quantities demanded are not as important as the relative changes in these two variables.

The tool that we use to measure relative changes between two variables is called *elasticity*. A general definition of elasticity is the relative amount one variable changes, given a change in another variable. Another way of saying this is by talking about the *percentage* change in one variable *per* percentage change in another.

Because the question immediately at hand involves price and quantity changes associated with demand, we define *price elasticity of demand* as

ELASTICITY is the RELATIVE amount one variable changes, given a change in another variable

or

$$\epsilon = \frac{\%\text{ change in } A}{\%\text{ change in } B}$$

PRICE ELASTICITY is the percentage of change (Δ) in quantity, given a percentage of change in price:

$$\epsilon_P = \frac{\% \Delta Q}{\% \Delta P}$$

Figure 4-7

the percentage change in quantity demanded, given one percent change in the price (see Figure 4-7). It is important to note that the *slope* of the demand curve is the ratio between price change and quantity change. *This is not elasticity*. Elasticity is the ratio of *percentage* changes in quantity and prices. *Elasticity is not slope.* As will be seen in an example at the end of this section, if two lines go through a point on a graph, then the steeper one will be less elastic than the flatter one. *Comparative* elasticities can be shown by *comparative* slopes on graphs with the same scales on the axes. But the slope of a line by itself does not measure elasticity.

Let us now return to the demand schedule for gloops. This is reproduced in Figure 4-8 with the addition of another column titled "Total Revenue." This is the total amount of money that would have been paid for gloops at different prices. It is arrived at by the process of multiplying the different prices by their corresponding quantities demanded. But, getting back to the arithmetic of elasticity, at a price level of $5.00, 2,000 gloops would be demanded. The *average price* between $5.00 and $4.00 is $4.50. The price change between the two points is $1.00. Hence, the *average* percentage change in this range is $1.00 divided by $4.50, or approximately 22 percent. The average quantity in the range of 2,000 to 3,000 is 2,500, and the total change in the range is 1,000. Hence, the *average* percentage change in quantity in this range equals 1,000 divided by 2,500, or 40 percent. The average elasticity of demand on the demand curve between prices of $5.00 and $4.00 is equal to the percentage change in quantity (40 percent) divided by the percentage change in price (22 percent), or approximately 1.8 (greater than one). In other words, in this range of the demand curve, a percentage change in price produced a *greater* percentage change in quantity demanded.

DEMAND & TOTAL REVENUE SCHEDULE FOR GLOOPS

Price	Quantity Demanded	Total Revenue
$5.00	2,000	$10 M
$4.00	3,000	$12 M
$3.00	4,000	$12 M
$2.00	5,000	$10 M
$1.00	6,000	$6 M

Figure 4-8

Now, look at the next range. Between $4.00 and $3.00, the average price is $3.50. The price change is again $1.00. The percentage change in price is about 29 percent. The quantities corresponding to these prices are 3,000 and 4,000 respectively, or an average quantity in the range of 3,500. The change in quantity is again 1,000 units. The percentage change is therefore equal to 1,000 divided by 3,500, or about 29 percent. On the average in this range, a percentage change in price produced an equal percentage change in quantity demanded. The coefficient of elasticity equals 29 percent divided by 29 percent, or 1.0. On another level, we see that in the range of $3.00 to $2.00, the average price is $2.50, the price change again is $1.00, which gives a percentage price change of 40 percent. Corresponding quantity changes are 4,000 to 5,000 for an average value of 4,500 units. The quantity change of 1,000 units produces a percentage quantity change equal to about 22 percent. The coefficient of elasticity now equals 22 percent divided by 40 percent, or about .55—*less than one*. In this case, a percentage change in price brought forth a *smaller* percentage change in quantity demanded.

These three examples illustrate the three ranges of possible price elasticity of demand. Where percentage price changes produce percentage quantity changes that are greater, the coefficient of elasticity is greater than one and demand is said to be in the elastic range. Where the two percentage changes are exactly equal, the coefficient of elasticity equals one, and we have what is known as *unitary* or *unit elasticity*. Finally, where the percentage change in quantity is less than the percentage change in price, the coefficient is less than one, and demand is said to be inelastic. There you have the mechanics of elasticity, but what does it all mean?

Let's return to the last column in Figure 4-8—the total revenue column. This is the total money that would be spent by demanders at different prices and also the total money received by suppliers at those different prices. Because we are talking about demand, a change in price will produce an opposite change in quantity demanded. Lowering the price increases the quantity demanded. Raising the price decreases the quantity demanded. Because total revenue is the result of multiplying price and quantity, total revenue could either rise or fall with a given change in price. Use a price decrease for an example. If price is lowered by 1 percent, and as a result the quantity demanded rises by more than 1 percent, then multiplying the new price and quantity demanded will yield a larger number than before. Total revenue will have *risen* with a *decrease* in the price. At prices between $5.00 and $3.50, this is precisely the case. In the elastic range of the demand curve, a lowering of the price will increase total revenue spent on the good. At unitary elasticity of demand, price and quantity changes exactly offset each other and total revenue remains constant. In the inelastic range, percent price decreases are greater than corresponding percentage quantity increases, and, therefore, total revenue falls. Of course, with talk about price increases rather than price decreases, the whole thing is reversed.

Figures 4-9 through 4-13 show the effects on total revenue of falling prices in a graphical manner. Figure 4-9 shows the total revenue as the area included between the axes, the $5.00 price line, and the 2,000 unit quantity line. Figure 4-10 compares the total revenues of the $5.00 and $4.00 prices. The drop in price causes a loss in revenue for the $5.00 box (the upper cross-hatched area), but a large gain in revenue results from the increase in quantity demanded from 2,000 to 3,000 units at the $4.00 price. In Figure

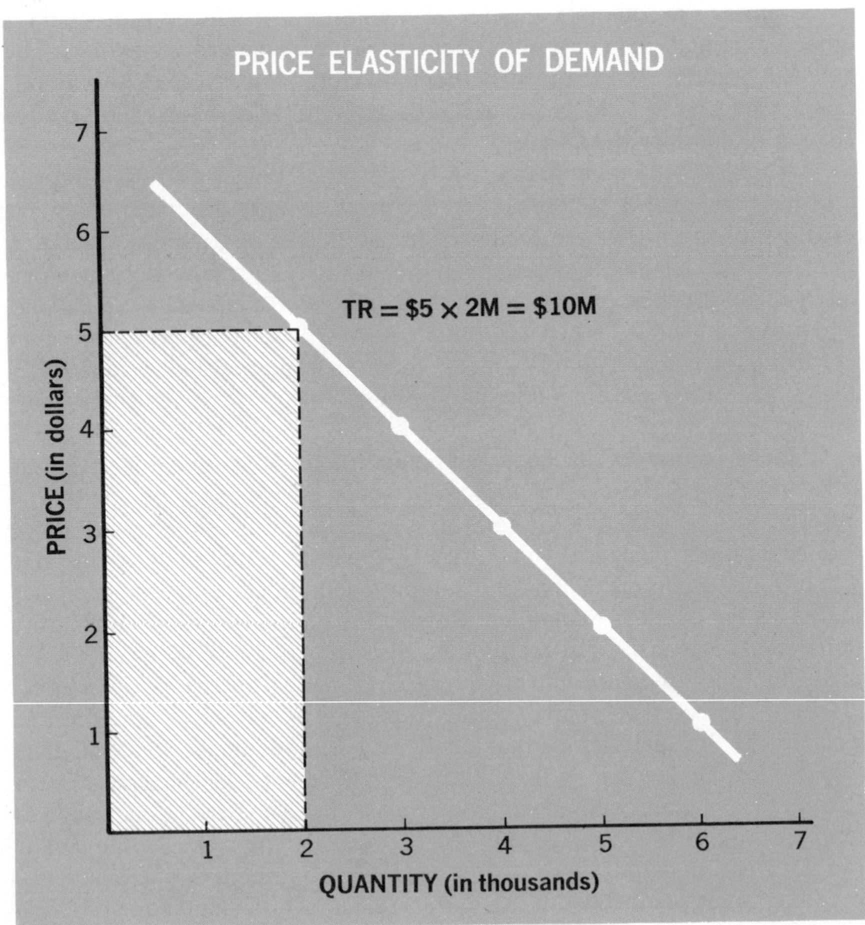

Figure 4-9

4-11, the price drop from $4.00 to $3.00 results in lost revenue of the same amount ($3,000) as is gained from the quantity increase (also $3,000). Decreases in the price from $3.00 to $2.00, and from $2.00 to $1.00, both result in larger losses than the gains picked up from increased quantities demanded, as in Figures 4-12 and 4-13.

Although it has been emphasized that elasticity and slope are not the same thing, it was also brought out that comparative elasticities could be determined from demand curves that passed through the same point on a graph. An example of this is shown in Figures 4-14 and 4-15. In Figure 4-14, the average elasticity of demand between $4.00 and $3.00 is 4.1; in other

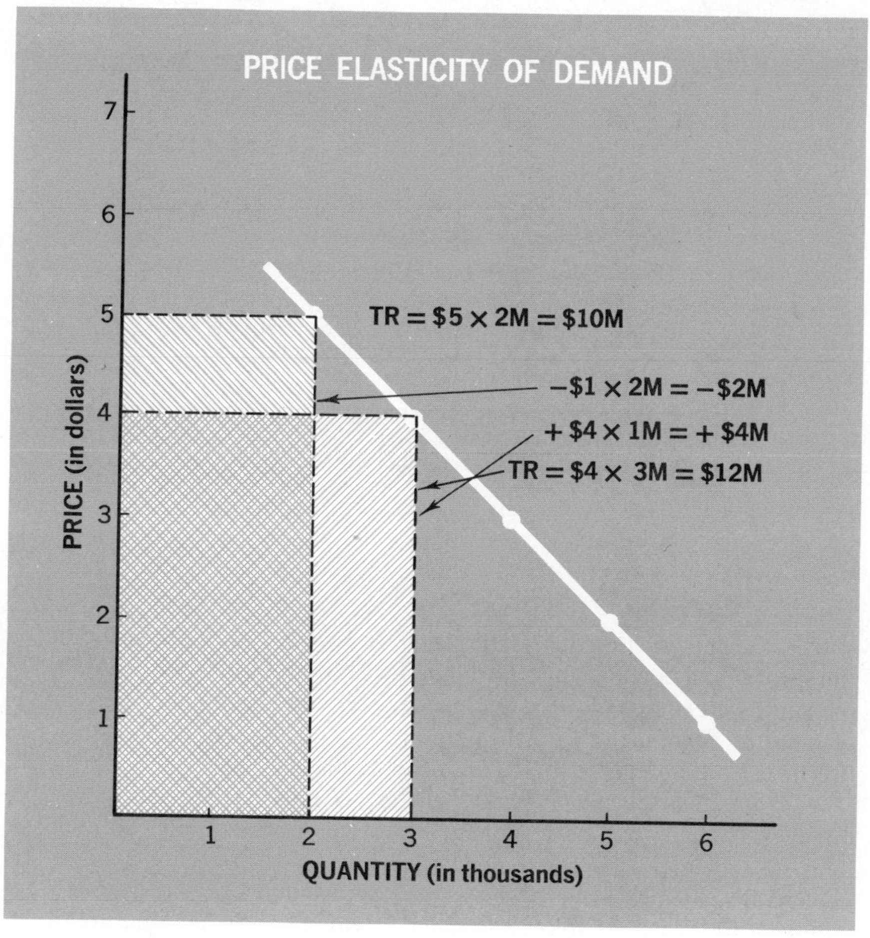

Figure 4-10

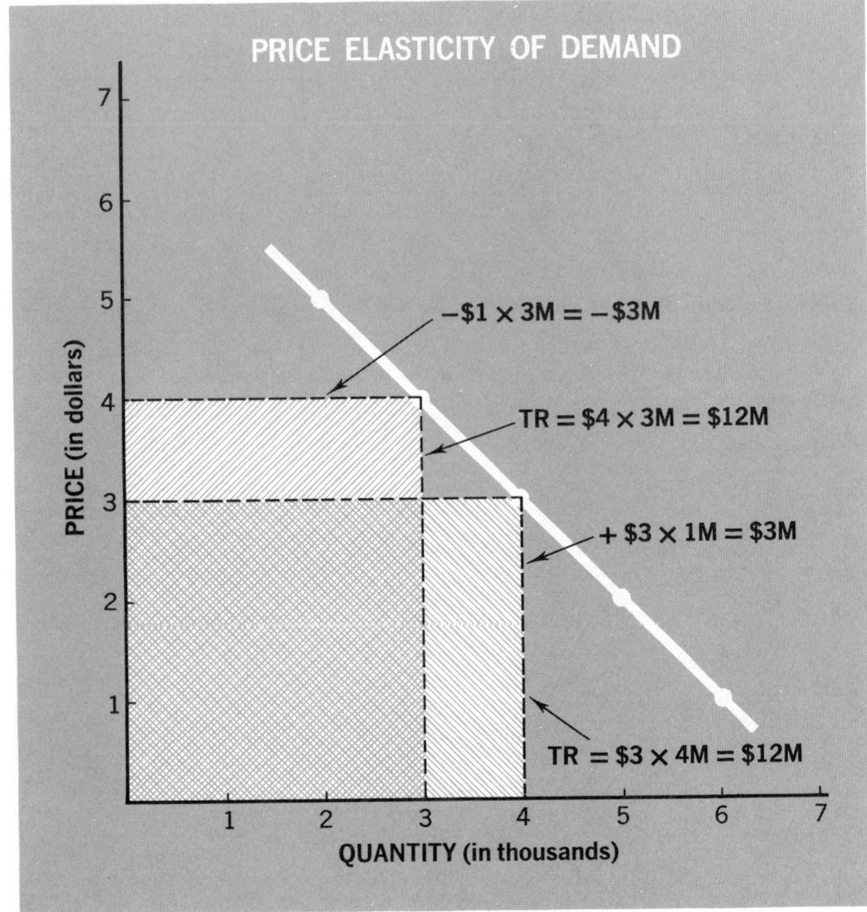

Figure 4-11

words, the demand is in the elastic range. In Figure 4-15, we have increased the slope of the demand curve through the $3.00 and 4,000 unit point. Now, the same percentage of price decrease (29 percent) results in a percentage of quantity increase of only 13 percent. Our coefficient of elasticity has dropped from an elastic 4.1 to an inelastic 0.45.

What does elasticity really tell us? It tells us just how sensitive quantity changes will be to changes in price. For example, an inelastic demand indicates that relatively large changes in price are going to be needed in order to bring about significant changes in the quantity demanded. By the same token, an elastic demand indicates that comparatively large changes in quantity demanded will take place with small changes in the price of the good.

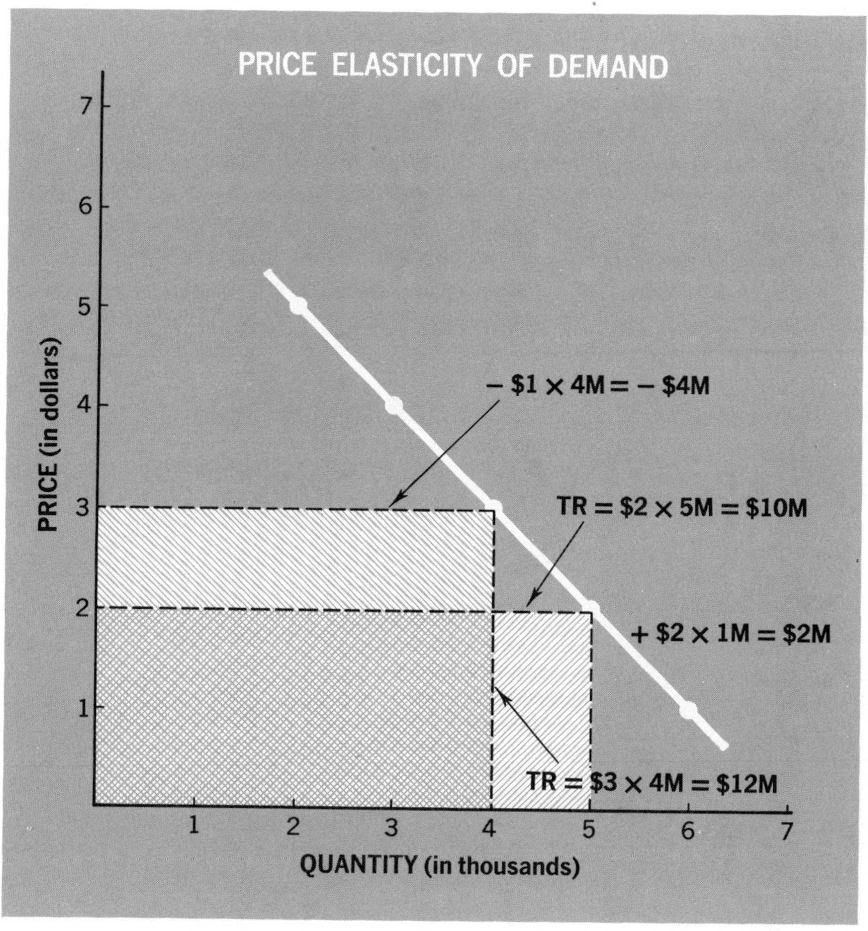

Figure 4-12

It is possible to identify some of the characteristics of goods that affect their demand elasticities. If a good is a necessity, say, drinking water in a desert, one would expect that people would be relatively uninterested in the price that they had to pay for enough water to stay alive. In other words, price could vary widely and they would still demand about the same quantity. Demand would tend to be inelastic, and so it is for most of the necessities of life. Goods that represent a very small portion of a person's total expenditures also tend to have inelastic demands. If the price of table salt rises from ten cents a box to eleven cents per box, this is a substantial *percentage* increase, and yet each person's consumption of salt probably will not change much. If the price of automobiles were to go up by 10 percent, say from $3,000 to $3,300, a significant drop in quantity demanded

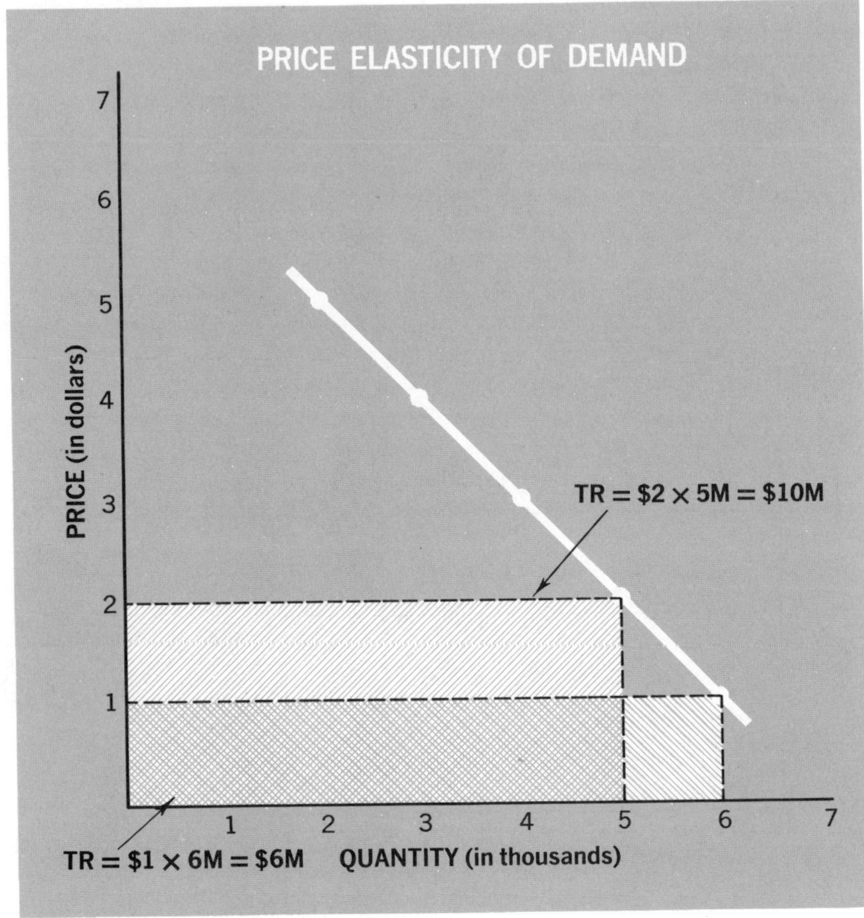

Figure 4-13

could be expected (*ceteris paribus*) because $300 is still a large amount of money.

Finally, the availability of many substitutes for a good will tend to make the demand for the good comparatively elastic. If blended whiskey is the only liquor for sale, one could predict that the quantity of blended whiskey demanded would be less affected by price than would be the case if good bourbon and scotch were available at similar prices. Increased availability of substitutes will also tend to decrease demand for the given good as well as increase the elasticity of demand for the product.

Before leaving the mechanics of elasticity, look at the demand curve with the particular shape found in Figure 4-16. We will be encountering this

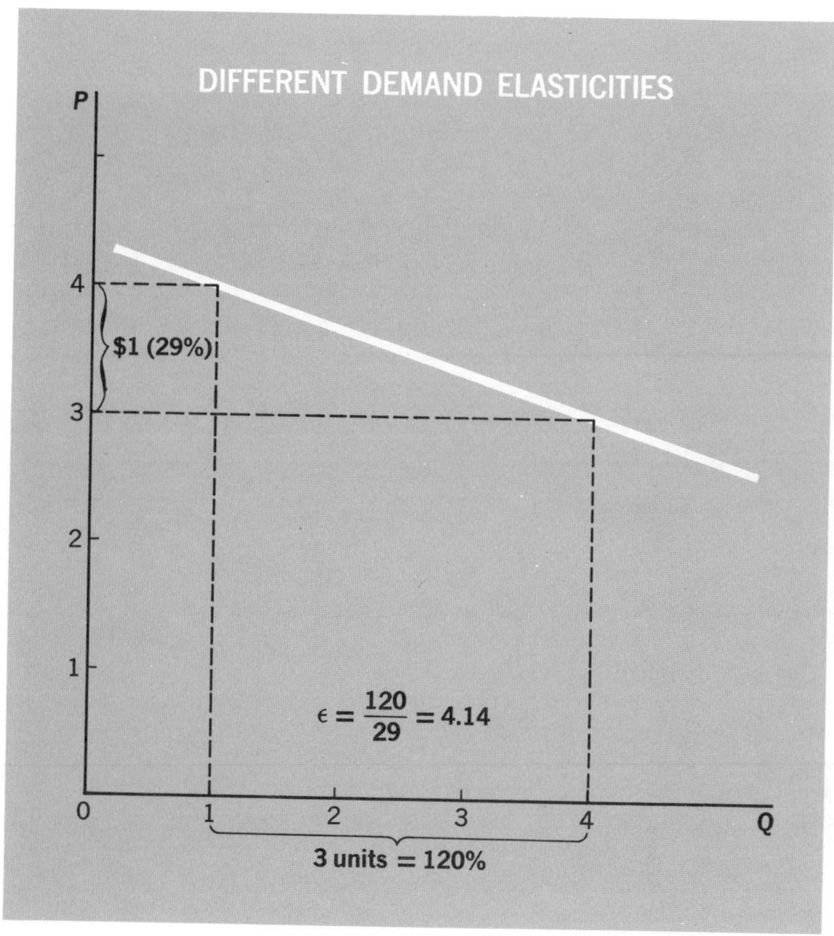

Figure 4-14

demand curve when we get to the subject of money. This is a demand curve with unitary elasticity along its entire length. This means that any time a price on the demand curve is multiplied by its corresponding quantity demanded, the result will be the same—a constant total revenue. From your geometry course, you may remember the *rectangular hyperbola* as shown in Figure 4-16. Geometrically, the area of any box, such as *Ofga*, will equal the area of any other box constructed under the curve, such as *Oehb* or *Odic*. Economically, this means that exactly the same total money will be spent on this product regardless of price. Lower prices will always generate just enough additional quantity demanded to keep total revenue or total expenditures exactly the same.

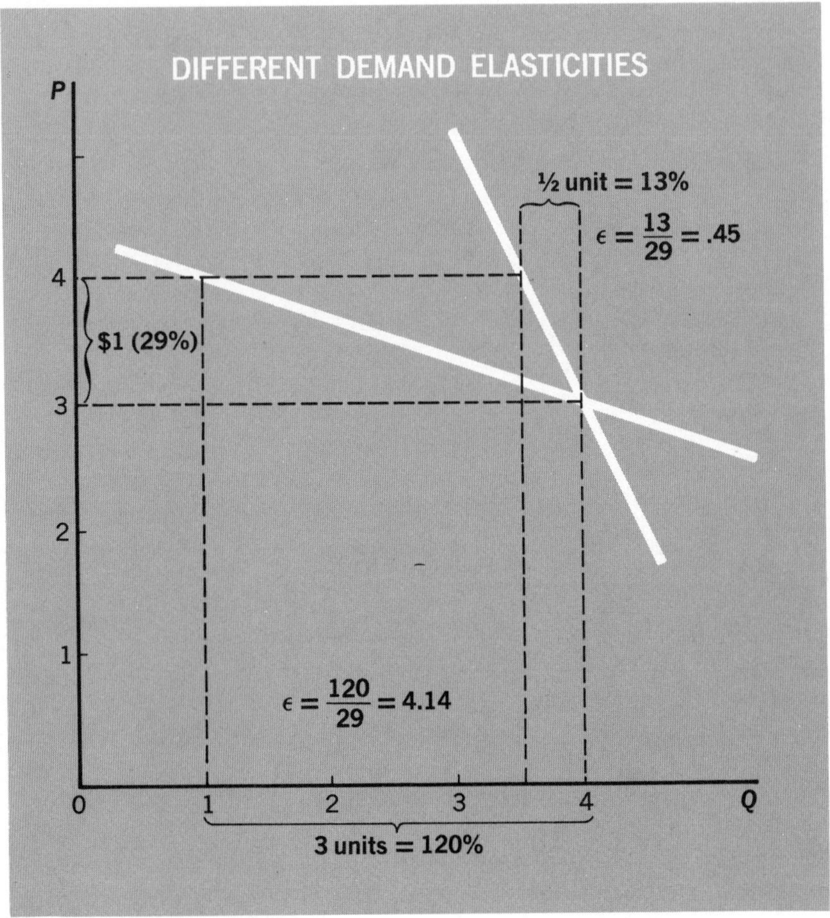

Figure 4-15

We will be talking about several other applications of the idea of elasticity as the book goes along, but if you understand price elasticity of demand, the rest will be comprehended easily.

QUESTIONS

1. Make a list of some items that you consider *needs* in your life, but which someone else might not.
2. How are needs or wants expressed in a market system? How might these be expressed in a system that does not use markets?

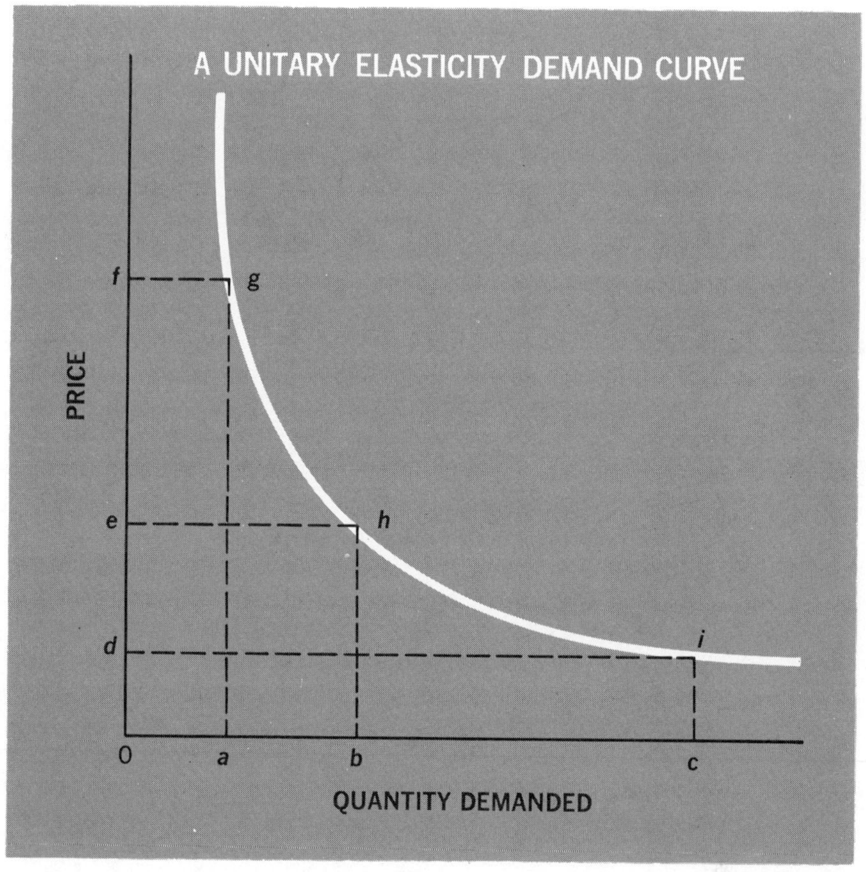

Figure 4-16

3. In the recent past, the price of beef has jumped considerably over previous levels. List ten products of which you would expect the price to rise and five other products for which you would expect price declines.
4. The actual purchasing power of people in the U.S. has been increasing for many years. List ten products for which you would expect an increase in price relative to other goods, taking this fact into consideration. What other factors might occur at the same time to reduce expected price rises?
5. This is probably the simplest question in the book, but one of the most important. Describe exactly the difference between a change in demand and a change in the quantity demanded.

6. List ten products that you have purchased recently for which you would expect the demand to be relatively *inelastic*. Explain why for each one. Now do the same thing for products that you would expect to have elastic demands.

5

Costs and Supply

OBJECTIVES

Essentially, the quantity of a good that people are willing and able to provide to the marketplace depends upon the cost *of producing that good. Costs are incurred because scarce resources called* factors of production *are used to make goods. Again, the concept of* opportunity costs *comes up. Factors of production include production and entrepreneurial labor; and capital goods can be broken down as producible, depletable, and energy. Costs and output (quantity supplied) can vary proportionally (constant costs); costs can increase faster than output (increasing costs); or less rapidly than costs (decreasing costs). The way costs and output vary can influence the nature of the industry as far as the degree of competition that may exist. The costs of firms in an industry can be aggregated to give a picture of the industrial situation. From industry costs, one can arrive, at least conceptually, at the relationship between the price suppliers can receive for their product and the quantity they will be willing and able to supply. With some important exceptions, it is assumed that increased prices will bring forth increased levels of output in most enterprises.*

INTRODUCTION

Demand comes from people's wants plus people's ability to get resources to spend satisfying those wants. Supply, very simply, depends one hundred percent on *costs*. At this level of analysis, we will look at the costs of individual firms within some particular industry and then add those costs up to obtain industry costs. There are some problems involved in handling costs this way, but it works out reasonably well.

COSTS

What sorts of costs go into the production of anything? That is a simple question in some ways, but its implications could fill volumes. Costs are generated because *factors of production*—those special goods that are used to produce other goods—are *scarce* and because they can produce something of value to someone. As recapped in Figure 5-1, factors are paid because they are *scarce* and because they are *productive*. In a market system, they are paid according to the value of what they produce. This repeats the opportunity cost idea. They will receive a wage *at least* equal to

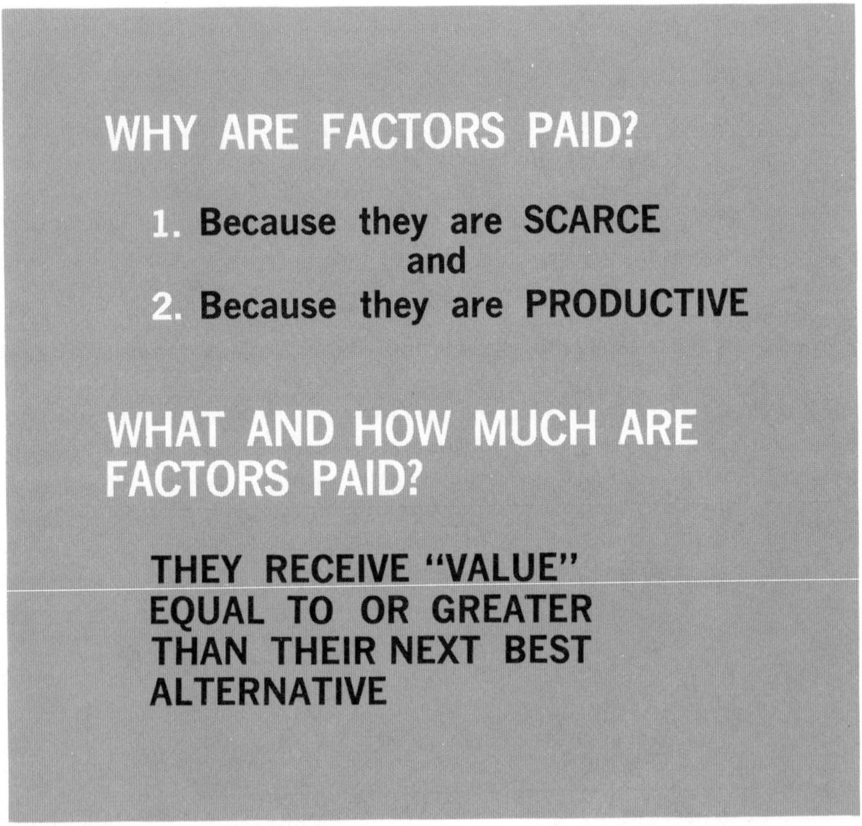

WHY ARE FACTORS PAID?

1. Because they are SCARCE
   and
2. Because they are PRODUCTIVE

WHAT AND HOW MUCH ARE FACTORS PAID?

THEY RECEIVE "VALUE" EQUAL TO OR GREATER THAN THEIR NEXT BEST ALTERNATIVE

Figure 5-1

or greater than the value of their next best producing alternative. Of course, *next best* means next best as they view the alternative. It does not necessarily mean next best in terms simply of money wages.

This idea can be illustrated by using the air example presented earlier. Without air (fresh or otherwise), we would cease to function as human beings in a very short time. Air, or at least oxygen, is essential to sustain life itself. In this sense, air is very *productive* indeed. However, in day-to-day living, there is generally plenty of air for everyone. It is not scarce in the economic sense of having to give up something to obtain it. Even if air were scarce in some absolute sense, we would be unwilling to give up anything for it unless it were to contribute to our life, health, or well-being in some form—unless it were *productive*. Productivity and scarcity, therefore, are the reasons why factors of production are paid. They are paid by the enterprise that employs them to produce. But, of course, the resources with which these factors are paid must ultimately come from those who buy the product of the firm. This assumes an absence of any kind of subsidy that could and would change this statement. With that exception, factors are paid from revenue received by firms in payment for the products of the factors.

How much they are paid will depend on their relative scarcity and productivity. It is safe to say, however, that factors that are free to move will never be paid a wage less than their next best alternative. Think about it in terms of your own experience. If you are working for a wage of two dollars per hour, the chances are that you have checked, at least to some extent, to find out if a better alternative exists (higher wages) for your particular skills and your particular desires for employment. This last phrase implies that *wages*, to you, include more than just money wages. This is the usual case. It is possible you could earn three dollars per hour if you were willing to take a job cleaning sewers. For at least some, however, the *disutility* of cleaning sewers is greater than the extra dollar per hour in money wages that could be earned in this job compared to operating a cash register in a supermarket. It is for this reason that the *what* factors received may be just as important as the *how much*. *Psychic income* must be included if alternatives are to be compared in a meaningful way.

In a productive operation, how and why does the pie get split among various factors? Assume that a technological innovation appears on the scene that makes some machine much more productive than labor. At first, there will be an attempt on the part of the enterprise's managers to substitute more capital for less labor. This will increase the quantity of capital employed, decrease the quantity of labor employed, raise the price of capital (demand for capital has increased), and lower the price of labor (demand for labor has decreased). Remember the whole discussion about demands for substitute goods in Chapter 4. The manager of the enterprise will constantly seek the combination of inputs that will yield the output he desires at the *lowest possible total cost.* The analogy to your own behavior as consumers is still useful. Each one of you tries to find that combination of goods that will yield you the greatest satisfaction for the smallest expenditure of your resources. When substitutes (as you evaluate the substitute) become cheaper, you will tend to use more of the cheaper item and less of the more expensive one.

Before going any further, let us look again at just what we are talking about when we use the term *factor of production.* There are several ways to break down factors into useful and logical categories. A simple one is to put everything together as either *labor* or *capital.* When this is done, one is then saying that all production takes place because of either human effort (labor), or more commonly, by this effort combined with something else that is useful in the production process (capital, in the broadest sense). Even this breakdown is not clearcut. In a very real sense, any kind of training that improves man's skills or ability to enjoy life represents an investment in *human capital.* Most of man's abilities come from just such investment. Latent or natural abilities are important, but without some kind of training, these talents usually do not count for much. In other words, much productive human effort can be viewed as resulting from human capital investment.

In most of our discussions we will use the term *labor* to represent productive human effort of any kind. But there are times in the discussions when it will be important to explicitly consider changes in the economy's "stock" of human capital. So, whether a person is working on an assembly line, programming a computer, or keeping the accounts of a major company, it all is labor as far as we are concerned.

In passing, it is a good idea to mention one special category of labor that is most important in any production economy. *Entrepreneurship* is the creative or innovative *function* that puts together other factors of production in a way that permits goods to be produced. In some businesses, the function is performed by the owner himself. In large corporate enterprises, the function is often difficult to pinpoint as being performed by a single individual or even a group of individuals, such as a board of directors or management team. But the function is essential. Even in firms operating in controlled economies, some one or some group must make the crucial enterpreneurial decisions of how much to produce and what combinations of inputs to use. Because the function is *necessary* and those able to perform it successfully are *scarce*, one would expect that an economy would provide incentives and rewards for those performing the function just like any other factor of production. And, so it is.

When it comes to capital, again it is very useful to break down the general category into subsets. The first of these is the most obvious and the most generally considered as capital. We will call it *producible capital.* It includes the normal run of factory buildings, machines, tools, road systems, electric distribution systems, warehouses, and stocks of finished goods held as inventories. They are producible capital because, given other resources, they can be replaced when used up or destroyed.

The next category we will call *depletable capital.* Sometimes this is also called *natural resources* but *depletable* catches the main characteristic of the group. Minerals, ancient forests, flowing water, flowing air, and the oceans of the earth are all part of this capital component. The most important thing about depletable capital is the fact that once used (or in the case of air and water, overused for the wrong purposes), it cannot be replaced.

A final category of capital that increasingly concerns us and often is included in the natural resource group is *energy sources.* In the past, much of this type of capital came from natural resources such as coal, oil, wood, water, and animal power. Now, with the advent of nuclear power and possibilities of solar power, there is reason to set it apart from the usual grouping of natural resources or depletable capital.

Figure 5-2 summarizes the breakdown of factors of production that will be used throughout the rest of this book. Again, remember that a good deal of arbitrariness goes into this or any other specification of factors.

COSTS AND SCALE OF OUTPUT

One thing that the economist is interested in knowing concerns the way in which costs vary as the output of either an industry or firms within an industry changes. Right here is a good place to clear up one potential misconception. If something of market value is being produced, then scarce resources are being used up in the production process. If this is the case, then increased output of the good *always* means that *total* costs of production will rise. Of course, some new method of production could come along (and it often does) that makes it possible to produce the same quantity of a good for less cost, but that is a different point. With a given method of production, producing *more* will cost *more*. How *much* more is one of the things to look at right now.

There are three ways that total costs can increase when a firm increases its level of production or output. First of all, increased units of output may cost just the same amount to produce as previously produced units had cost. The first unit of output might cost a dollar, the second a dollar, the third a dollar, and so forth. The cost of producing one more or one less would stay the same at any *level* of output. In Figure 5-3, this type of cost is illustrated by curve *A*. The cost curve is actually a straight line, and the straight line runs through the origin of the graph. Another way of

WHAT ARE FACTORS OF PRODUCTION?

SPECIAL GOODS USED TO PRODUCE OTHER GOODS, INCLUDING:

LABOR
Production
Entrepreneurial

CAPITAL
Producible
Depletable
Energy

Figure 5-2

describing this type of cost function is to say that total costs increase *proportionally* with increases in output. A doubling of output will cause a doubling of costs. A tripling of output will triple costs. This type of cost function is called *constant costs*. Again, constant costs certainly does *not* mean that total costs stay the same with increases in output. It says that the *rate of change* in total costs will be the same as the *rate of change* in output. The cost of producing an *additional* unit of output will be the same as the one produced just before it.

Curve *B* illustrates another possibility. In this case, costs are again increasing as output increases, but the rate of cost increase is greater than the rate of output increase. Costs are increasing *more than proportionally* to output increases. Output can be increased only if the firm is willing to spend more to produce additional units than it did in producing units at lower levels of output. This type of cost function is called *increasing costs*.

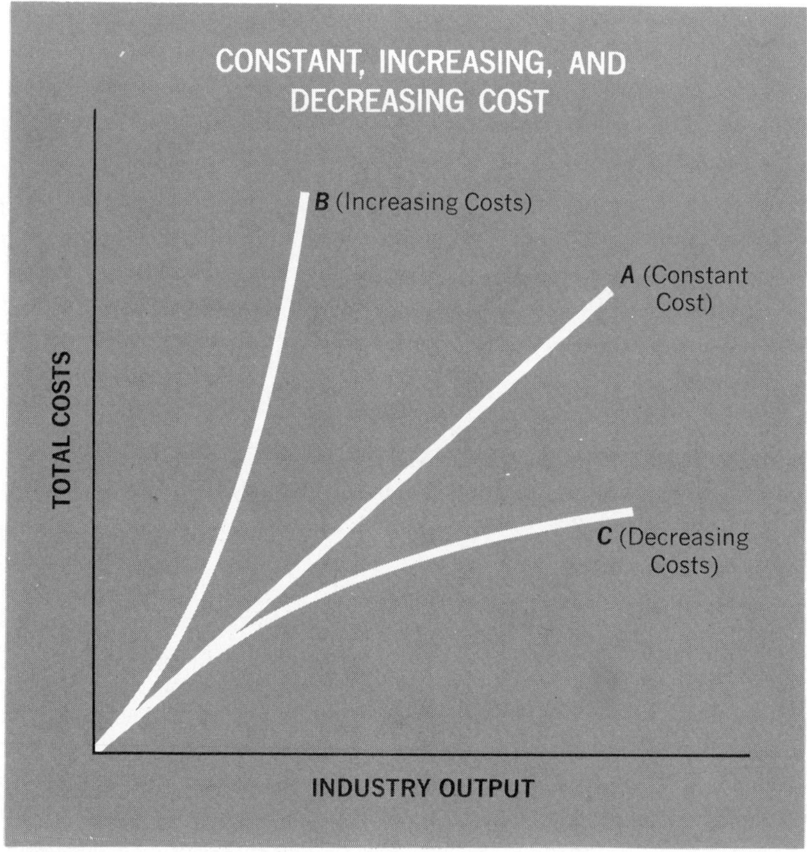

Figure 5-3

Finally, the third possible type of cost function is illustrated by Curve *C*. In this instance, an increase in the level of output will again increase total costs, but the increase will be proportionally less than the increase in output. The cost of producing additional units will be less than the cost of previously produced units. For example, if the firm doubles output, it will *less than* double total costs.

What, then, does the cost curve for a typical firm look like? We can get some interesting insight into the answer to that question by asking what would happen to a firm and the industry in which the firm is operating, given different cost conditions. In the first place, assume that each firm in an industry is faced with *decreasing costs* throughout the range of outputs that would be marketable. This would mean that any firm that got a little bigger than any other firm would be able to produce more cheaply than its competitors. In other words, whichever firm could get the biggest the most quickly would take over the entire industry. No new entry would be possible or practical unless the new firm could begin operating at a scale larger than that of the existing firms. This type of cost situation would lead to a *natural monopoly*. It is *natural* because of the technological nature of the cost function. The bigger the scale, the cheaper are additional units produced, and, therefore, the cheaper would be the average cost of producing all units. A quick look around would show that there are very few industries or firms within industries that exhibit that kind of behavior. Only in industries like electric power generation or communications do we find this kind of a cost situation. Even in these cases, there is some question whether decreasing costs exist throughout the *entire* possible production range. Even in these industries, there is evidence that very large scale leads to *increasing costs* at some point.

How about a firm that had increasing costs throughout its entire range of possible production? Increasing costs throughout the entire output range would mean that if one firm could get *smaller* than its competitors, it would produce its output at a *cheaper* per unit cost. Competition, in this case, would cause *firms* to get smaller and smaller until they all virtually disappeared. The only way the industry could survive would be to have some kind of protection from the competition. Again, a look around would indicate that this type of cost function is probably not very typical either. Many firms *do* exist in most industries, and there does not seem to be any major trend for them to get smaller and smaller.

Typically, the total cost curves for most industries and also for most firms within those industries probably exhibit all three types of costs. Most likely, firms operating at relatively low levels of output will be able to increase that output at a *cheaper* cost for additional units. In other words, at low levels of output, most firms would be in a decreasing cost range. But as the output of the firm increases, sooner or later it is likely that some factor will either be less productive or cost more. In this case, the firm will run into an increasing cost situation. Figure 5-4 illustrates what we are talking about. The firms's total cost curve is shown as *Ocde*. Between output levels *O* and *Oa*, costs of producing additional units of output are decreasing. But at point *c*, the firm runs into increasing costs and at all levels above output *Oa*, the costs of producing additional units increase.

Notice that there is a line drawn through the origin of the graph and tangent to the total cost curve at point *d*. The *slope* of this line is significant in that it represents the *average cost* of producing any level of output along the line. Average cost is *total cost* (the vertical axis) divided by the level of output (the horizontal axis) that produces the given total cost. So, at point *d*, the total cost of output level *Ob* equals *Og*. The average cost of each unit of production at level *Ob* equals *Og*/*Ob*, which is also the slope of line *Of*.

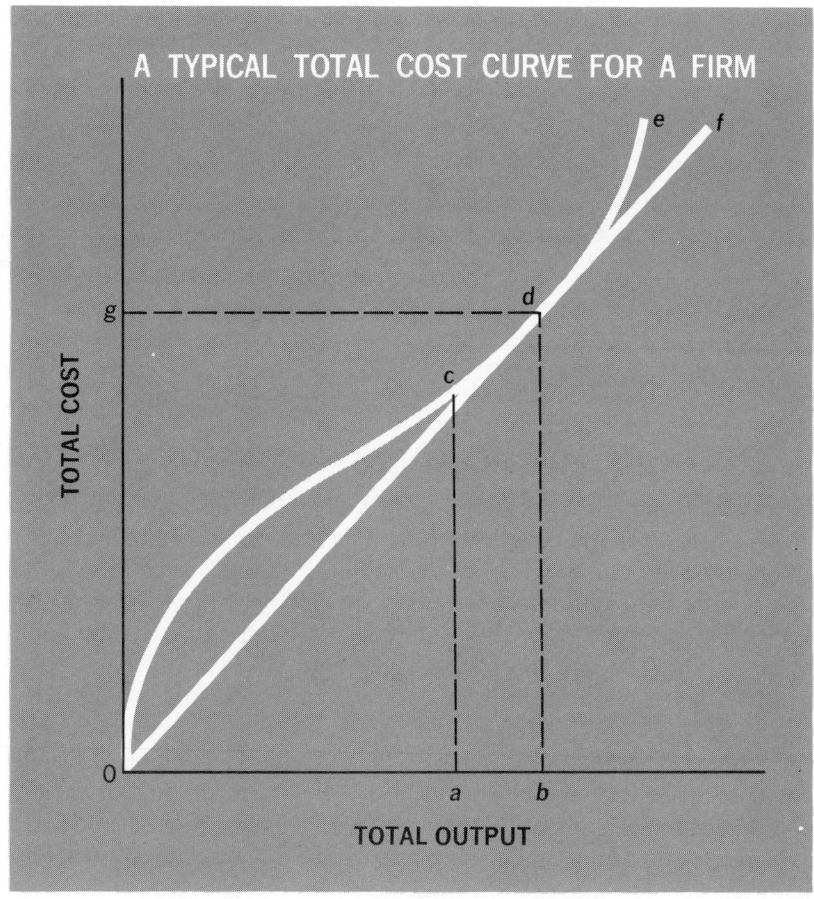

Figure 5-4

If you draw any other line through the origin that *intersects* the total cost curve, you will find that the slope of such a line will be greater than that of *Of*. This is no graphical accident.

The economics of this geometry goes like this. As long as a firm is in an output range of decreasing costs, then the *average* cost of producing all of the units will be falling. Assuming that higher output levels will put the firm in a range of increasing costs, then at some point after those increasing costs begin, the average cost of producing total output will begin to rise. Just before that development, the average cost of producing the total output will be at a *minimum*. That is the output level *Ob* in Figure 5-4. Any line through the origin that would intersect the total cost curve to the left of point *d* would have a greater slope than line *Of*. Average costs would be higher. Any line intersecting the total cost curve to the right of point *d* would also have a greater slope (higher average cost). The slope of tangent line *Of* is as low as possible, indicating the lowest possible average cost for the cost function illustrated. At output level *Ob*, total cost equals *Og*, and *Og*/*Ob* is the lowest possible ratio.

The significance of this lowest average cost output level will be explained in the upcoming chapter on pricing and output. But at this point, it can be seen that if something would force firms to operate at minimum average cost levels, then the resources used in the production of *all* units would be minimized.

PROFIT AS A COST

This section will use the word "profit" in a special way. Included as part of costs will be a certain amount of what accountants call *profit*. If a businessman is asked for a simple definition of profit, he will probably say that it is the difference between what he takes in and pays out. If, over the long pull, he manages to sell his product for a bit more than it costs him, he figures that he has made a profit. The trouble with this simple idea is that there are many things entering into the public's calculation of profit that the economist would not put there. There is also one thing that usually *does not* enter into that same calculation of profit that the economist *would* put there.

In the first place, some businesses, particularly small businesses, are owned and run by people who have a substantial amount of their own capital invested in the firm. They may own their own buildings, tools, and so on, and not owe anyone else a nickel. If, in this case, they consider just the difference between receipts and expenditures as being profit, they are ignoring the fact that their investment probably has an alternative use from which they could earn some type of return. In other words, the opportunity cost of their own capital used in the business must be considered and deducted from the simple definition of profit. Of course, if they have borrowed the resources to purchase their capital, then the opportunity cost becomes an out-of-pocket cost in the form of interest paid to the lender. Similarly, many small businesses include any labor supplied by the proprietor or his family in profit. Here, again, the individual's opportunity cost—that which he could earn working outside of the business—must be deducted from the excess of receipts over expenditures. In other words, costs must include the full costs of the operation including the opportunity cost of all factors used, not just those that are actually paid for.

This idea of including opportunity costs in with the total costs of a firm needs to be carried one step further. In a market economy, some profits are made. If one firm makes more profit in one endeavor that another firm makes in an alternative endeavor, there is automatically an incentive set up for factor movement into the more profitable operations. Every business enterprise needs *profit* to survive as an enterprise even if this profit might be in nonpecuniary form. There are many farmers who refuse to move to much higher paying jobs in an urban setting because the life style they possess as farmers provides a profit greater than the monetary advantages an urban job would offer. Many students work at part-time jobs. They could earn much higher per-hour wages at full-time jobs, but then they could not carry the course loads that they desire. The "profit" in the lower paid part-time employment consists of being able to carry on a university program and still earn enough to survive through the school year.

The economist, then, includes as a necessary part of costs the *minimum* return that firms require to keep them producing in their given operation. The amount of this profit is such that were it to be reduced, the firm would either stop producing the given level of output or would go into some alternative employment of their productive resources. Any profit greater than this minimum, we call *excess profit* or *economic rent.* From this definition, one can see that when it is said that firms are operating at a point where total revenue and total costs are just equal, at this point firms *will* be making some profit. Again, they will be making just the minimum level of profits that they feel they must have to maintain the productive activity concerned. The total cost figure we are *defining* includes this minimum level of profit.

Some may ask just what percentage this minimum profit actually is. The answer will vary from firm to firm and from industry to industry. Obviously, it will depend on the amount of risk involved in the operation. It will also depend on the expectations of the entrepreneur or business management. And, most assuredly, it will depend heavily on the alternative opportunities for employment of the resources being used. If these opportunities are very good, higher minimum profits would normally be expected.

To summarize, profit is defined as the difference between total revenue received by firms and the total cost of those firms.

$$\text{Profit } (\pi) = \text{Total Revenue } (TR) - \text{Total Costs } (TC)$$

Total costs will be assumed to include the opportunity costs of the factors of production and the minimum profit necessary to keep the firm operating. Thus defined, π becomes excess profit or economic rent.

COSTS AND THE LENGTH OF THE RUN

Everyone has heard people talk about things "in the short run" or something else being the case "in the long run." What does this short run/long run mean? As with some of the other everyday words that we have been using, these phrases mean something quite specific in economics.

When we talk about the "short run," we are talking about a time period that is sufficiently short so that something is *fixed* or cannot vary. As an example, let us say that you buy a car and decide to drive it until it literally falls apart. We will assume also that the time period needed to accomplish this self-destruction is two years. Further assume that the number of miles you actually drive will not change the fall-apart date. If you paid $3,000 for the car, then you will face an average cost of $1,500 each year of the car's life. But once you have bought the car, as long as you do not sell it, this cost of owning is a *fixed cost*. There is nothing you can do about it. If you drive one mile, the cost of just ownership will not be one bit different than if you drive it 100,000 miles. Put another way, the cost of driving additional miles will be some amount based on the gasoline, oil, tire wear, maintenance, and so on associated with additional miles driven. These represent *variable costs*—costs that vary with the output of the car. But the $1,500 per year ownership cost will not change one cent as miles driven (output) varies. This *fixed cost* remains the same.

In our example, the two-year period of ownership represents a *short-run* time period because, during that time, a fixed cost exists. Notice that the only costs that will influence your decision to drive more or less miles will be the out-of-pocket (variable) costs of doing so—the gas, oil, tires, and so on. Once you have made the commitment of the purchase itself, then this cost of ownership does *not* influence the decision of how much output you are going to get out of the car.

Now how about the *long run*? As you can guess, the long run is that period of time that is sufficiently long so that *all* costs—all factor use—become variable. You see, in our example, at the end of two years, you have another decision to make. At that time, the car must be replaced if you are to continue driving. Therefore, at that time, the *fixed cost* of owning the car becomes a variable cost. It becomes a cost that you can either incur again or forego. To drive an additional mile means that you must again spend $3,000.

It should be obvious that long run and short run do not refer to specific periods of time. The short run might run for years in some cases and the long run might happen every day. In the short run, something involving a cost will not vary with output. As a result, in the short run, there will be fixed costs that will not affect *short run* output decisions. In the long run, there are no fixed factors and, hence, there are no fixed costs. *All* costs influence output decisions in the long run.

FROM THE FIRM TO THE INDUSTRY

At least at first glance, going from the costs of individual firms in an industry to the total cost for the industry seems like a simple and uncomplicated process. All there is to do is add up the levels of output of all the firms and add up the total costs associated with each of the summed outputs. Figure 5-5 illustrates a simple example. Assume we have a two-firm indus-

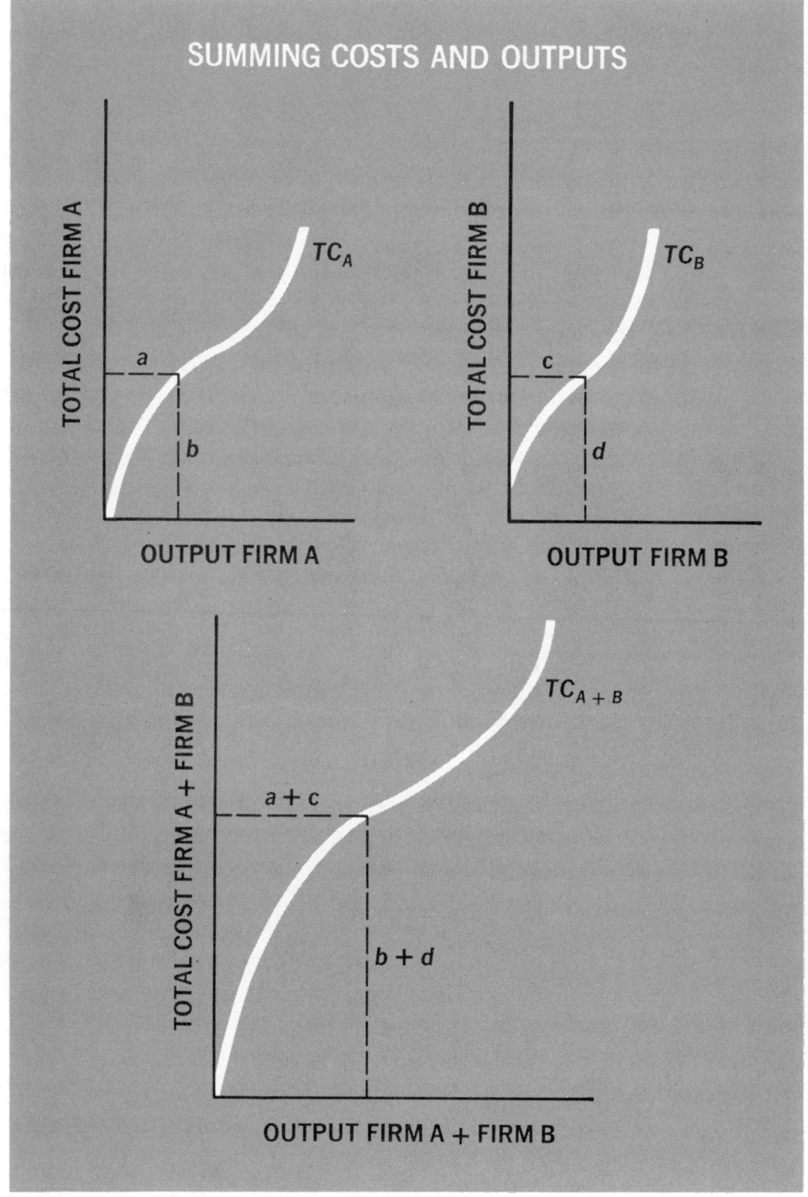

Figure 5-5

try consisting of Firm A and Firm B. With Firm A producing output level a, and Firm B producing output level c, the output for the two-firm industry will equal $a+c$. For Firm A, the total cost of producing this level of output equals b but for Firm B, the total cost is d. Therefore, the cost *for the industry* of producing output level $2a$ will equal $b + d$.

There are some strongly weighted assumptions behind this simple aggregation of firm costs into industry costs.

1. If all the firms face exactly similar cost functions, then there is no problem. As you will see in the next chapter, this means that each firm will operate at the same level of output and will have the same average cost of production, if the industry is perfectly competitive.
2. This method also assumes that the firms in the industry, as they increase their hiring of needed factors of production, do *not* bid up the wages of those factors. What this implies is that the entire industry represents only a minute demander of those factors of production when compared to total demand for the factors.
3. There is another kind of external effect that is also assumed away in this cost aggregation. Think of a river in northern Wisconsin on which there are four small papermills. Their use of the river water does not exceed the river's ability to dissipate, transport, and effectively get rid of the industrial wastes of the plants. But now, we double the number of plants on the river that are also using the water. This overloads the river's waste disposal capabilities and the result is pollution—degradation of the flowing water as well as the bodies of water into which it flows. In this case, increasing the size of the industry also introduced costs that are greater than those of the previously operating plants. Of course, the reason the costs are greater is that previously the plants had been able to use the river *as though* it were a free good. The expanded industry may also be able to use the river as though it were a free good, but in doing so, they will impose *unreimbursed* costs on the environment and life in that environment.

Although this discussion of industry costs derived from firm costs has been brief and incomplete, the idea of an industry cost function is understandable. It comes both from the costs of the firms themselves plus the impact of the aggregate industry.

FROM COSTS TO SUPPLY

At the beginning of this chapter, the statement was made that the quantity of goods that suppliers would be willing and able to supply in a given market depended completely on *costs*. Now it is time to look at just how this statement works out. First, the *price* of the good in the market place is going to have some influence on the quantities that potential suppliers will be willing and able to supply. But how is the price of the good itself a *cost* to potential suppliers? It has to do with the now familiar idea of *opportunity cost*. The price that a potential supplier can get for his good in the market also represents the amount per unit that he will *forego* if he decides *not* to produce the good. It is this opportunity cost of *not* producing that he must weigh against the actual costs if he *does* produce. As the price of the good *increases,* then the cost to the potential supplier also increases on an everything-else-being-equal basis. If production costs remain the same, and the price of the good increases, then there will be additional incentive for resources to move from the production of alternative goods into the production of this good. The result will be to *tend* to increase the level of output of the given good *both* because it is more profitable for existing suppliers to increase their outputs *and* because new sources of supply will now find it more profitable than other goods they were previously producing. Just as with demand, we are talking about *ceteris paribus* again. Everything else being equal, an increase in price generally will bring forth an increase in the quantity of a good supplied.

Whenever possible, it is a good idea to try to think of these ideas in terms of one's own experience and actions. Again, take the example of a working student. At the present, the bookstore pays student help $1.85 per hour for part-time clerking. They manage to get all of the help they want for that wage, but no one is clamoring to get a job at that rate. Now, assume that they decided to go on a three-shift operation and wanted a full staff for each shift. Even if it were just as desirable to work the night shifts as the day shifts, they would probably have to increase their wage rate to get the additional help. Increasing the wage rate *would*, in fact, increase the quantity of this kind of labor that the students would be willing and able to supply.

With demand, we could talk about a *law of demand*. With supply, the relationship between the price of the good and the quantity supplied of the good is not quite as general. We cannot talk about a law of supply in which the quantity of a good supplied always increases as the price of the good increases. *In general,* this statement is true, and, for the purposes of this book, we will assume it to be true. But there are important exceptions, particularly in the supply of labor and capital, that prevent the use of the idea of a *law*.

As with demand, when we talk about supply, we are not just talking about a single quantity supplied. *Supply is the series of prices and quantities that people will supply at those prices*. It is a *schedule*, not a single price and quantity.

A second variable that will affect the quantity supplied is the overall cost of production structure facing firms. This consists of all of the things discussed earlier in the chapter that are paid out to scarce and productive factors. As has been seen, an increase in any of the costs of production decreases the profitability of supplying the good, and the quantity supplied will be reduced *for any given price*. Related to this cost structure is the element of *technology*. Technological changes generally mean that production costs are reduced. Hence, improved technology also *shifts* the relationships between prices of a good and the possible quantities supplied.

Suppliers face a set of costs that have the same name as a category facing demanders—ICP costs. We could leave this category as part of the rest of the cost structure. However, this group of costs has special significance when analyzing the markets for negative goods, so it is useful to put it into the supply function as a separate variable. As with the ICP costs facing demanders, suppliers' ICP costs are fairly evident. A supplier must have information about the kinds of services or disservices his product provides for demanders of the good. Information about different market potentials—one city versus another, one suburb versus another, one country versus another—can be obtained only at a cost. As the costs of information needed by a supplier increase, the effect on the schedule of prices and quantities he is willing and able to supply is the same as any other cost increase. At any given price, quantity supplied will decrease. Contractual costs act the same way. If the records a seller is required to keep, say, for tax purposes increase, *supply* will be decreased because of the increased cost of record keeping. The costs incurred by suppliers in policing property rights associated with their enterprises and products will affect supply in a similar manner.

Again, as with demand, the expectations about future events also will affect the present actions of suppliers. These expectations include estimates of future product prices, factor prices, states of the economy, war or peace, and all of the other things that concern people.

Figure 5-6 lists the specific relationships that will be considered in analysis of supply. Quantity supplied is a function of the price of the good (p), the costs of production (C), the state of technology at the time (T), the ICP costs facing suppliers (ICP_S), and finally the expectations of suppliers (E_S). This is the *supply function*. This function is primarily concerned with *quantity supplied* (the dependent variable). Our demand function was basically concerned with quantity demanded. The supply and demand functions have only one independent variable in common—the *price* of the good concerned. This is no mathematical accident. The common argument (price) is precisely what we are interested in as the adjusting mechanism that will bring quantities supplied and demanded into balance. More on this in the next chapter.

Supply, then, is the relationship between the price of a good and the

The QUANTITY of a good SUPPLIED depends upon (is a function of):

1. the PRICE of the good
2. the COSTS of production
3. the TECHNOLOGY used
4. TRANSACTIONS COSTS
5. EXPECTATIONS of Suppliers

or

$$q_s = f(p, C, T, ICP_s, E_s)$$

This is a SUPPLY FUNCTION

Figure 5-6

quantity supplied, holding all other variables constant (*ceteris paribus*, again). Figure 5-7 lists a hypothetical supply schedule for the gloopmakers. At one dollar per gloop, it will not be worthwhile for them to produce gloops. As the price increases, they will be willing and able to produce increasing quantities until at the price of five dollars per gloop, they will be willing and able to produce 8,000 units. This schedule holds true only when the variables other than price in the supply function are at specified and constant levels. Figure 5-7 also graphs the relationship shown in the supply schedule, and we see the typical *supply curve* sloping upward and to the right. As prices increase, *quantities supplied* increases—a direct relation-

SUPPLY SCHEDULE FOR GLOOPS

Price per Gloop	Quantity Supplied (thousands)
$4.00	6
$3.00	4
$2.00	2
$1.00	0

HELD CONSTANT:

1. $\overline{C}$
2. $\overline{T}$
3. $\overline{ICP}_s$
4. $\overline{E}_s$

SUPPLY CURVE FOR GLOOPS

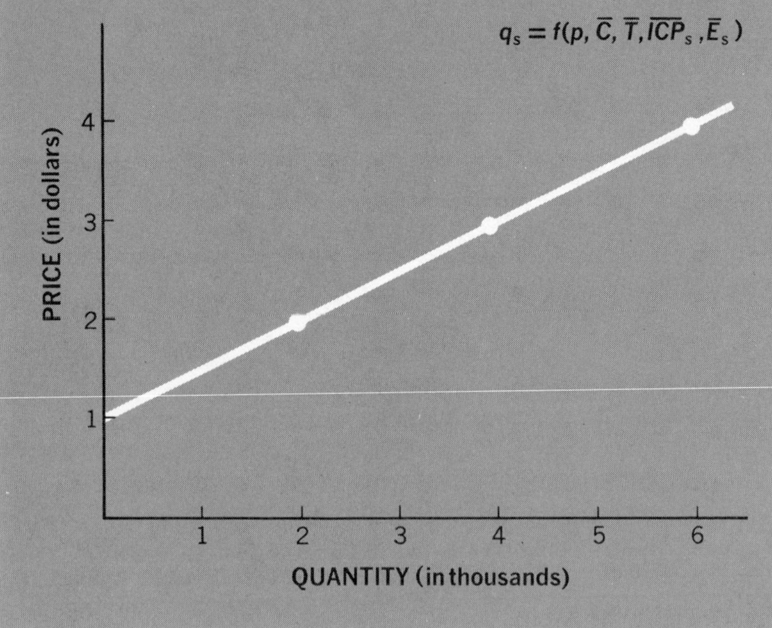

Figure 5-7

ship. Notice that supply is opposite to demand in the way price and quantities vary. It should be remembered that in the case of demand, price and quantities were *inversely* related producing a downward-to-the-right sloping demand curve.

As with demand, if any of the arguments in the supply function change, then the supply curve itself will shift. In Figure 5-8, the cost of one of the factors used in making gloops—the cost of steel—rises. This change means that for any given price of gloops, the supplier will now be willing and able to supply *fewer* than before. Alternatively, any given quantity of gloops will be supplied only at a *higher* price. Supply has decreased. The

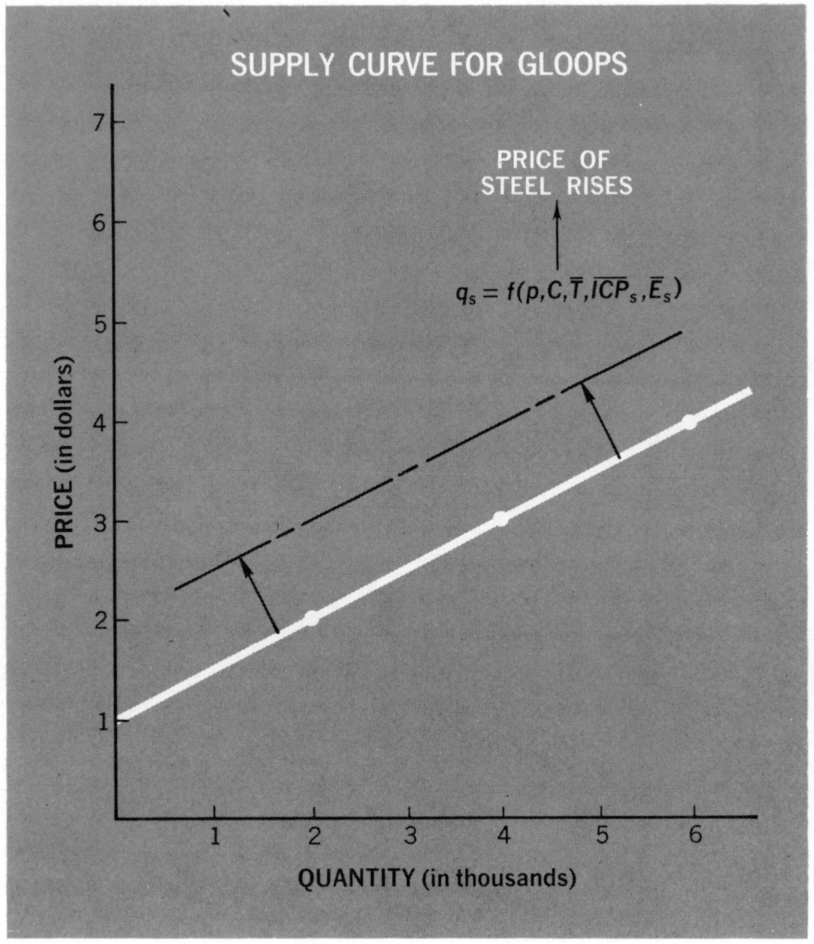

Figure 5-8

supply curve has shifted upward to the left. If we assume a technological breakthrough in the automated production of gloops, a shift in the supply curve such as illustrated in Figure 5-9 could be expected. Here, supply has *increased*. At any given price, the gloopmakers in the country will be willing and able to produce a larger quantity of gloops, *or* the same quantity of gloops can now be produced for a lower price.

Remember that there are two ways in which the quantity supplied of any good could be increased with increased prices. Producers already in the gloop-making business could increase their levels of production and or producers of other goods who had not felt there was sufficient profit in

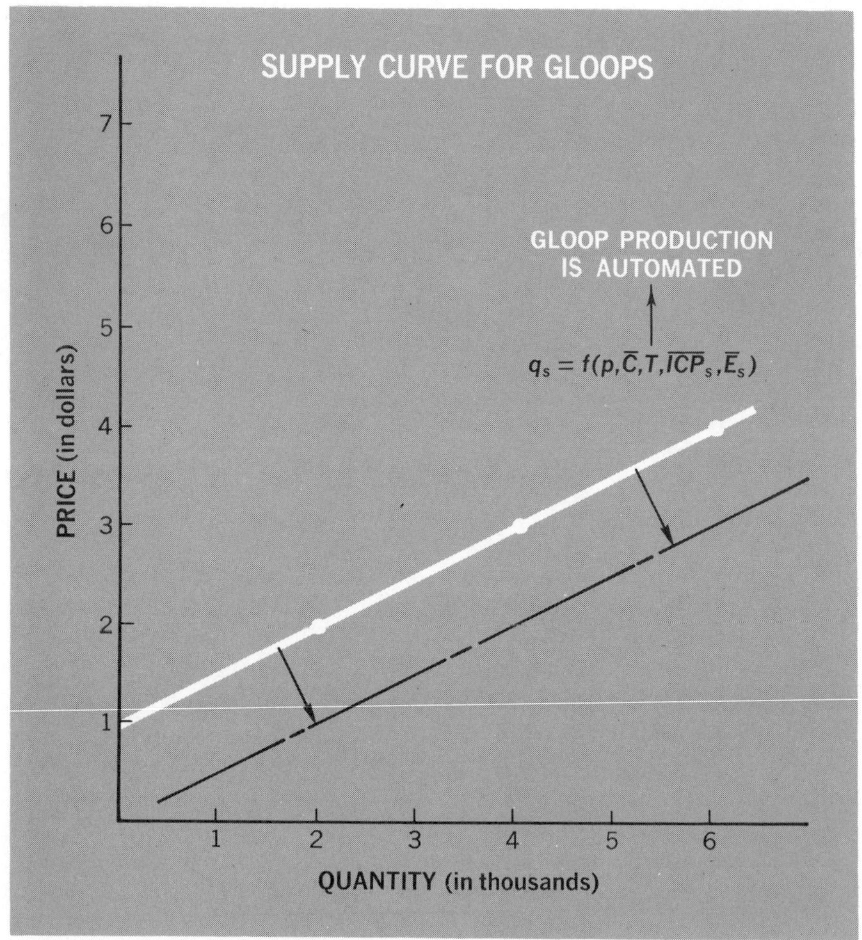

Figure 5-9

gloopmaking may change their minds with the increased revenue potential and enter the industry. Similarly, lower prices may cause some producers to restrict their production, and also, low prices may force some producers out of business.

ELASTICITY OF SUPPLY

The relative responsiveness of prices and quantities supplied can be discussed in the same way as in the case of demand. In the case of supply, price elasticity is the percentage change in quantity supplied caused by a given percentage change in the price of the good. A very small reaction on the part of quantity supplied to a change in price means a comparatively inelastic supply and, of course, the converse means a relatively elastic supply. A completely vertical supply curve means that the price of the good and the quantity supplied are completely independent. The supplier would deliver a certain quantity, no more, no less, regardless of price. A completely elastic supply curve takes the form of a line horizontal to the horizontal axis. At the given price, suppliers will supply any amount from zero to infinity.

QUESTIONS

1. List and assign money values to the opportunity costs of spending your time reading this question. Is it really worth it?
2. Can you explain the fact that occasionally a group of workers get paid for their labor while other workers who are just as skilled in the same trades are unemployed? Does this mean that the unemployed workers are "free goods"?
3. Compare human capital and non-human or physical capital. In what ways are they the same and in what ways are they different as far as creation and use are concerned?
4. Explain why fixed costs will not affect the level of a firm's production in the short run. Define short and long run in the answer.
5. How can the price of a certain thing be considered one of its "costs"?
6. Is the supply of Rembrandt paintings completely inelastic? Why or why not?

6

Competition and Monopoly

OBJECTIVES

Combining supply *and* demand *for a given good results in the operation of a* market. *If* price *can move freely, then quantities supplied and quantities demanded will be brought into a stable equilibrium by price changes. If price cannot change freely, then* economic shortages *or* economic surpluses *will be created. If* prices *cannot adjust in a market,* quantities *will. In their everyday lives, firms and individuals try to maximize* net benefits—*the difference between total benefits minus the cost incurred to obtain those benefits. For a firm, this involves maximizing the difference between total revenues and total costs. In a competitive industry, competition is maintained by the ability of firms to enter and leave the industry. Any individual firm is thus prevented from making more profit than the minimum needed to keep him in business. Monopolies can develop when the entry of new firms is barred or restricted. In this case, a monopoly can choose that level of output which will result in the largest* excess profit—*profit over and above the minimum needed to keep it in business.* Oligopolies *occur when there are only a few producers of a given similar product in an industry.* Monopolistic competition *takes place when firms within an industry attempt to differentiate their basically similar products through advertising and minor product changes. Both of these industrial organizations tend to reduce the competitive nature of an industry.*

THE MARKET

Figure 6-1 pictures the ideal supply and demand curves together on the same graph—again, referring to our thriving gloop industry. We can put both of these functions on the same set of axes because both contain the variables of *price* and *quantity*—quantity *demanded* and quantity *supplied*. Remember that one of the questions an economic system must answer

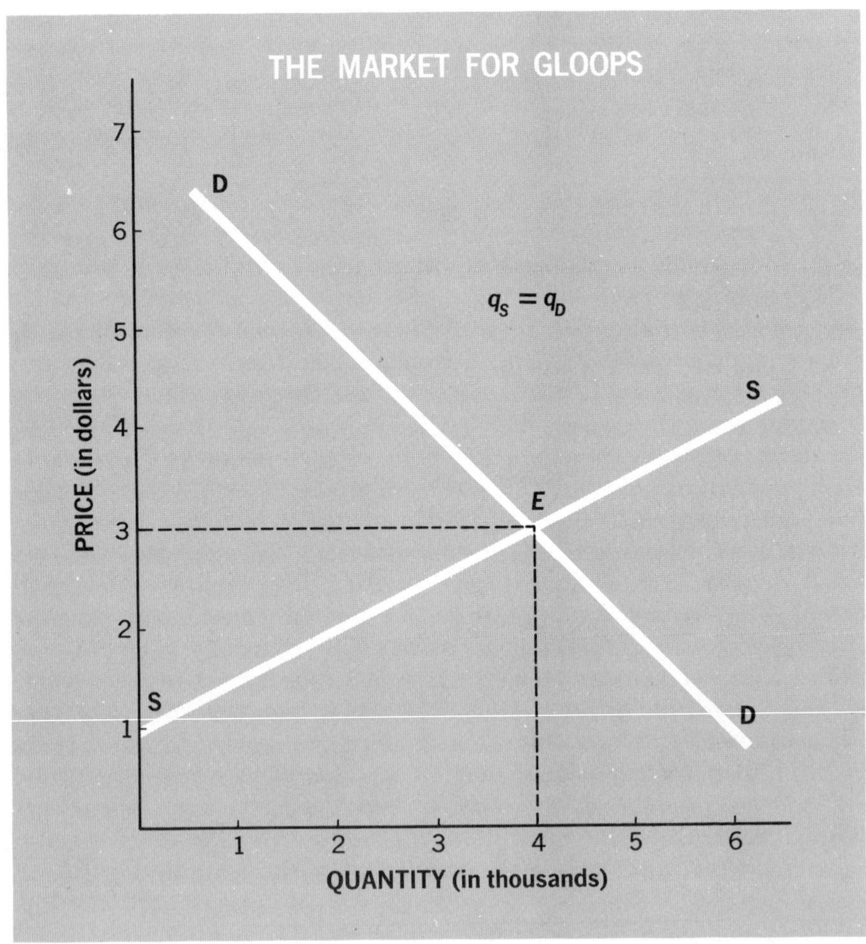

Figure 6-1

is how the desires of the producers of scarce goods and the consumers of scarce goods are going to be reconciled. How is quantity supplied going to be equated with quantity demanded? Clearly, price is the thing that will perform this function if buyers and sellers can bargain in some sort of market operation. Our graph illustrates an equilibrium position at which the price and quantity values are the same for both suppliers and demanders. In this case, the point is a price of three dollars per gloop and a quantity marketed of 4,000 units. This merely says that at a price of three dollars per gloop, suppliers are willing and able to supply 4,000 gloops and demanders are willing and able to purchase 4,000 gloops. Do not forget all of the things that are being held constant. In the case of demand, there are the prices of related goods, the incomes of demanders, transactions costs, tastes, and expectations. For suppliers, all types of costs, technology, and expectations are constant. This is a "flashbulb" picture of a moment in time that represents desires for quantities associated with various prices. At this price, and *only at this price*, the desires and abilities of the two groups are reconciled. At this point, quantity supplied equals quantity demanded ($q_s = q_d$).

What will happen if the price is other than three dollars? Two possibilities exist. First, should the price in the market be too low (below the equilibrium level of three dollars), say two dollars, suppliers will be willing to produce and/or sell only 2,000 gloops (see Figure 6-2). On the other hand, demanders will be willing and able to purchase a higher quantity than they would at the higher equilibrium price—in this case, 5,000 units. Thus, we have what is defined as an *economic shortage* of 3,000 gloops. Quantity supplied is *less than* quantity demanded by 3,000 units. If this shortage develops in a free market, the result is simple and automatic. Some people are willing and able to pay a higher price for gloops. This is precisely what our demand curve tells us. Because there are not enough to go around at the two dollar price, those who want gloops the most and/or are the most able to pay for them, will start bidding for the limited quantity available. As with any bidding process, the price will be forced up, and, as it increases, two things take place. First of all, higher prices give more incentive to suppliers to increase their output—quantity supplied goes up. Secondly, as prices increase, the quantity people are willing and able to purchase—quantity demanded—goes down. Both of these occurrences help to reduce and eventually eliminate the economic shortage. When the equilibrium price is reached again, quantity supplied and demanded will again be equal.

It is important to understand that during the process of changing prices, *demand* has *not* changed. *Quantity* demanded has changed. During the process of changing prices, *supply* has *not* changed. *Quantity supplied has changed.* A change in either demand or supply would have meant a change in one of the variables being held constant with the resultant shift in

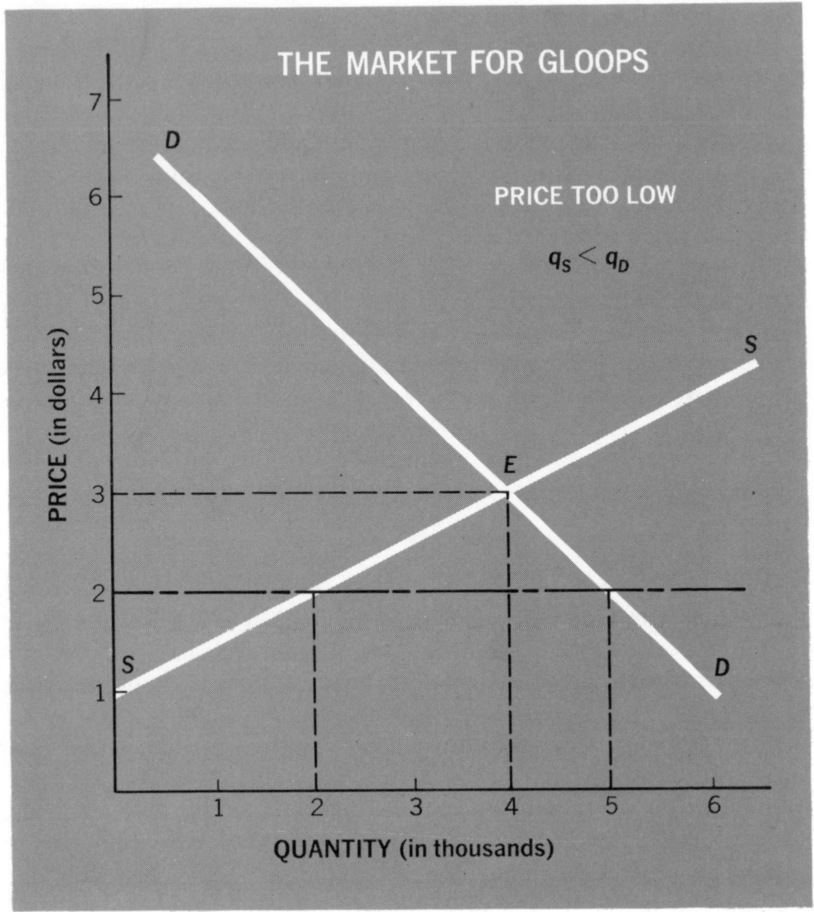

Figure 6-2

either the supply or demand curve. That is not what happened. Prices changed in response to an economic shortage that, in turn, adjusted the quantities back to equilibrium.

The opposite situation is illustrated in Figure 6-3. Here, we start with a price above market equilibrium, say four dollars. At this high price, suppliers are willing and able to produce *more* units than at equilibrium (6,000 units instead of 4,000), but demanders are willing and able to purchase only 3,000 units—1,000 less than at equilibrium. This produces an *economic surplus* of 3,000 units. Again, if the market is allowed to function without interference, suppliers will find that they are unable to sell their entire production at the four dollar price and will be forced to reduce this

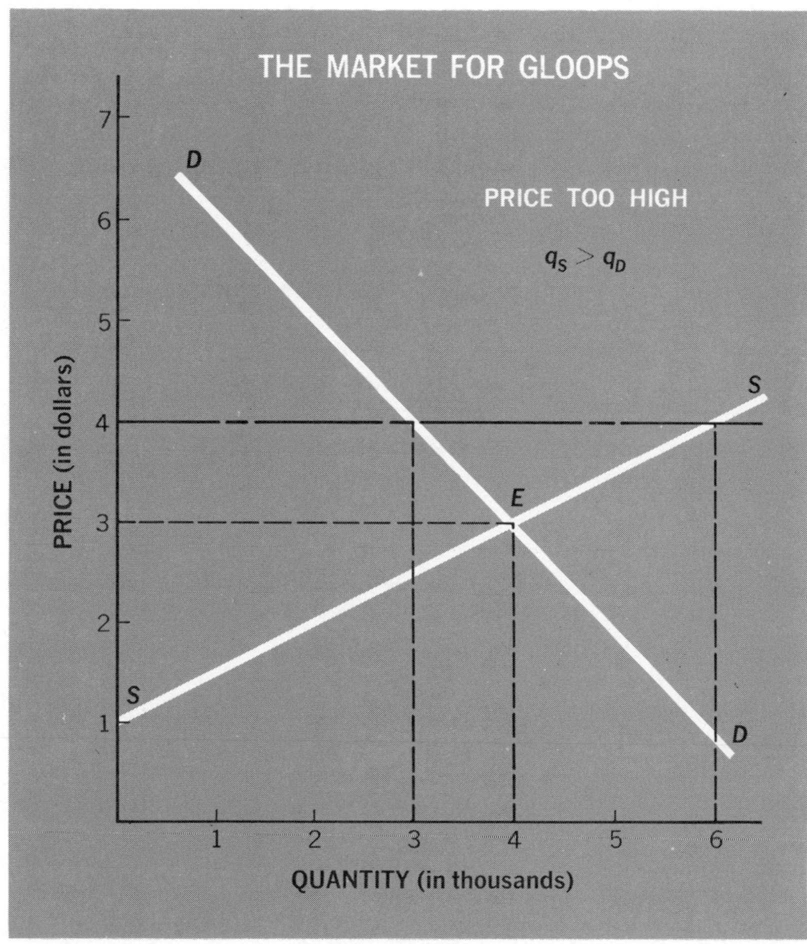

Figure 6-3

price to tempt more persons to purchase more of the product. As the price is reduced from the four dollar level, we again have a two-fold reaction. At the lower price, quantity demanded will rise *and* quantity supplied will fall. Both of these reactions work in the direction of restoring equilibrium and eliminating the economic surplus by lowering the price of the product. Again, neither supply nor demand changed during this process, only quantities supplied and demanded. The movements toward equilibrium have been *along* the supply and demand curve and not shifts of the curves themselves.

ANOTHER LOOK AT COSTS AND REVENUES

From the fairly simple and modest beginning above, we can begin to put many of the pieces developed thus far into their respective slots. In Figure 6-4, we have taken the demand schedule and curve for gloops and, just below the demand curve, we have graphed *total revenue*. At the high price end of the demand, we have an elastic range in which decreasing prices increase total revenue. At the $3.50 price and 3,500 quantity point, demand is of unit elasticity; and, at all prices below $3.50, demand is inelastic and price decreases produce decreases in total revenue.

Corresponding to these elasticity ranges, we find total revenue rising from zero at prices of $7.00 and above to a maximum of $12,250 when the price is $3.50 per gloop and the quantity demanded equals 3,500 units. At output levels greater than 3,500 units, the price decrease needed to sell gloops is proportionally greater than the increases in quantities demanded and, therefore, total revenue falls. Finally, at a zero price, people will demand 7,000 but total revenue received by suppliers would be zero. As a free good, people would demand 7,000 units.

Consider the situation in which our gloopmaker would remain in the Navy and continue the production of gloops using GI material and GI labor. Assume that, as a result, his costs of production were literally zero. Of course, we must also assume that his time was also without value—zero opportunity costs for other uses, including leisure. We will also assume that he has no competition from any source whatsoever, including competition from close substitutes. He can choose any level of output he wishes. The question then becomes, "What level of production will he decide to produce?" To answer this question, it is necessary to make one more assumption. We will assume both here and throughout the book that firms act *as though* they were trying to maximize profit. We assume that they are trying to make the *difference* between total revenue and total cost as large as possible—to maximize what we have defined as *excess profit*. Remember that we have defined profit as

$$\pi = \text{TR} - \text{TC}$$

where π equals profit, *TR* equals total revenue, and *TC* equals total cost. Remember also that *TC* includes the minimum profit needed to stay in business.

Some people will argue that businesses today do not really try to maximize profit. They argue that firms have other goals as well, such as community responsibility, public service, or power consolidation. Actually, none of these other goals need necessarily conflict with the

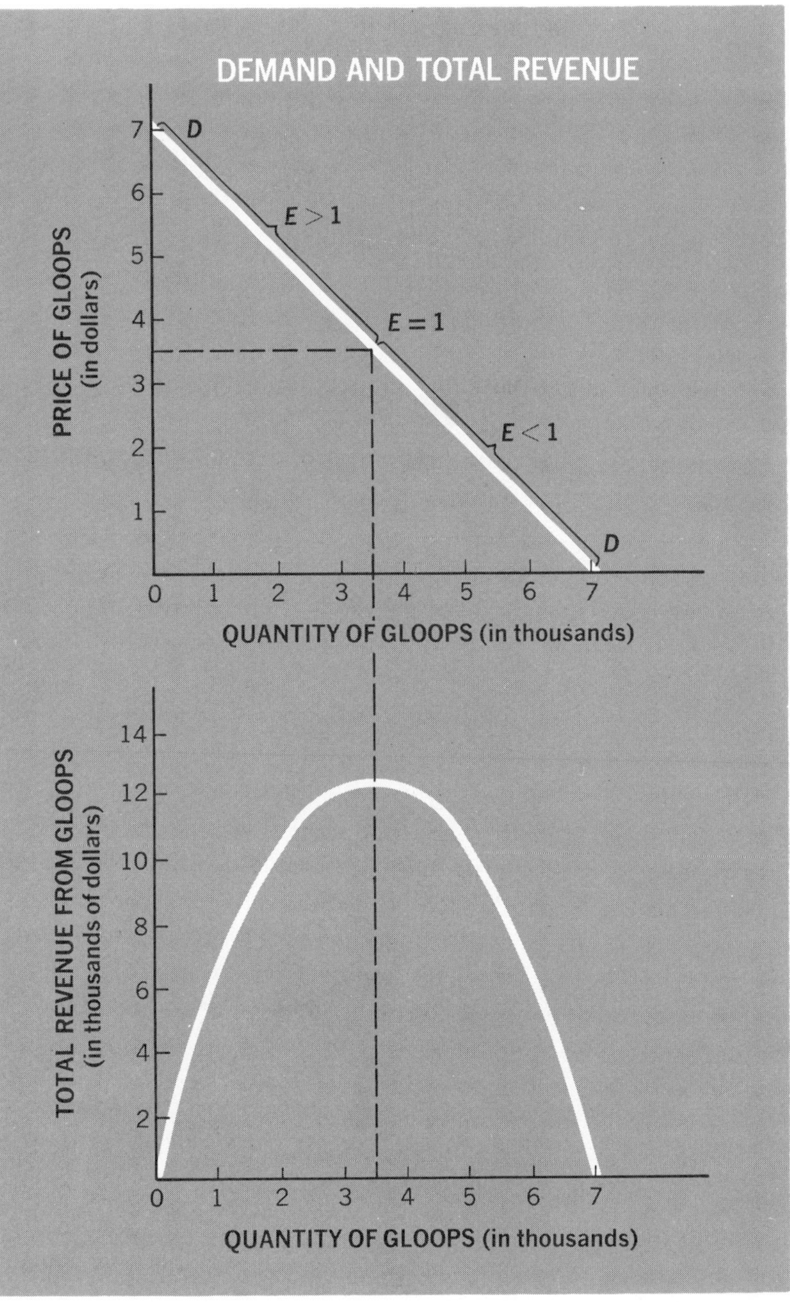
DEMAND AND TOTAL REVENUE
PRICE OF GLOOPS
(in dollars)
7
6
5
4
3
2
1
D
E > 1
E = 1
E < 1
D
0
1
2
3
4
5
6
7
QUANTITY OF GLOOPS (in thousands)
TOTAL REVENUE FROM GLOOPS
(in thousands of dollars)
14
12
10
8
6
4
2
0
1
2
3
4
5
6
7
QUANTITY OF GLOOPS (in thousands)

Figure 6-4

profit-maximizing assumption. Usually, businesses have these other goals as part of a long-run desire to maximize profits. This may mean that the telephone company spends hundreds of thousands of dollars on public service advertising trying to convince the public of how conscientious they really are. But the long-run reason is also to convince people that their public service commissions, whose job it is to regulate telephone rates, should give more favorable treatment to the enterprise. The company contribution to the community chest also will not hurt the corporate image. And *not* giving to the community chest, along with all the other community charities, could certainly have negative effects on business. Anyway, the assumption that firms act *as though* they are trying to maximize total profits will be used here.

Because our gloopmaker has no costs, then, using the formula

$$\pi = \text{TR} - \text{TC}. \quad \pi = \text{TR} - 0, \ \pi = \text{TR}.$$

In other words, to maximize profit, he will choose that level of output at which price times quantity (*TR*) is the greatest. A look at Figure 6-4 illustrates just where that point will be. If he sells less than 3,500 units, he can get a higher price than the $3.50 per unit the market will support at the 3,500 unit output level. But because the demand is elastic above 3,500 units and $3.50, *total revenue* will be reduced if less is sold. On the other side of the coin, reducing the price and increasing the output can be done, but this action too will reduce total revenue. Put another way, the gloopmaker will produce and market a level of output that will meet demand at the point of unit elasticity because that level will maximize total revenue. Because there are zero costs, total revenue is the same thing as total profit.

There are a couple of most important points illustrated by this example. First of all, notice that the monopolist will *not* charge "the highest possible price" for the product. He is still constrained by *demand.* The price people are willing and able to pay for the product has little or nothing to do with the fact that the seller is a monopolist or a competitor. True, there might be some people who would reduce their demand if they knew that the seller was a monopolist, but basically, demand will be the same whether the industry consists of a single seller or many firms competing with each other for the business. As will be seen again in a few paragraphs, what the monopolist *can* do is adjust his *output.* This is where he gets a big advantage over a competitive firm. By adjusting output, he can influence market price, and thus maximize total revenue and total profit.

Before getting into this issue further, let us see what happens when costs are introduced into the picture. Figure 6-5 graphs the situation. First of all, up until this point, we have been using a supply curve for gloops that

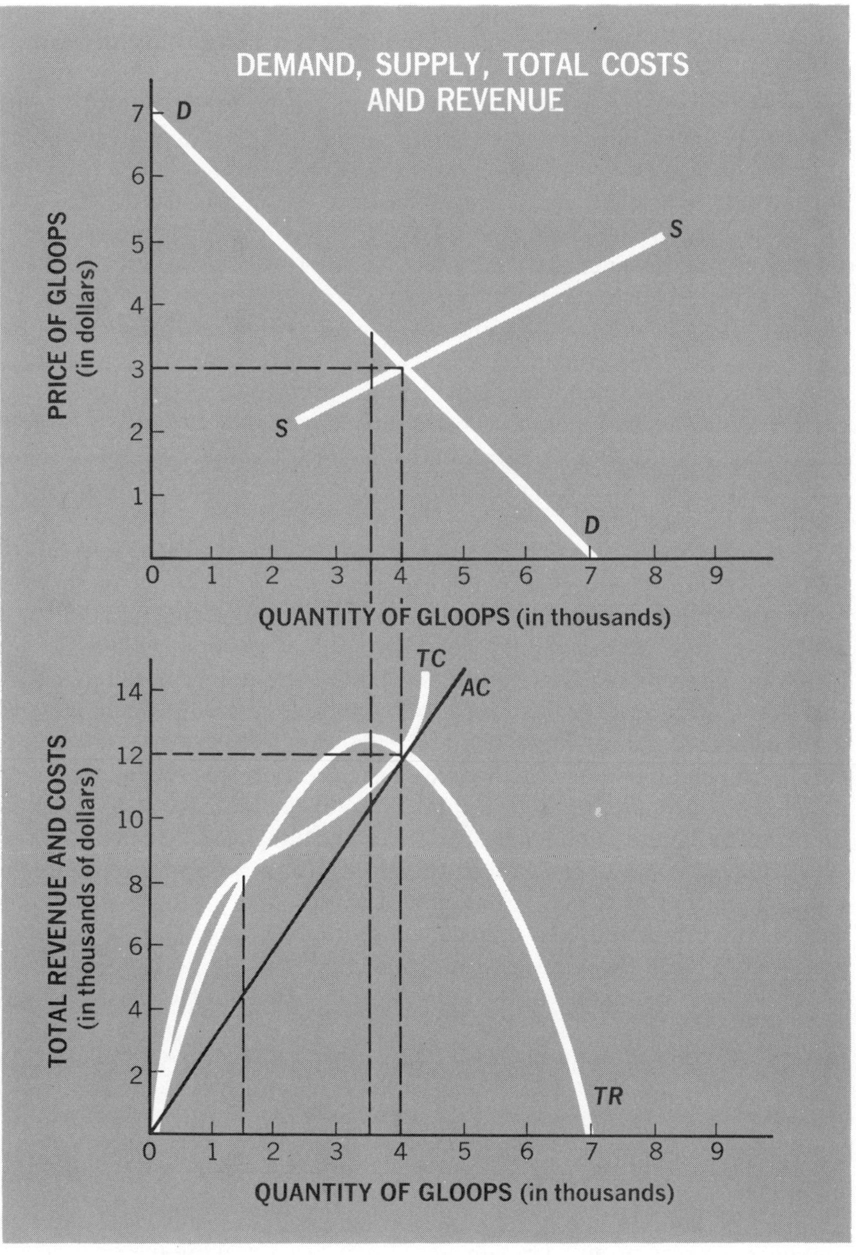
DEMAND, SUPPLY, TOTAL COSTS AND REVENUE
PRICE OF GLOOPS (in dollars)
7
6
5
4
3
2
1
0
D
S
S
D
1
2
3
4
5
6
7
8
9
QUANTITY OF GLOOPS (in thousands)
TOTAL REVENUE AND COSTS (in thousands of dollars)
14
12
10
8
6
4
2
TC
AC
TR
0
1
2
3
4
5
6
7
8
9
QUANTITY OF GLOOPS (in thousands)

Figure 6-5

reflected *increasing costs* throughout the range involved. Each gloop cost more than the one produced just before it. But now we want to illustrate costs using the more general case described in Chapter 5 where firms and the industry have cost functions containing decreasing, constant, and increasing ranges. This is not too important for this level of analysis, but to keep things accurate, we have cut off the supply curve to show only that portion that is in the increasing cost range.

There is a tremendous amount of information and insight that can be obtained from this figure, so let us take it point by point. First of all, the industry will never operate in any range where total costs exceed total revenue. If all firms have the same cost functions and are all the same size, then when the *TC* is greater than *TR* for the industry, it will be greater for all firms as well. The opposite is true in the industry's range where *TR* is greater than *TC*. In Figure 6-5, the industry will never operate at output levels less than 1,500 units nor greater than 4,000 units. In both of those ranges, total costs are higher than total revenues, and firms in the industry would be losing money.

Now let us assume that the industry has an output level of 1,500 units. Total costs and revenues are equal to each other, which means that the firms are neither making an excess profit nor are they losing money. They are making just the minimum level of profit they need to prevent moving into some alternative resource use. We have an equilibrium, but it is not a *stable* equilibrium. If firms reduce their outputs, they will lose money, so movement in that direction will not take place in the long run. On the other hand, firms, both in the industry as well as others outside the industry, can see that if they increase their outputs *or* enter the industry as a new firm, there will be excess profits to be made. So, two things can take place. Firms in the industry can expand their outputs and/or new firms can enter the industry. Either of these two actions will increase the level of industry output. But this increased output can be sold *only* if the price of the product is reduced. Price falls and, as it does, at first, the pie gets bigger. Total revenue actually increases as long as demand is in the elastic range. Simultaneously, costs are rising as well, but, initially (in the example illustrated), excess profits increase. Total revenues are rising faster than total costs. At some point just to the left of maximum total revenue, excess profits will be at their highest point. Firms in the industry are making the maximum excess profit possible. Total revenue minus total cost is at its highest level.

Why, then, do the firms not keep their outputs at this level and thus maximize excess profit? The answer is that those making the best profits would want to see that happen—at least, to his competitor. A single firm could still increase its output and raise the volume of its own total profits even though the profit *rate* for the firm might be reduced. If one firm expands its output, there would not be much (if any) impact on price. But the same incentives to expand apply to *all* firms in the industry, and if a large number of them try this expansion, then output for the industry does increase significantly, forcing the price of the product still lower. Of course, that excess profit is also signaling other firms outside the industry to continue their entrance into this moneymaker. Here are three of the most important characteristics of a competitive industry.

1. No single firm can significantly influence total market price by varying its own output.
2. Entry and exit into the industry must be possible in response to signals in the form of profits and losses.
3. Information must be readily available as to alternative resource employment opportunities.

So, output in the industry continues to expand as long as there are larger profits to be made in this endeavor than in alternative occupations. The total cost curve is really a measure of the next best alternative employment for the factors used, including entrepreneurial talent. Finally, either costs start rising faster than revenue or revenue actually starts to fall as the inelastic portion of demand is encountered. In this illustration, this soon brings the industry to an output of 4,000 units. This was the equilibrium point in the supply and demand analysis presented earlier in this chapter. The point has many important characteristics, among which the following are of particular interest at this stage.

1. The equilibrium is a *stable* equilibrium. As long as cost and revenue functions stay the same, forces are created to maintain this level of output. If output exceeds the given level, then costs exceed revenues and firms lose money. This will either force firms to cut output or to leave the industry for better alternatives. Either way, output falls back toward the equilibrium point again. If output falls too far, then excess profits again are generated, inducing an increase in output back towards the stable level.

2. At this output level, resources paid to the industry for its product exactly equal the payments by firms in the industry to their factors of production. Additionally, these payments are the *minimum* payments required by the factors to maintain their employment in this, as opposed to alternative employments. Firms in the industry will take in $12,000 in this example. But their costs at this output level are also equal to $12,000. Again, these costs include the minimum return or profit required to maintain output. But the point is that no *excess* profit exists. All the fat has been trimmed away by competition.

3. Notice that in the illustration, the average cost line is

tangent to the total cost line at this point as well. From the discussion in the last chapter, it will be remembered that this means average cost is at its minimum level at this point. On the average, gloops are being produced as cheaply as possible, and resource use is minimized.

4. The price of the product is as cheap as possible if users of the product are going to pay the resource value of the product. At any lower price, the value of resources used in production would exceed the value paid in. This is just another way of saying that total costs would exceed total revenues. So here again, customers for gloops are not having to pay inflated prices to get their product.

5. Output of the product is as large as possible, given demanders' preferences as expressed through demand and cost conditions. Here again, this assumes that people pay for what they get. Total revenues equal total costs.

MONOPOLY

Much of what can be said about monopoly price and output decisions has already been alluded to in the previous discussion of competition. Figure 6-6 will be used for the discussion. It is similar to Figure 6-5 in most ways. We have seen that competition will result in an industry output of 4,000 gloops at a price of three dollars each with total costs exactly equal to total receipts from the sale of gloops.

Now let us see what happens when one firm in the industry takes over the rest of the firms in the industry. Such an action would seem to establish a monopoly, but it does not. That is only one thing that would have to happen to create a monopolized industry, at least one that would *stay* monopolized by a single firm. Two other things must also be accomplished. First of all, *entry by other firms must be prevented.* As will be seen, the monopoly will generate excess profits that will serve as an incentive for other firms to enter this industry. Unless this entry can be stopped, the monopolizing firm soon will lose its singular position. The other thing that must take place is the elimination of all close substitutes for the product. If close substitutes exist, then, when the monopoly raises the price of its product, demand for the substitutes will increase at the expense of the given product.

If we assume that our new monopoly has accomplished both of these necessary conditions for establishing and maintaining a monopoly position, what will happen next? More assumptions are needed before the question can be attacked. One of these is that the *costs* facing the monopoly will be neither greater nor less than those facing the industry in its competitive form. In other words, the total cost function for the industry stays the same. This is a fairly strong assumption because there are many reasons to think that the cost function would indeed change *either* up or down, depending on conditions.

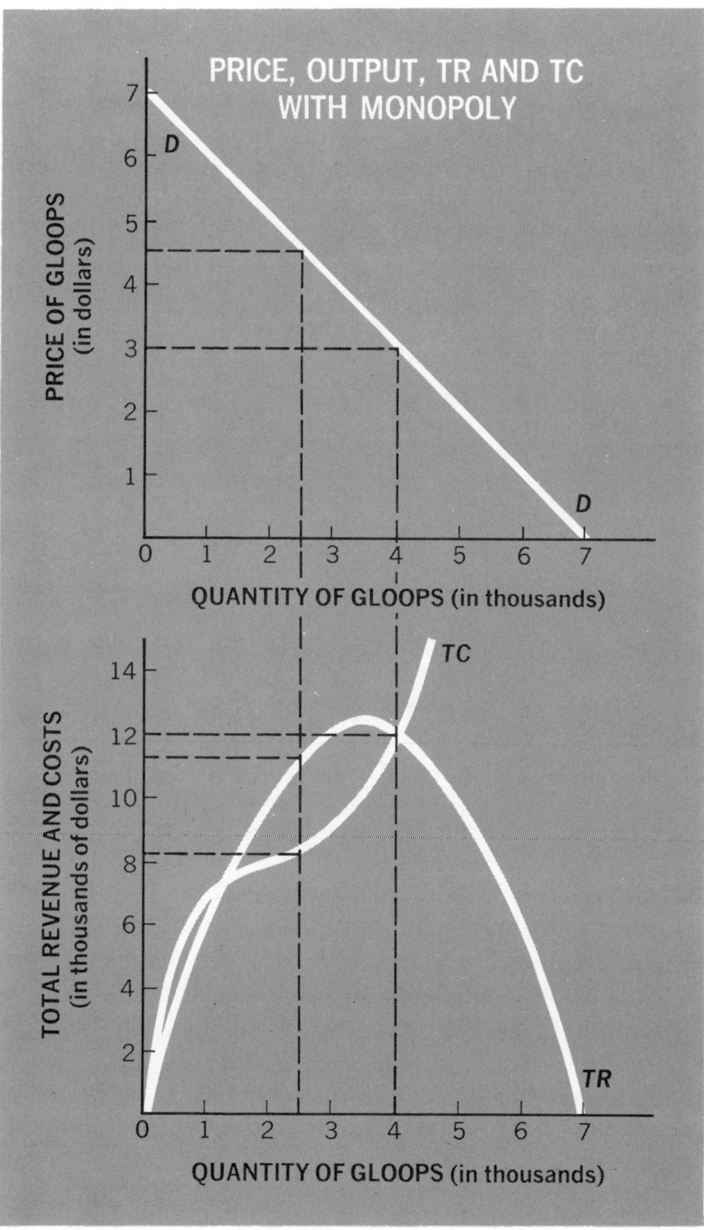

PRICE, OUTPUT, TR AND TC
WITH MONOPOLY
PRICE OF GLOOPS
(in dollars)
D
D
7
6
5
4
3
2
1
0
1
2
3
4
5
6
7
QUANTITY OF GLOOPS (in thousands)
TOTAL REVENUE AND COSTS
(in thousands of dollars)
TC
TR
14
12
10
8
6
4
2
QUANTITY OF GLOOPS (in thousands)

Figure 6-6

We also assume, as stated before, that the demand facing the monopoly is the same as the demand facing the industry when it was competitive. This assumption is quite reasonable except to the extent that some people might prefer buying from non-monopoly type firms. Thus, the total revenue curve, as well as the total cost curve facing the monopolist will remain the same as they were under competition.

Given these conditions, our new monopolist will try to operate *just as all of the competitive firms had tried to operate*. He will try to maximize the difference between total revenue and total cost. He will try to make *TR - TC* as large as possible. But there is a big difference in the result of this maximizing behavior as compared to the competitive case. He is in a position to control the level of output of the industry (he *is* the industry) and, as a result, he can choose that level of output that will yield the greatest excess profit. In Figure 6-6, output is reduced from 4,000 units to about 2,500 units. As the output is reduced, the price of the product can be raised. In our example, price goes up from $3.00 per gloop to about $4.50. Now, costs of production equal only about $8,250 and total revenue equals about $11,250. Thus, the monopolist has been able to attain a $3,000 excess profit.

A couple of other points are of interest. Notice that the output level chosen is *to the left* of the point of maximum total revenue. It is in the elastic portion of the demand curve. Of course, this makes perfectly good sense. As long as demand is *inelastic,* then a decrease in output would increase total revenue. *Any* decrease in output will also decrease total costs. As a result, no monopolist would ever operate in the inelastic portion of demand. Competition might or might not force output up into the inelastic range. In this example, the competitive industry was, in fact, operating in this range.

Notice that we have eliminated a supply curve in Figure 6-6. This is because now the conditions affecting the quantities supplied and demanded are no longer independent of each other. Now, the price of the product affects not only quantity supplied through changing opportunity costs, but it also affects quantity supplied because of the impact on total revenue.

There is another way of putting this. Graphically, the demand curve facing a competitor is *completely elastic.* He can sell any quantity he wants to at *the* market price without materially affecting that market price. In Figure 6-7, this is illustrated. Regardless of his sales, the price of the product will remain the same. A competitor is a *price taker.* On the contrary, a monopolist faces whatever the industry demand curve is, and, most generally, this will have something less than perfect elasticity. Therefore, the monopolist can influence price by changing his output. The monopolist is a *price maker*, or, at least, a price influencer. For the

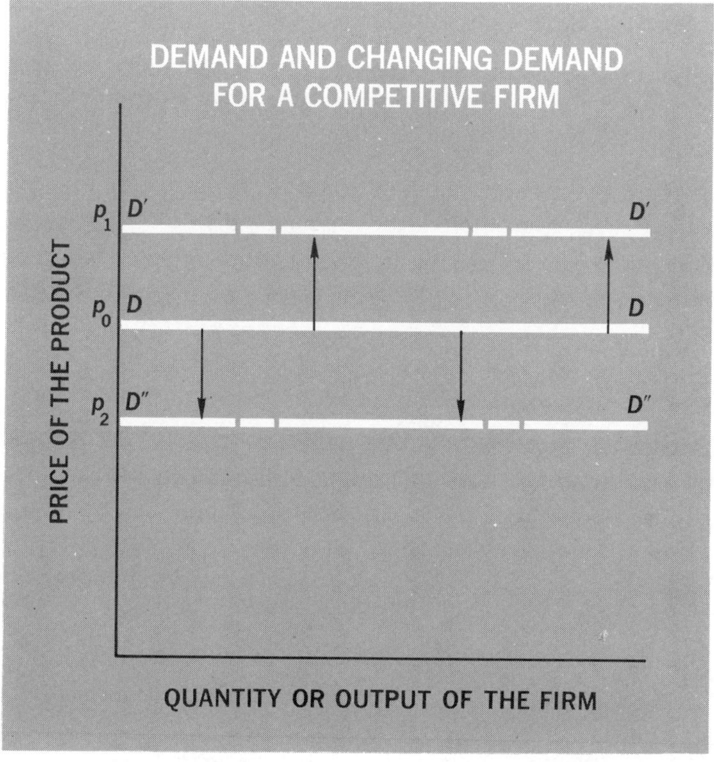

Figure 6-7

competitor, a change in the market price is a shift in the perfectly elastic demand curve he faces. Thus, in Figure 6-7, $D'D'$ is the increase in the demand he faces that results in an increase of the market price from p_0 to p_1. Similarly, $D''D''$ shows the downward shift in demand associated with a decrease in the market price from p_0 to p_2.

To recap, then, the differences between pure competition and pure monopoly under conditions of similar demand and costs are as follows.

1. Monopolies will sell their products at a higher unit price.
2. Monopolies will produce and sell a smaller quantity than would be the case under pure competition.
3. Monopolies will generate excess profits. The resources taken in from revenues will be greater than the minimum necessary to produce the same level of output under competitive conditions.
4. Monopolists will be price makers rather than price takers.

NEITHER FISH NOR FOWL

Thus far, we have discussed how price and output decisions are made in two extreme models of industry. We have also pointed out that examples of pure competition or pure monopoly are practically impossible to come by. In fact, most industries in most market economies lie somewhere in between these two perfect models. There is generally more than a single firm in the industry, but there are not enough firms to fulfill the stringent conditions for perfect competition. Why, then, do we not spend our time looking at the theory of so-called imperfect competition instead of wasting time studying abstract models that do not even exist in the real world?

The answer to this question is manifold. First of all, even though perfection in the real world is nonexistent, many industries come sufficiently close to the competitive or monopolistic picture to allow analysis using the abstraction. Secondly, most industries contain elements of both models that can be understood by reference to the two benchmarks. Finally, there is no really satisfactory single theory of imperfect competition. There are many hypotheses and a few good empirical studies, but, for the most part, we must use descriptive material and the use of the two extreme models of competition and monopoly for predictive purposes.

OLIGOPOLY AND MONOPOLISTIC COMPETITION

There are two kinds of imperfect competition that overlap each other but nevertheless have some different characteristics. The first of these is called *oligopoly*—a few sellers. Industries such as steel, cement, pharmaceuticals, and so on, fall into this group. Entry into the field is difficult, but not impossible. Firms cannot completely control prices by varying their separate outputs, but, at the same time, their individual output decisions *do* influence market price. A second type of imperfect competition we call *monopolistic competition*. This is characterized by firms that produce very similar products, but manage to differentiate their products slightly—either in the minds of the customers or in actual fact. This is the whole business of brand names and the thousands of permutations and combinations of models and accessories possible in any particular brand of automobile. Products competing with each other in this arena depend heavily on advertising to trumpet the real or imaginary differences in their characteristics from those of their close substitutes.

Analytically, one difference between a pure competitor and an oligopolist can be seen in the comparative demand curves of Figure 6-8. Remember, a competitor is a *price taker*. He views *the* market price as something that is given and feels that changing it is something beyond his

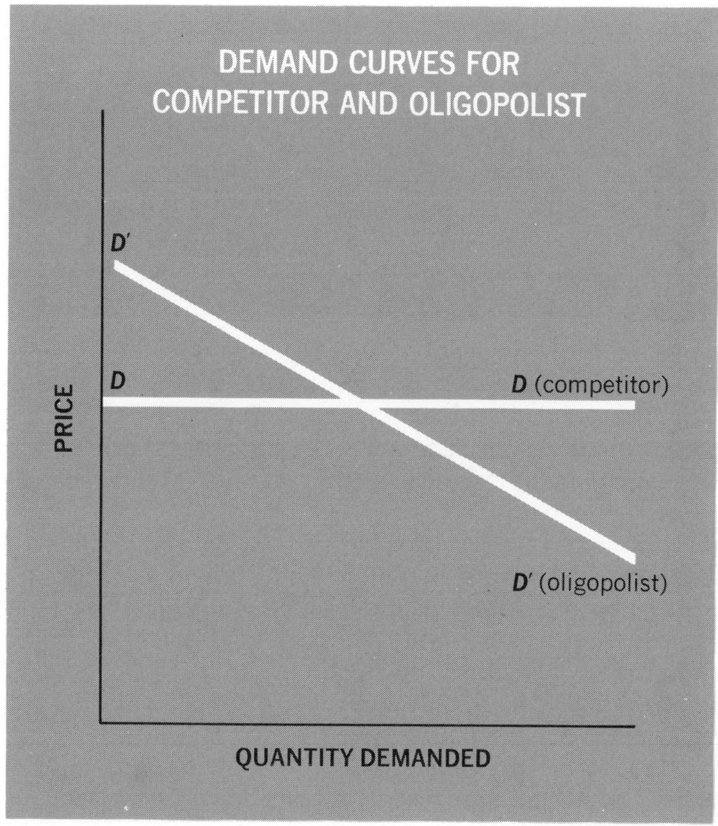

Figure 6-8

control. In other words, as he views his demand curve, it is completely elastic. Whatever his output decisions, the market price will not be affected. Even though the industry demand curve is downward sloping, as an individual competitor, he can and will ignore this fact. On the other hand, an oligopolist must recognize the fact that the firm demand curve he faces has some price responsiveness. It is *not* perfectly elastic. Being one of only a few sellers in the industry, his own output decisions will affect the market price. Lowering his output will tend to raise the total market price and increasing his output will tend to lower market price. Of course, the more firms and the smaller each firm's share of the total market, the more elastic will be each firm's demand curve. As a limit, with many firms and all of them roughly equal, the oligopoly approaches pure competition with its perfectly elastic firm demand curves.

One of the big problems in developing any consistent theory of oligopoly is that a great deal depends on *reactions* of one oligopolist in response to some action of another. For example, if one firm lowers its product price, will the others follow suit, or will they maintain their original prices and suffer the decreased volume of business that is likely to follow? On the other hand, if one firm cuts its prices, will the others start a price war in which one firm undercuts the other which then undercuts the first until everyone is losing money? Why? Because if there are some financially weak firms in the industry, this action may wipe them out. Thus, the strong become larger and presumably stronger, too. Price wars are *not* examples of pure competition in action. On the contrary, they are clear symptoms of oligopoly.

In monopolistic competition, there is generally easy entry to and exit from the industry concerned. But, in this case, firms do their best to convince customers that their non-unique product really is unique. Unlike the oligopoly, there may be many sellers in the market, but each will try to attain a semi-monopoly position for his particular brand of soap or automobile or what have you.

There is an interesting analogy to be made here between the attempt of Bayer aspirin to convince its customers that Bayer's product is unique (or at least better than others) and the action of heroin pushers on users. Sellers of both products are trying to get their customers hooked on their particular product. Of course, the heroin pusher has more going for him because heroin is physiologically addictive. The ad man for Bayer aspirin does not have that characteristic to help his sales. He must create the image of Bayer, the first, the original, the obviously better quality, the benefactor of mankind. The ad man's job is made doubly difficult by the fact that a five grain aspirin tablet is a five grain aspirin tablet, no matter who makes it and who puts a label on it.

Graphically, advertising for differentiated products is attempting both to *increase* demand by increasing the public's tastes for the specific brand, and also to make that demand less elastic—less responsive to price changes. In Figure 6-9, the attempt is not only to increase demand from say, DD to $D'D'$, but also to rotate the demand as in $D''D''$. In this way, the firms will be able to raise the prices of their products without losing as much business as would otherwise be the case.

Monopolistic competition and oligopolies are both likely to lead to many different forms of *nonprice competition*. The savings and loan associations, which have legal maximums on interest rates, now try to entice new customers with a shiny popcorn popper or new blanket. Because they can buy items at lower cost than most individuals, it looks like more of a bargain than it really is. But it still is just one way of getting around the interest ceiling.

Trading stamps are another way of making very small price conces-

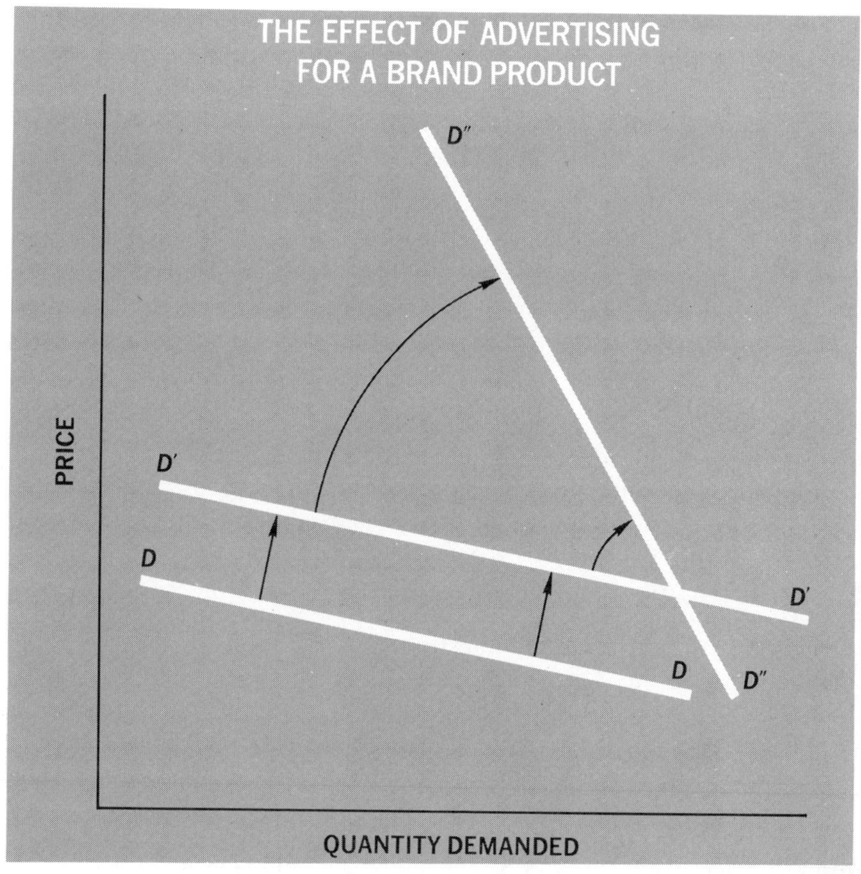

Figure 6-9

sions that end up looking bigger than they really are. All this gimmickry takes resources. The supermarket employee is made responsible for the trading stamps given out as well as the cash taken in. The distribution system of the trading stamp gifts is possibly a bit less expensive than that of a department store, but it still costs money. Who is going to pay these costs? The same answer applies. Both customer and merchant will share in the cost of making these nonprice "price reductions." It is interesting to note that the current trend is away from the use of trading stamps and back to the alternative of actually making prices a bit cheaper. From an efficiency standpoint, and from the standpoint of making the market work better, this is a healthy sign.

A look at the kind of advertising carried out by a firm can give some clue as to the kind of market position it occupies. If the advertising takes the form of pure market information about price and service characteristics, this is evidence that the firm may well be operating in a basically competitive setting. If the nature of the advertising is pushing the total product, then the firm may well be monopolistic. As an example, Bell Telephone companies advertise the joys of telephone service with relatively little emphasis on Bell's particular services. (Incidentally, in 1969 there were still about nineteen hundred telephone companies in the U.S.) Of course, what Bell is trying to do is increase the demand for *total* telephone service. If it can do that, then Bell will come in for a large share of the increased business. As far as increases in long distance demand, Bell would capture almost 100 percent of the business.

On the other hand, if the advertising is primarily pushing some particular brand of soap, cigarettes, cars, nonprescription drugs, and so on, then one can be reasonably sure that some kind of monopolistic competition is going on. Consider the actions of some of the major soap companies who spend millions of dollars pushing several brands of basically the same product. Are they competing against themselves? Not really. Their attempt is to establish dedicated groups of different customers who will stick to Cheer or Oxydol no matter what, even higher prices.

How concentrated is U.S. industry? There are many alternative ways of measuring the answer to this question. One is to measure the percentage of industry shipments that are accounted for by the largest companies in the industry. For example, it will come as no surprise that 92 percent of motor vehicles are made by the 4 largest companies in the field (1967 figures from the Bureau of the Census). Ninety-eight percent were manufactured by the largest 8 companies, and 99+ percent by the largest 20 companies. In the field of aircraft manufacture, the percentage figure ran 69, 89, 99, and 99+ for the largest 4, 8, 20, and 50 firms respectively. On the other hand, ready-mix concrete firms were concentrated with percentages of 6, 9, 16 and 24 respectively. In the case of cigarettes, 100 percent were produced by the top 8 tobacco companies.

What does all this mean? It means that at the very least, industrial concentration is something that must be watched carcfully if the free market system, or anything approaching it, is to survive. With concentration also goes both economic and political power that can be used to further consolidate monopolistic positions. And, of course, this concentration and attempts at attaining monopoly power are not confined to business and industry. Members of labor unions, trade associations, professional associations, and even faculties within our universities all try to get more rewards for themselves by limiting competition. Often it is done in the name of *maintaining quality* or *order and stability*. In spite of the not-to-be-believed, high-flown phrases, everyone tries to escape the constraints that a competitive market structure places on the operations of us all.

One slightly more optimistic note should probably conclude this discussion of imperfect competition. Much of the efficiency associated with competitive industry can still be obtained with less than perfect competition. As long as entry into an industry can take place, a monopoly position will be difficult to maintain unless, as pointed out in the last chapter, decreasing costs exist in the industry. Even the oligopolist or monopolistic competitor is kept somewhat honest by this threat of entry. Perfect competition may not exist, but *effective* competition may still produce outputs and prices close to the perfect model. Freedom of entry and good information on alternatives are, again, the keys in seeing that such effective competition exists.

QUESTIONS

1. List all the conditions that would be necessary to establish a perfect monopoly.
2. Will the total revenue paid for products of a monopoly always be greater than for the same goods produced by a competitive industry? Why or why not?
3. How are excess profits and production incentives related under conditions of monopoly and under competition?
4. Do you hold any monopoly powers yourself? Are you trying to develop any monopoly or monopolistic power?
5. Under what conditions would the output of a monopolistic industry be greater than that of a competitive industry?
6. Think of some ways in which monopolies could be "controlled." What side effects might your suggested control measures generate?
7. If the demand for a good were perfectly inelastic and the supply were perfectly elastic, would the equilibrium quantity change if supply increased? Would the price change? If demand increased and supply remained constant, what would happen to equilibrium price and quantity? Explain your answers.
8. In economic units, "bigness is the same as badness." Discuss this proposition from the economic standpoint as well as the standpoint of social and personal values.
9. Compare competition as it is found in the telephone, steel, soap, and wheat producing industries. In what ways would these industries vary from the models of pure competition and pure monopoly presented in the preceding chapters?
10. Take a copy of your daily newspaper and actually measure and compare the column-inches of advertising that you consider informational with that which attempts to increase sales with little or

no new information about the product presented. How much does the latter type of ad actually influence your own buying habits?

11. Discuss the proposition that advertising is a waste of the nation's resources. Be sure to include such elements as opportunity cost and alternative uses.
12. Obtain a list of ten drugs from your local pharmacist that are marketed under a brand name and also sold either generically or by a smaller company. (Make sure that they are the same pharmaceutical item.) What differences in price exist between the brand drug and the non-brand drug? What steps might be taken to make these differences smaller?
13. Discuss oligopolistic organizations *outside* the field of business.

7

Issues and Problems of the Market

OBJECTIVES

This chapter sets forth some examples of the use of economic tools in examining a wide range of problems. Some of these problems deal directly with money and money prices. Rent controls and minimum wages are examples. The operation of an uncontrolled market is said to "optimize welfare" and a simple look at this proposition is illustrated. Demand elasticity is tied into the discussion to show a practical application of this most important concept. The markets for illegal drugs are discussed and the pot market is compared with the heroin market, with the latter presented as an illustration of a discriminating monopolist. Environmental quality is used to show how difficult it is for the market to solve pollution problems. Finally, subsidies and taxes are examined using the simple tools of supply and demand.

INTRODUCTION

At this point in our course, we can talk about more relevant things than brontosauri and gloops. Using the simple tools developed thus far, we can gain an amazing amount of insight into some of the pressing problems of the day. Most of these involve some kind of interference with market mechanisms in attempts to change the outcomes of market operations.

PRICE CEILINGS BELOW MARKET EQUILIBRIUM

Assume that a politician is either morally or politically concerned about the fact that many of his constituents in the inner portion of the largest city in his district are poor. By anybody's definition, they are poor. One of the major expenses that they still have is rent paid out for housing. The landlords are stealing from the people by charging rents that none of the people can afford.

There is one solution that is so simple *and so visible*, that he wonders why no one had thought of it before. All that has to be done is to pass a law fixing a *maximum* price (rent) that landlords can charge, and setting that price well below the levels currently being charged. A rent *ceiling* will be imposed below the market equilibrium rent. Poor people will be relieved of the excessive rent payments they have been making because the landlords cannot charge them the previous exploitive rates.

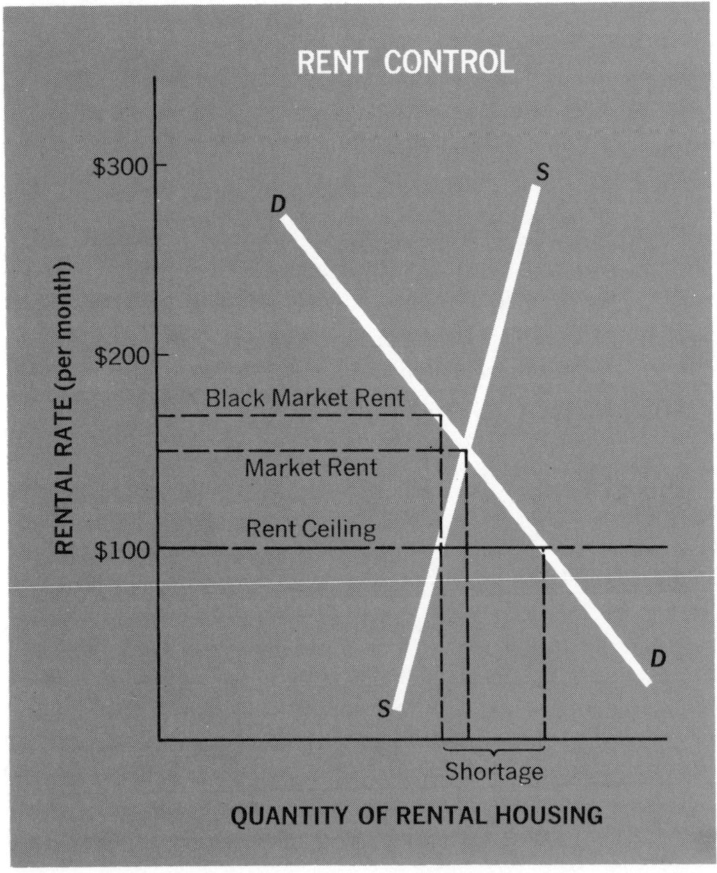

Figure 7-1

Figure 7-1 shows the result of this course of action. Assume that the market rate before the ceiling was imposed averaged out to $150 per month for typical housing units. Assume further that the ceiling imposed amounted to $100 per month. Any rent higher than $100 per month was now illegal. At the lower rental rate, two things happened. Suddenly, people who had been living elsewhere clamored for the cheap housing. The quantity of housing demanded rose. At the same time, many of those landlords now claimed that renting was no longer worthwhile so they withdrew their units from the market. Quantity supplied went down. Both of these events contributed to a brand new *housing shortage*. But another interesting thing also happened. The politician was amazed to find that many of his poorest constituents were the ones who were literally out in the cold because of the housing shortage. When he checked into it further he found that something called a black market had developed in the rent-controlled housing. At the reduced quantity supplied, there were those who were willing and able to pay a rental rate that was even *greater* than the previous equilibrium rate. These, generally, were those least poverty-stricken among the poor. Rather than take their chances on a waiting list, they were going to the landlords with cash "under the table" in return for the assurance of a place to live. As a result, the actual rent they paid was higher than previously charged, but now there were people with no place to live.

Of course, there were attempts to crack down on the black marketeers. These cost the community resources, but did succeed in stopping *some* of the undercover payments. But another strange thing began to happen, too. The housing had never been well maintained by the landlords, but now they really let things go. They insisted they did not have the resources anymore to keep the buildings in repair. Finally, some builders, who had been considering the construction of some low-cost housing, moved out of town the day the rent control act was imposed. They claimed that there was no longer any way that they could come out ahead on such a housing project.

The point of this vignette is not to support either the tenants or the landlords, but to point out how the market will react to this kind of policy. The market has no politics, only people. And people, given free choice, are going to act in about this way. Imposed ceilings that are below free market levels generate the kinds of forces just described. This still might be a relatively cheap way of accomplishing desired goals of cheaper housing for the poor. But to ignore the ramifications of rent control is shortsighted. There have been many examples of this type of policy, including rent control in the U.S.'s largest city—New York. The things described here actually happened and, in some areas, are continuing to happen.

What will determine the magnitude of the bad effects of such controls? Elasticity. If supply is very inelastic—if there is almost no response in quantity supplied to a change in price, then this will reduce the potential shortage. Similarly, if demand is highly inelastic, there will only be a slight increase in quantity demanded when the artificially low price is imposed.

PRICE FLOORS ABOVE MARKET EQUILIBRIUM

Now, take a look at an example of manipulating the free market operation in the other direction. In this case, we will also carry some side effects into other markets to demonstrate the interdependency of certain markets.

Ever since the 1930s, this country has had *minimum wage legislation*. The federal government and many state governments have enacted laws that make it illegal for employers in certain fields to pay less than some specified hourly wage rate. The avowed purpose of the legislation had been to aid the poorly paid worker whose bargaining power vis-à-vis his employer was weak. The comparative weakness is said to often lead to exploitation of the worker in terms of the employer's receiving a disproportionately high share of the total receipts from production. This might be in the form of either excess profits or excess return on his invested capital. The last two sentences are filled with value judgments that are poorly defined at best. What is "poorly paid"? What is a "fair return" or a "fair wage"? For the moment, forget about these very important questions and just look at the economic analysis of the impact of minimum wages on workers.

Figure 7-2 illustrates hypothetical supply and demand curves for workers in the country who are unskilled by some generally accepted standard—for example, sixth grade education and no technical training. The demand curve in this case is called a *derived demand*. Essentially, this means that the employer demands the labor as a required factor of production in producing his product. The greater his (or the industry's) output, the more labor he will require. Labor will be hired *only* if it is profitable for the employer to do so. It is probable that this derived demand will be similar to demand for other goods because at lower prices (wages) larger quantities will be demanded and vice versa. On the supply side, it is probable that the higher the wage offered, the more labor will be willing to work. Workers will be prepared to work more hours, *or* persons currently not working will be enticed into the market. Thus, the general shapes of our supply and demand curves seem to be reasonable. In our example, a market equilibrium wage is established at $1.60 per hour, and the six million people willing to work *at this rate* are employed. Similarly, employers find it profitable *at this wage* to hire the six million workers willing to work. The market wage has brought the quantity supplied and quantity demanded into equilibrium.

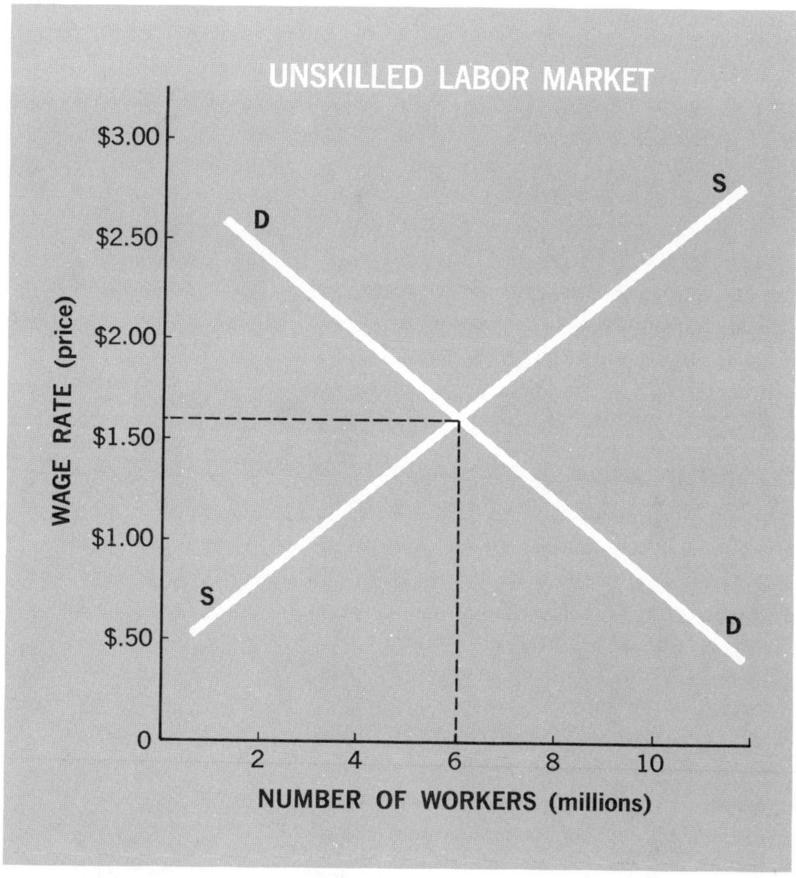

Figure 7-2

Now, let us impose a minimum wage *above* the free market equilibrium rate, say $2.00 per hour as shown in lefthand graph of Figure 7-4. At this higher wage, employers, whether they are exploiting or not, will find it profitable to hire only four million workers (*0f* in Figure 7-4) — two million less than equilibrium quantity (*0b* in Figure 7-4). Unfortunately, this is not the only effect. At the higher wage, more people are willing to work more hours than was the case previously — eight million (*0g* in Figure 7-4) versus six million. If *unemployment* of labor is defined as persons unable to find employment at the going wage rate (as generally it is defined), our minimum wage has produced unemployment of four million workers.

Granted, this is a very simplified analysis of the minimum wage issue, but the results are precisely those that have occurred when minimum wages *over* the market equilibrium have been imposed. True, workers remaining in their jobs have improved *rates* of pay. This may or may not

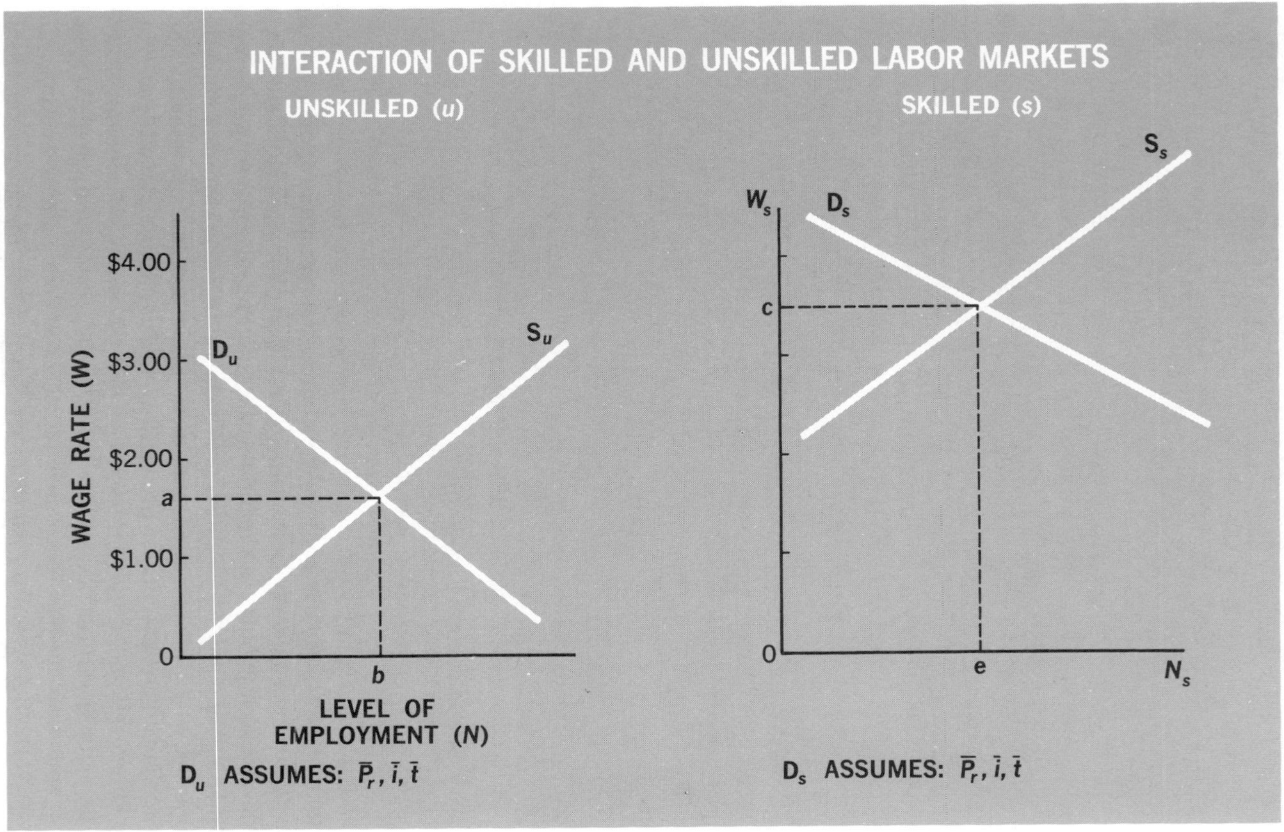

INTERACTION OF SKILLED AND UNSKILLED LABOR MARKETS

UNSKILLED (u)

WAGE RATE (W)
$4.00
$3.00
$2.00
a
$1.00
0
D_u
S_u
b
LEVEL OF EMPLOYMENT (N)

D_u ASSUMES: $\overline{P}_r, \overline{i}, \overline{t}$

SKILLED (s)

W_s
D_s
S_s
c
0
e
N_s

D_s ASSUMES: $\overline{P}_r, \overline{i}, \overline{t}$

Figure 7-3

mean that they have improved *incomes*. If they are working fewer hours, their incomes may actually be reduced. Some workers, however, will be out of a job. Does this mean that minimum wages are bad? Some workers gain while others lose. Some unemployment will occur, but again, the degree of this unemployment will depend upon the elasticities of supply and demand. How long this unemployment might last is another issue. If job retraining is possible, it might be able to help in moving workers into jobs where their potential earnings would be higher in the future. We look at the gains and losses once again in the forthcoming welfare discussions. But the main point of this presentation is that although the initial intent of a minimum wage policy is to help the poorly paid worker, the results are not without some ill effects on the very group that was supposed to be assisted.

The discussions thus far have implied that many markets are interrelated. We have said, for example, that the *demand* for a particular good will depend upon the *prices* of complements and substitutes. Our minimum wage analysis provides an opportunity to study one such interaction. In Figure 7-3, two markets are shown, the supply and demand for unskilled labor and the supply and demand for skilled labor. There are certainly problems in breaking down the labor force into these two categories, but conceptually, it is easy to imagine. Let us assume that the wage rate for unskilled laborers in a free market would be $1.60 per hour again, and that the wage rate in the skilled market would be $3.50 per hour. This latter wage is clearly above the minimum wage suggested in the previous example, so it would seem unlikely that representatives of skilled workers, such as their unions, would be very concerned about increasing the wages of their unskilled (and nonunion) fellow workers. One could suggest that unions are motivated by ideals of better pay and working conditions (another form of pay) for all men who earn their bread by the sweat of their brows. This is possible. There is, however, a very good economic reason for such unions to support increased minimum wages. Remember that the supply and demand curves in this example are constructed *ceteris paribus*, including the prices of substitute goods. Are skilled and unskilled workers substitutes for each other? Most assuredly there are many cases in which any appreciable substitution would be almost impossible. An untrained floor sweeper would probably have a difficult time performing the job of a precision toolmaker without a substantial investment in time and training. In many jobs, however, substitution is possible *if* the less skilled person can be hired for a lower wage. Although his productivity is lower, the wages paid to him would also be lower.

Our initial demand curve for skilled labor was constructed holding the wage of unskilled labor at the $1.60 per hour rate. If a minimum wage of $2.00 per hour is imposed, its direct effect will be felt only in the unskilled market because the equilibrium wage in the skilled market is already above the new minimum. Again referring to Figure 7-4, we see the unemployment effect of *fg* (four million). Employers of unskilled labor will demand quantity *0f*. Unskilled workers are willing to supply quantity *0g*, and an unemployment of *fg* will result. For those still working, however, the wage has increased to the $2.00 minimum. Employers in the skilled market are now faced (again, at least to some degree) with a substitute for skilled labor that is more expensive. If these employers are also employing some unskilled laborers, they are now paying a higher wage for their services. The price of the substitute good has risen, and, therefore, the *demand* for the skilled workers will increase. This is actually quite a reasonable result. If the employer is forced to pay higher wages, he will try to substitute (or retain) workers with the greatest possible productivity. This substitution results in an increase in the demand for skilled workers—in our example, D_S'. With this new demand, both the wages and quantity hired of the skilled labor will increase. For the skilled types, that has to be the best of all possible worlds.

Again, it is important to emphasize that the "goodness" or "badness" of minimum wages is not the issue in this case. The analysis merely points up some of the expected effects that have been known to be ignored at times by politicians and protesters. In recent years, there have been various movements to boycott California grapes that were supposed to help the plight of harvest laborers in that state's grape-growing area. It is of interest that in listening to many arguments on both sides of the issue, one never heard any mention of the potential effect of the boycott on the long-run demand for grapes. Nor was the effect on the derived demand for grape harvesters discussed. There was no consideration that the demand for grapes is related to the demands of other fresh fruits. It was never suggested that *increasing* rather than decreasing the demand for grapes might be one method of raising the potential wages of the harvesters. Above all, there was *never* a suggestion that increased wages gained through the formation of a union might create unemployment among a portion of the workers. Whether the union *should* be formed or whether the workers *should* receive higher wages is not the issue. These may be perfectly legitimate goals, but their impact should be considered in total and not just those effects that fit the interests of the conflicting parties.

THE MARKET AND WELFARE

A freely operating market will bring the quantity demanded by buyers into balance with the quantity supplied by sellers via a freely moving price. How do we know that this price is *optimal*, and how do we define optimal? To answer these questions, it is necessary to agree on some method of

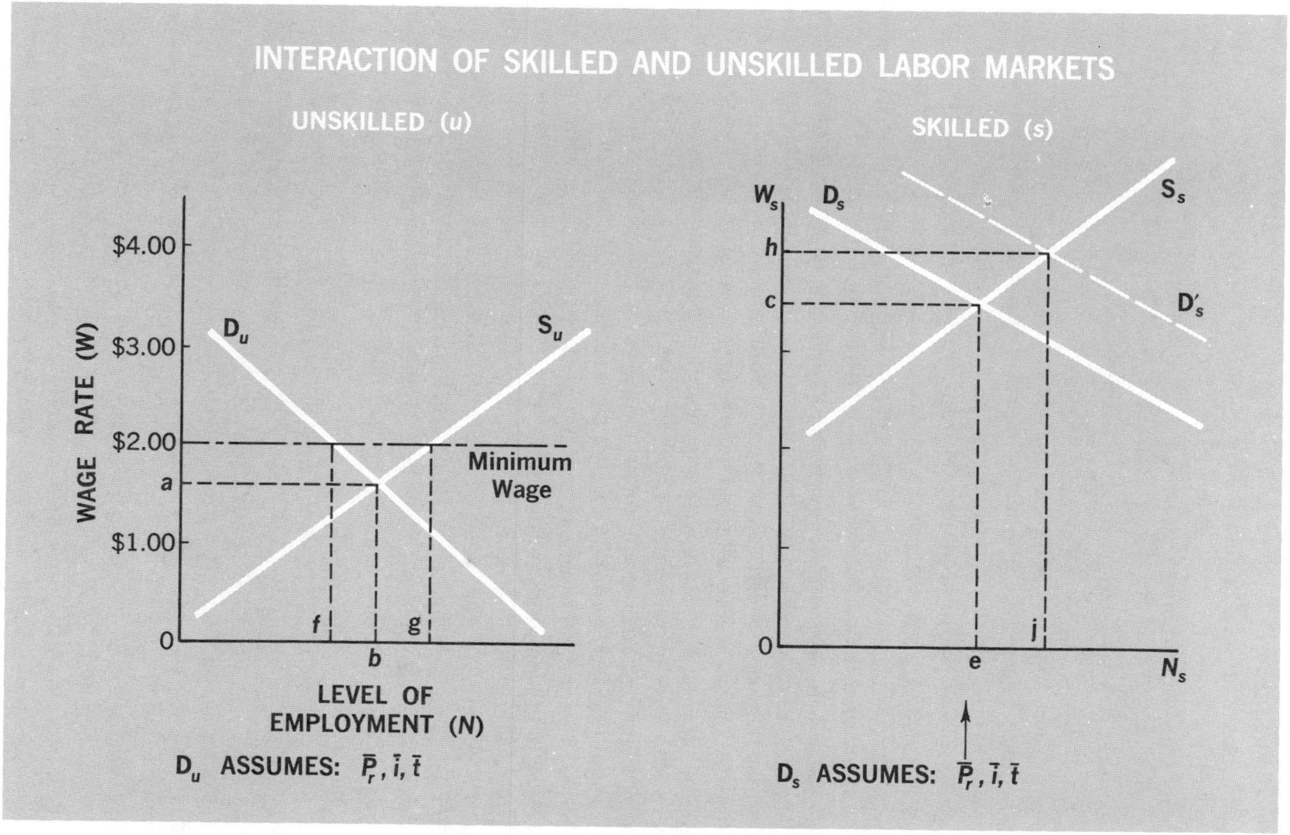

INTERACTION OF SKILLED AND UNSKILLED LABOR MARKETS

UNSKILLED (u)

WAGE RATE (W)

$4.00

$3.00

$2.00

a

$1.00

0

D_u

S_u

Minimum Wage

f

b

g

LEVEL OF EMPLOYMENT (N)

D_u ASSUMES: $\bar{P}_r, \bar{i}, \bar{t}$

SKILLED (s)

W_s

h

c

0

D_s

S_s

D'_s

e

j

N_s

D_s ASSUMES: $\bar{P}_r, \bar{i}, \bar{t}$

Figure 7-4

determining the *welfare* gains and losses that a society, or groups within a society (such as buyers and sellers), can be expected to accrue under different market conditions. We will use the concept of welfare in a rather narrow sense and define it as carefully as possible.

It has been pointed out several times now that economists, *as economists*, try to separate analysis from value judgments. Even though the general concept of welfare usually includes many subjective evaluations, most economists will agree on one criterion. If one person or entity can be made better off without making another person or entity worse off, then society's total welfare has been *increased*. If one person or entity is made worse off without another person or entity being made better off, then welfare in the society has *decreased*. The catch comes in the next statement. If one person loses something of value and another person gains something of equal value, society's welfare has not changed. The analysis that follows makes that assumption, *but it is an assumption*, and, in essence, it amounts to a value judgment in itself. It is impossible to say, for example, that one dollar taken from a millionaire and given to a ghetto welfare recipient will result in no change in the society's total welfare. It is equally impossible to state with any degree of certainty that the dollar will make the welfare recipient "happier" (increased welfare) to a greater extent than it makes the millionaire "unhappier" (decreased welfare). By assuming that *redistribution effects* cancel each other out, we can be on dangerous ground. However, such an assumption does give us a benchmark that makes analysis possible. The results of the analysis can be modified to whatever extent the user may feel is justified, by substituting other subjective evaluations of redistribution effects. With this note of caution, let us investigate one type of welfare produced by the price system in both free and controlled markets. Figure 7-5 presents supply and demand curves for some particular commodity in some particular market. At the moment, the only important assumptions made are that the demand curve is downward sloping and that the supply curve is upward sloping, both from left to right. In other words, *ceteris paribus*, demanders will purchase larger quantities at lower prices, and suppliers will supply larger quantities at higher prices. In a free market, a price of *0c* will serve to equate quantities supplied and demanded at quantity *0d*. Consider for a moment that portion of demand represented by segment *ab* of the demand curve. What is the meaning of that portion of demand where some quantities of the good *would be* purchased at prices higher than the equilibrium price? As with most concepts in economics, ask this question of yourself. There are undoubtedly some goods that you purchase in your daily life for which you would pay a higher-than-market price if you had to. That does not mean you *like* to pay higher prices, but it means you would pay on an "all or nothing" basis. Presumably, if you did pay a higher price, your

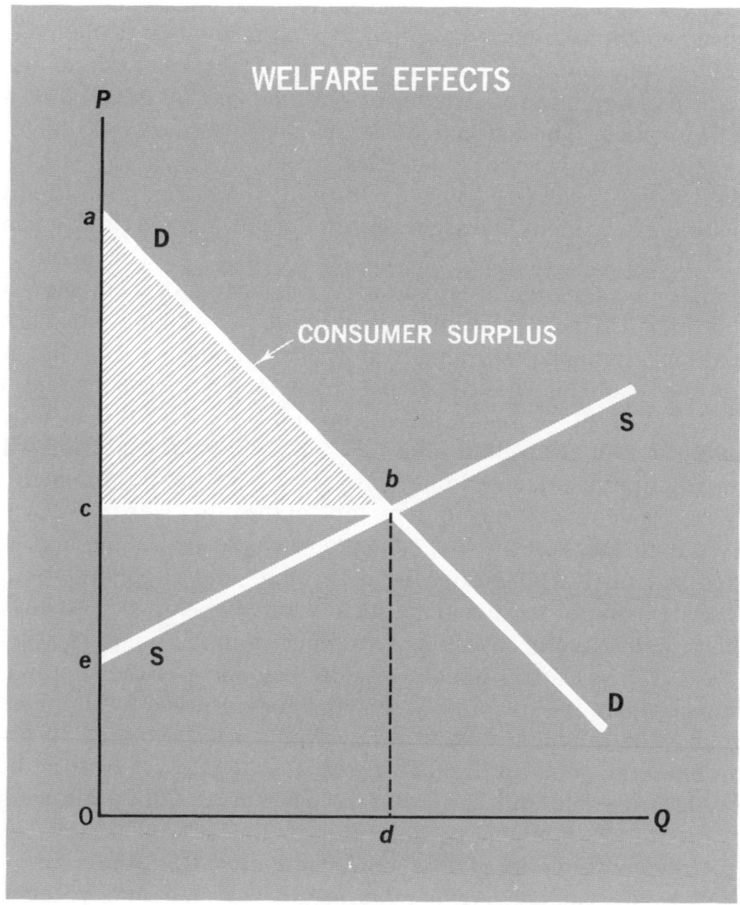

Figure 7-5

welfare would decrease because you would then have less money to purchase other goods you desire.

Take a college education as an example. Assume that a student is paying tuition of $300 per semester at the moment. There are some who probably would drop out of college if the tuition (price) were raised at all. Those people are "at the margin." They are just willing and able to pay the $300 and not one cent more. But others probably would stay in school even if the price were raised to $350 per semester. Fewer still might remain if the price went to $500, and so forth, until finally the price would be raised so high that no one would demand an education at that institution. Those who are willing and able at this time to pay *more* than the actual price are really receiving a "bargain." The operation of the market has made it possible to receive a good at a cost *less than* that which the student would have been prepared to pay on an all-or-nothing basis. This demonstrates that the demand curve implies the existence of some demand for the product above the market price. The amount of money that people would have been willing and able to pay above the market price represents a "savings" of sorts. Economists call this *consumer surplus*. On the graph in Figure 7-5, this amount can be identified as the area under the demand curve and above the price line. It is triangle *abc*. Demanders actually paid an amount equal to the price times the quantity marketed, or the area of rectangle *0cbd*. If each one had paid the maximum he would have been willing and able to pay on an all-or-nothing basis, then an additional amount equal to the area of triangle *abc* would also have been paid by demanders. The amount of this "saving" or surplus is a measure of consumer welfare. It is not the *only* measure of consumer welfare, but it is a useful one in analyzing why the market solution of price and quantities, in one sense, is "optimal."

Leaving demand for a moment, look at the other side of the picture—supply. At the market price *0c*, suppliers would be willing and able to produce a quantity of *0d*. Notice, however, that *some* suppliers would have been able to supply smaller quantities at prices below *0c*. At least one supplier would have been willing to supply an initial quantity at a lower price of *0e* (or just a hair above *0e*)—the beginning of the supply curve. Here again, there is a quantity of money being received by suppliers *over and above* the minimum amount they would have required to produce quantities of the good up to quantity *0d*. It is the area *ecb*. It is the area below the price line and above the supply curve. On an all-or-nothing basis, producers would have accepted an amount of money equal to *0ebd*. At the market price, they received a total of *0cbd*, the same amount paid out by demanders. Again, this means that suppliers received *ecb* more than the minimum they would have accepted to produce the quantity marketed.

Figure 7-6 illustrates these two areas together. Triangle *abc* gives a measure of consumer welfare, obviously for consumers involved in this market. Triangle *ecb* gives a measure of the welfare of producers in this market. Adding the two triangles together gives us a measure of the welfare of everyone, producers and consumers, associated with this market. The total triangle *abe* is often called the welfare triangle.

To analyze the effects on welfare of prices and quantities *other than* the market solution, we will see what happens to the size of these areas when other prices are imposed on the system. In the first example, go back to rent control, or ceiling prices imposed below the market equilibrium. Assume that the government imposed a rent ceiling in the housing market equal to *0k* in Figure 7-7. Without the ceiling imposed, the market equilib-

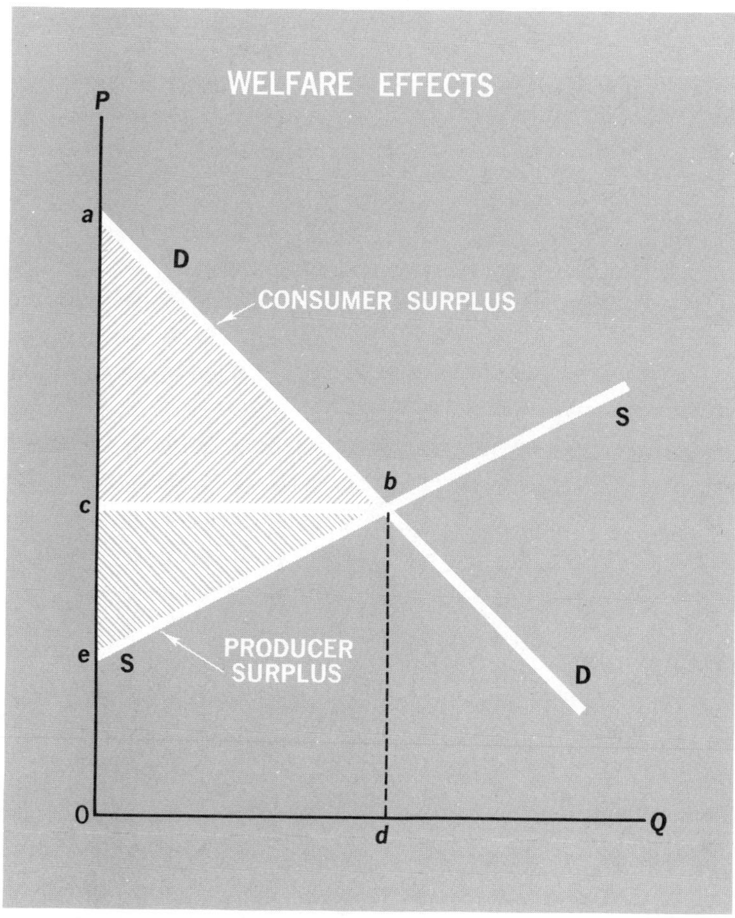

Figure 7-6

rium rent would be $0c$. From the previous discussion, consumer surplus would equal the area of cab, the area above the price line and below the demand curve. Producer (landlord) surplus would equal the area below the price line and above the supply curve, triangle cbe. We will assume that the imposed ceiling is successfully enforced, and, as a result, the quantity supplied drops from the equilibrium level $0d$ back to $0g$. Of course, at the low price, quantity demanded has risen to $0h$ thus producing an economic shortage of gh. But with only $0g$ now available, the quantity demanded does not really matter. There is only $0g$ available, no matter what quantity is demanded. $0g$ will now be the quantity marketed. Of course, price will no longer perform its rationing function and some other way is going to have to

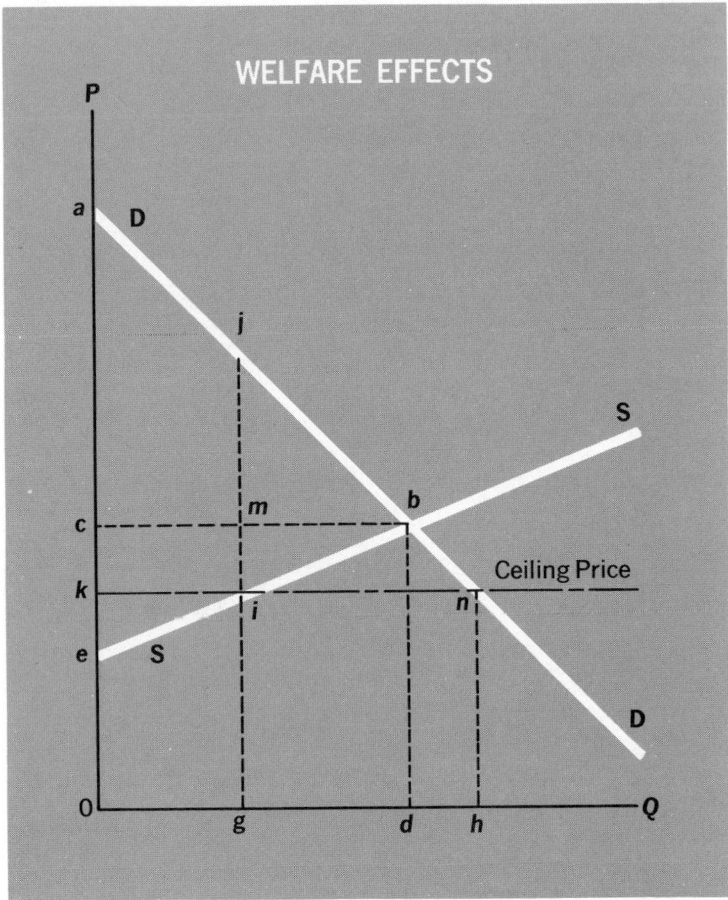

Figure 7-7

be employed to decide who gets what. It may be coupons, or first-come-first-served, or some other criterion set up by a planning board. This is all old hat by this stage of the game, but let us see what has happened to consumer and producer surplus.

In order to determine the new consumer surplus, it is necessary to know *who* among all of the potential demanders actually ended up with the limited supply. Who among the demanders, represented by *0h*, actually received the quantity available, *0g*? Assume for the moment that those people who were willing and able to pay the highest prices (represented by demand curve segment, *aj*, actually received the housing. In this case, consumer surplus would be reduced by triangle *jmb* because of the reduced quantity available, but it would also be increased by the rectangle *cmik* as the result of the lower ceiling price. Producers would lose surplus in the amount of *cbik* because of both the lower price for those that are still renting their housing, and also because some suppliers are no longer renting any units. But, as you can see, part of the landlord's losses are redistributed as gains to tenants who are still able to rent the short supply. Again, this group is actually paying less for its housing, which represents a clear gain to it. This is a clear transfer of purchasing power from the landlords, who were getting it from the tenants in the form of rent, to the tenants who are no longer having to pay this money in rent.

Now to recap the gains and losses. First of all, there is no way that a ceiling price below equilibrium can produce gains for the producers, in this case, the landlords. They are bound to lose in every way. First, as a group they lose by the fact that some landlords have withdrawn their properties from the market, and those properties previously yielded surplus equal to *mbi* in Figure 7-8. Those landlords still in the market are getting less for their properties by the amount of *cmik*. Consumers, the tenants, both gain and lose. Those who are no longer able to find housing because of the shortage have lost *at least* the triangle *mbj*. Again, this assumes that those most willing and able to pay for the short supply actually get the short supply. If this is not the case, the losses for consumers become even larger. So tenants lose by at least *mbj*, but those still renting gain by *cmik*, the redistribution from the landlords. Whether tenants *as a group* gain or lose will depend on the relative size of the loss triangle, *mbj*, and the gain rectangle, *cmik*. This, in turn, will depend on the elasticity of supply. If supply is highly inelastic, then the loss triangle will be small compared to the gain rectangle, and consumers as a group will gain. If supply is relatively elastic, then the loss triangle will be large compared to the gain rectangle. Study this from several angles and you will see how it works out.

This makes sense in other ways than the geometry. If supply is inelastic, this is saying that an enforced decrease in price will not make much of an impact on the quantity supplied. Even though legal rents are cut, landlords will continue to supply the housing units. There will not be a very large housing shortage, and those with housing will do very well at the expense of the landlords. With the inelastic supply, society's minimum welfare loss, the area of triangle *jbi*, will also be comparatively small. Most of the impact of the ceiling will be to transfer surplus (buying power) from the landlords to the tenants. But the impact on long-run supply may still be there. If it is no longer profitable to build or rent housing, the long-run supply will decrease thus accentuating any shortage developed by the ceiling.

One interesting point, however, needs to be made. Unless supply is *completely* inelastic, society as a whole must lose at least some welfare by

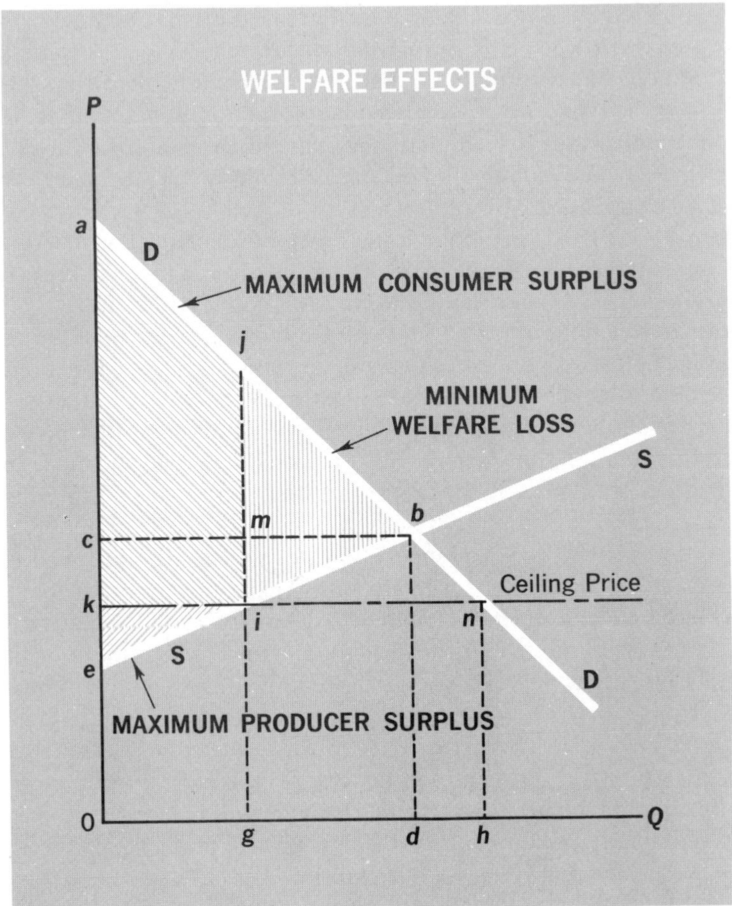

Figure 7-8

the imposition of the ceiling. The minimum welfare loss triangle *jbi* will still be there, no matter how small.

Now let us take our other example of market interference and see how that works. In the case of the minimum wage imposed above market equilibrium, what effects would one expect? The mechanics are similar to those of the ceiling price. In Figure 7-9, we have graphed the situation. Without the minimum wage, the wage rate would be *0f* in the free market and the level of employment would be *0b*. Consumer surplus would be *fhk*, and producer surplus would be *dhf*. Consumers in this case are the people who are hiring labor—labor's employers—and the producers here are the laborers themselves.

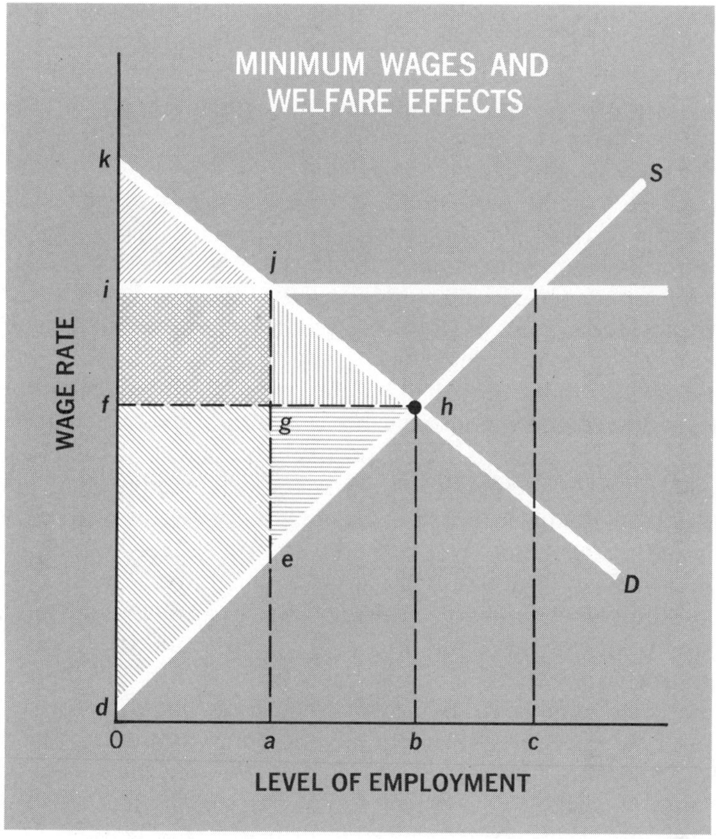

Figure 7-9

Now, impose and enforce a minimum wage above the equilibrium wage, say *0i*. At this wage, the number of people wanting to work rises from the old equilibrium level *0b* to a new high of *0c*. But, unfortunately, employers are willing and able to hire *fewer* workers than before. They will only hire *0a*. Obviously, quantity demanded is less than quantity supplied, and, as always, when these two quantities are different, the smaller of the two is the one that counts. With a ceiling price, it was quantity supplied that was the quantity marketed and with a floor price, it will be quantity demanded that is marketed.

Of course, we end up with unemployment equal to *ac*. Of this total unemployment, *ab* represents workers who had a job before and now do not. For comparison purposes, this is the unemployed group that we are interested in. In the free market, this group had had a producer's surplus equal to *ehg* and this has been wiped out. Incidentally, their only job alternatives now are to try to find a job at the minimum wage somewhere outside this market or to find a job in some employment not subject to the minimum wage law. At the higher wage rate, employers will have laid off the *ab* group of workers. Employers had been getting *ghj* of consumers surplus from this group, and now they have lost that surplus. In addition, employers are paying a higher wage to those workers still employed and this increased expenditure amounts to *fgji*. On the other side of the coin, workers who still have jobs are, in fact, being paid the higher wage, and this group is receiving *fgji* more money than before. In other words, employers (consumers of labor) lose, no matter how the effect is figured, by a total of *ijhf*. Workers (producers of labor) as a group lose by *ehg* but gain by *fgji*. If this latter rectangle is larger than the loss triangle, then *as a group*, they have done well. On the other hand, if the area of the triangle is greater than the area of the rectangle, they have lost *as a group*. What will determine the relative sizes of these two areas? In this case, it will be the elasticity of demand for the services of the workers. If the demand is highly inelastic, then all of the potential losses from the minimum wage law will be comparatively small. If the demand is elastic, losses will be large. Again, it makes sense. An inelastic demand will mean a comparatively small cutback in employment with an increase in the minimum wage so that the losses from unemployment will be small. Figure 7-10 illustrates the point. With a comparatively inelastic demand, such as demand curve *D*, imposing the minimum wage only reduces previous employment by *ab*—very little in this case. Workers in the unemployed group now only lose *ehg* of producer's surplus and employers lose only *ghj* of surplus from the employees they laid off. On the other hand, the size of the redistribution from employers to workers is relatively large again, *fgji*. For workers as a group, they have clearly gained. The rectangle is much larger than the loss triangle *ehg*.

What this rather long and tedious exercise points out is that, given our definition of welfare, the free market will produce the greatest welfare possible. Any attempt in either direction to forceably change the free market price will lead to shortages or surpluses and some loss of welfare for society as a whole. This does not mean that floors and ceilings should not be used. It does mean that caution should be exercised with this sort of policy. If the elasticities concerned are wrong, then it is possible to do more damage than good and do the damage to the very group to be helped. There are alternatives to these imposed prices that involve redistributing income *before* it is spent in the marketplace and then letting the free market take over. This will be covered in detail when national tax policy is discussed in Chapter 13.

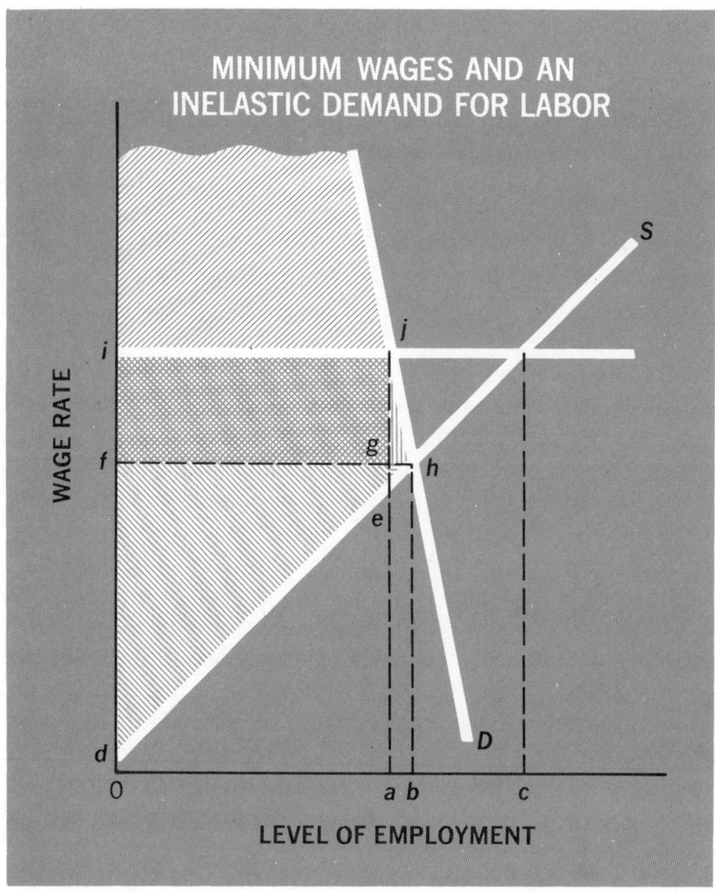

Figure 7-10

ILLEGAL DRUG MARKETS

The tools developed thus far can also be used to describe market operations that society has labeled as illegal or immoral. Consider two of these markets—the market for marijuana and the market for heroin. The market for both pot and heroin can be described with the usual supply and demand curve with a free market equilibrium price and quantity that would exist in the absence of government restrictions. Remember, both supply and demand curves are drawn on the assumption of free choice by both consumers and producers. In the case of these two products, society has decided that individuals should not be given the free choice to either produce or consume the goods. Previously, we have shown the results of government intervention through the media of minimum prices above equilibrium and ceiling prices below equilibrium. In the case of these two commodities, the government operates on *quantities* rather than prices. In general, the attempt is made to prevent *any* quantity from entering the market (except for small quantities for research). As one might expect, the attempt at thwarting individual desires to use drugs involves substantial policing costs that tend to keep society from "going all out." It is too expensive. As a result, the effort is only partially effective and substantial quantities of both goods do reach consumers. Thus, quantity is reduced below the free market equilibrium quantity as shown in Figure 7-11 for pot and Figure 7-13 for the heroin market. The effect of this enforced reduction in quantity is analytically similar in some respects to the imposition of a ceiling price. *Producers* (not necessarily *suppliers*) would be willing to produce the limited quantity at a lower-than-equilibrium price, and a few demanders would be willing and able to pay a much higher-than-equilibrium price. Look now at the pot market shown in Figure 7-11. As with a ceiling price, the stage is set for the operation of a *black market.* There will be a market incentive for people to go into the illegal distribution business. These people will purchase the limited quantities at the low price offered by producers (*0e*) and sell to buyers at a price of *0f*. This will produce a return to the distributors equal to the size of rectangle *ejhf.* You could call this revenue *profit*, but it really is not. The distributor is actually performing a useful function and taking considerable risk in doing so. True, society does not view his activities as a service, but the person buying the pot certainly does and is paying for it.

In effect, making the pot illegal raises the costs of production and distribution *as viewed by the customer*, which means that, from his standpoint, the supply curve has shifted upward to the left. Supply has decreased as shown by the shift from *SS* to *S'S'* in Figure 7-12. Incidentally, because one of the risks involved in the distribution process includes going to prison, it is to be expected that the kind of person most likely to get into the business would be someone for whom prison held relatively less fear than for others.

Most information available suggests that there are many amateurs in the pot distribution business and that there is usually a fairly competitive market available to a potential user. In other words, the potential buyer of pot could go to several, if not many, sources to obtain the product. If one seller tries charging more than the market price, the buyer can find another seller willing to sell at the market price. Because of this competition, there will tend to be a single price for all demanders in the market.

Now, let us shift our attention to the heroin market illustrated in

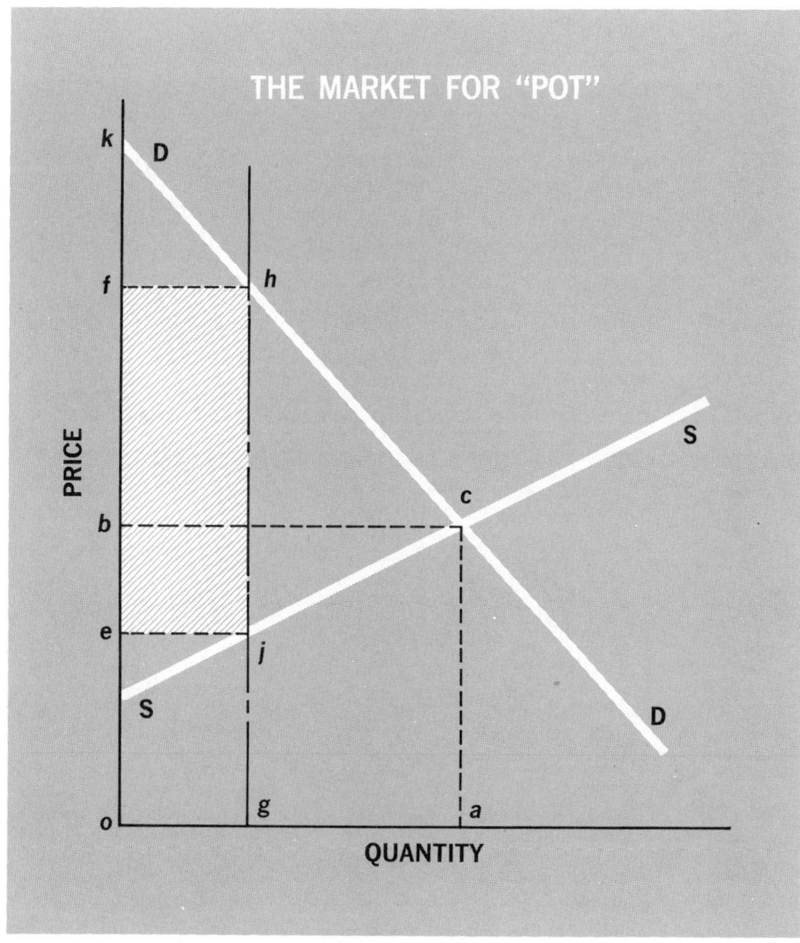

Figure 7-11

Figure 7-13. The analysis is similar to that in the pot market *up to a point.* The limited quantity that escapes the authorities (*0g*) is purchased from producers at price *0e* by the refining and distributing organization. This quantity is then sold to customers for a price of *at least 0f*. This "at least" represents a large difference in the character of the two markets. Unlike pot, the marketing of heroin seems to be almost exclusively in the hands of professionals, and there is substantial evidence that they are organized into a highly effective monopoly. This monopoly either handles directly or effectively controls all stages of the refining and distribution processes from the opium poppy grower to the ultimate user of heroin. Even the "pusher" at the final customer level generally has his specified (and pro-

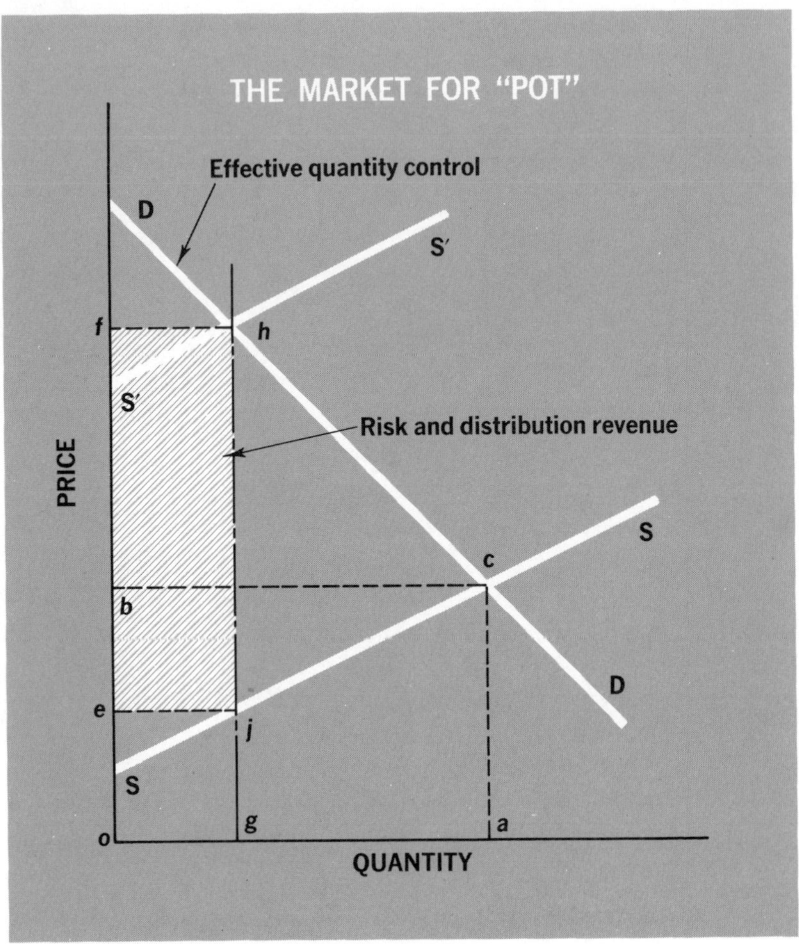

Figure 7-12

tected) area, or, at least, specific customers who must buy from him if they are to obtain the drug. This fact changes the potential profitability of the distribution process. Assuming that he has personal knowledge of his customers and their degree of addiction, the pusher can capture the consumer surplus of each of his customers. Some of his customers would be unwilling to pay a price greater than $0f$ in Figure 7-13. A few may be willing to pay as much as $0k$, and, assuming the pusher knows that fact, he can charge that particular customer $0k$ because the addict has no other source from which to buy. If the pusher knows each of his customers, he will be

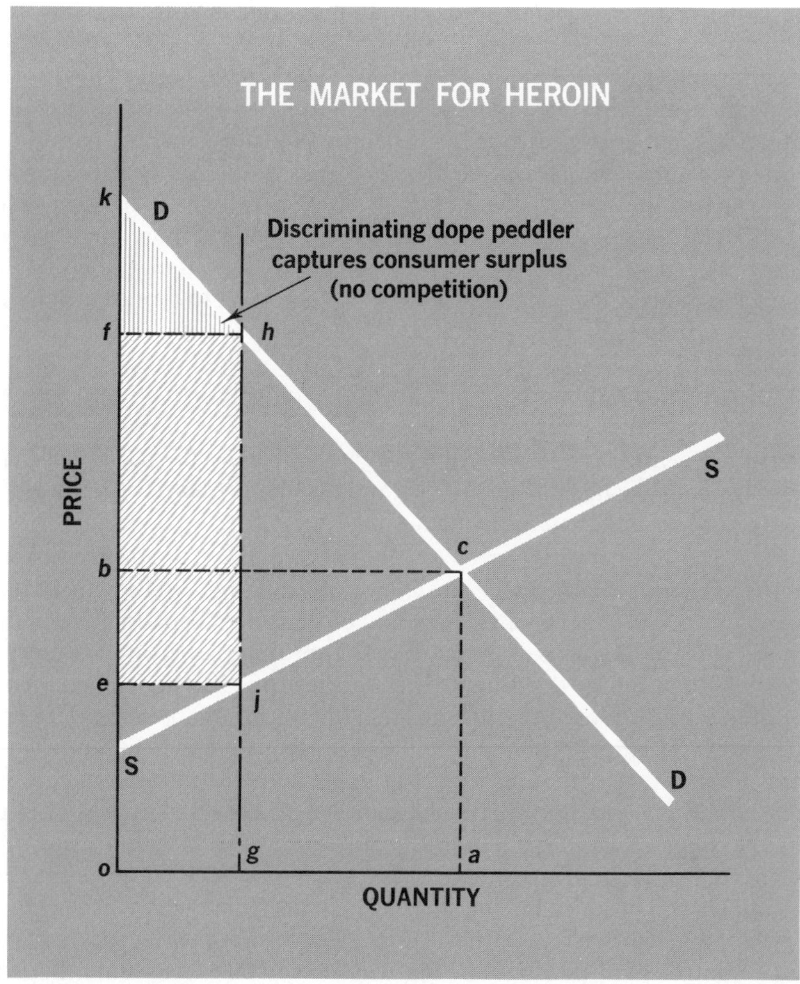

Figure 7-13

able to charge each one the maximum the person is willing and able to pay on an all-or-nothing basis. In this way, the operation is able to collect not only *ejhf* for risk and distribution, but the consumer surplus *fhk* besides.

One loophole might exist that could dampen this scheme. One person is willing and able to pay *0k,* the top dollar for a "fix." Another customer is willing and able to pay only *0f* for a fix. What is to prevent Demander Two from buying a fix at *0f* and then selling it to Demander One for *0k*? The answer is "nothing," as long as the amateur seller did not get caught by the professionals. In this case, he might find himself cut off from further supplies, or even be found dead. The prevention of resale is an essential ingredient if a discriminating monopolist is going to be successful.

As an aside, there are other semi-monopoly operations that use discriminating pricing. For example, the electric industry generally has different rates for different uses of electricity. For example, the per-kilowatt charge for heating purposes is generally less than that for lighting. The reason for the cheaper rate for heating is the existence of more competitive fuels for this purpose. The reason they can get by with multiple pricing is the fact that it is difficult for some enterprising person to buy electricity at the low rate and resell it at the high rate. Electricity is difficult to store and distribute, at least for the would-be small operator. Doctors, too, can get away with differential pricing. They claim to charge less to the people who cannot afford their regular rates. Of course, this implies that those regular rates are high enough to balance the cut-rate service to the poor. But they can do this because it is difficult to buy and resell their services. How does one go about reselling an appendectomy?

There is another difference between the two illegal goods just discussed. It is generally agreed that pot is not physiologically addictive. It is universally agreed that heroin is *very* addictive—the most addictive of the opiates. This implies that after some period of time, a heroin customer's willingness to purchase the drug will become less and less dependent on the price of the drug. In other words, his demand for heroin becomes less and less elastic. Actually, his demand curve is rotating as shown in Figure 7-14. As this happens, the amount of consumer surplus the pusher can capture increases sharply and, thus, his profits can also be expected to rise. This, of course, explains the willingness of the pusher to offer his product to new customers, or potential customers, at very low prices. He knows that his free samples will produce paying customers in the future who will be willing to pay increasing price levels for the dope. There are other factors, such as ease of control over production, but it is reasonable to assume that the addictive quality of heroin provides strong incentive for distributors to monopolize the market. The increasing consumer surplus that addiction implies makes much more profit potential than in the case of pot.

This example of an illegal activity that is supported by a significant part of the population brings out some interesting points. The *cost* to society of making dope illegal does not stop with the cost of ineffectually harassing drug traffic, traffickers, and users. By far the largest portion of dope gets through the net, and even the most avid enforcer admits that it always will. The economic incentives are so strong, and the basic nature of distribution so simple, that any reasonable level of resources spent on enforcement is not likely to do much good. But the largest cost of keeping this traffic outside the law lies in two other areas. First of all, by far the largest amount of street crime today is connected with the need to support

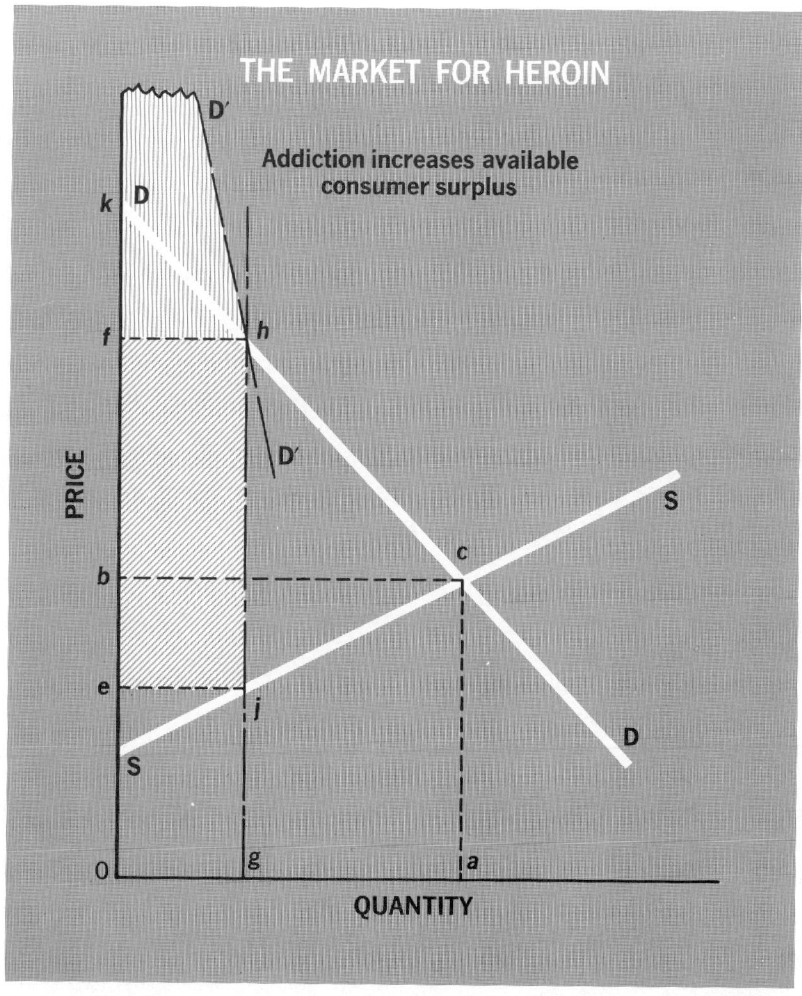

Figure 7-14

addictive habits. There are very few ways one *legally* can earn sufficient funds to support a $200 a day habit. In fact, to net this much from stealing, the thief will have to steal five to ten times that much in merchandise. Either that, or go into the pushing business himself. The costs of this illegal activity in heroin are staggering.

The second poorly recognized cost comes in the incentives that exist to hook the young and the inexperienced. The school yards of the country would not have their own pushers for long if the profitability of illegal heroin were eliminated.

Does all this mean that heroin should be legalized? Does it mean that any addict should be able to go to his doctor and get a fix any time he needs it? Society should be aware of the costs it is imposing on itself when it uses the law to enforce basically moral beliefs. Having all of the information, if the decision is the same, so be it. But not having good information on costs and benefits as well as alternatives can be fatal for a society based on individual action.

ENVIRONMENTAL QUALITY

It seems as if it happened overnight. Amid spectacular productivity and prosperity, pollution has begun to take over the world. Economics has something to do with the creation of the pollution monster, it has something to do with the present levels of pollution, and some of the cures will take place *only* if those economics are understood both by the policy maker and the voting, buying, and taxpaying citizen. We will not go into these economics in great depth, but some insight into the problem may be gained by following the next pages carefully.

One common myth is that if only the right people had control over the property rights of the thing being polluted, then everything would be pristine pure and clean. The myth says that if you and I owned the air over Gary, Indiana, we would stop all the impurities from going into the air tomorrow. On the other hand, if U.S. Steel owns the air over Gary, then it is going to pollute to its heart's content as long as polluting means it can produce cheaper steel. The strange thing is, as far as the *level of pollution* is concerned, it might not make any difference at all who actually owned the air rights. We are assuming for the moment that whoever owned the air rights could actually enforce those rights without cost. This is a big assumption, as we will see.

If you and I started off with these air rights, probably the first thing that would happen is that we would tell U.S. Steel to *stop* all emissions of impurities into our air. *That* really is going to be expensive. In fact, given present technology, the only way that can happen is for U.S. Steel to shut down completely. Not only are U.S. Steel and the stockholders going to be unhappy, but the thousands of workers in Gary that work for U.S.S. are also going to be upset. They may try the next best thing which would be to try to *buy* the right to pollute the air, at least a little bit. As economists, we could appreciate this approach but where will this end? The answer is that given our assumptions of zero cost enforceability of property rights and a zero cost transaction between U.S.S. and ourselves, the level of pollution that U.S.S. was producing before will probably go *down*. There will still be some, but it will be sharply reduced when compared to the situation in which U.S.S. was able to use the air as a free good. Now, what happens if the wrong person gets the property rights? What happens if U.S. Steel owns the rights to the air around its plants, and we do not? One thing that could happen is that you and I move out of Gary. This is one way to reduce the pollution *problem*, not pollution, but the problems associated with it. Get away from it! This is precisely what many people have done in the past few decades by moving farther and farther away from metropolitan centers in which industry and the municipalities themselves have lowered environmental quality. But if we do not want to leave Gary, we still have an alternative *if* we have command over sufficient resources. In the same way that U.S.S. bought the privilege of polluting, we can buy off U.S.S. to *reduce* their polluting. Given our assumptions, this will work, and pollution will be reduced to the same level that it would have been when we held the property rights. As long as the right to the resource being polluted can be *defined, assigned*, and *enforced* without major costs, then the *level* of pollution will not change by changing the ownership of the resource. No matter who owns it, the holder will be faced with *opportunity costs*. When we own the air, we face the opportunity cost of having a customer willing and able to buy some of our rights. When U.S.S. owns the rights, they face the opportunity costs of having citizens willing and able to pay *them* to reduce their levels of pollution.

A look at Figure 7-15 may help with the understanding. This set of supply and demand curves are a little different. Instead of quantity, we will talk about percentage of pollution control, or, conversely, percentage of pollution. The scale runs from left to right for pollution control (0-100%) and from right to left for level of pollution (again, 0-100%). Our demand curve says that the sufferers of pollution will demand a higher percentage of control for lower prices of control and lower percentages of control if prices of control rise. It is the same law of demand with a little twist. Similarly, the suppliers of pollution control—in this case the polluters themselves—will be willing and able to provide larger measures of control (lower levels of pollution) if the price of doing so goes up.

If property rights do not exist or are not defined nor enforced for the air we are considering, then potential polluters will use the air as though it were a free good. Pollution will stand at the 100 percent level, or, in other words, there will be no attempt at control. Let us say that property rights *are* assigned, and U.S.S. gets them. At first, they continue to pollute as before. But for 100 percent pollution, the sufferers are willing and able according to the demand curve, to pay a price of *ae* for at least a little control. It is only going to cost U.S.S. a small amount to provide that control as shown by the supply curve. As a result, it will pay U.S.S. to provide some control and take our money. As long as the price we are willing and able to pay (our demand) is greater than U.S.S.'s cost of providing additional control, it will pay them to accept our payments and

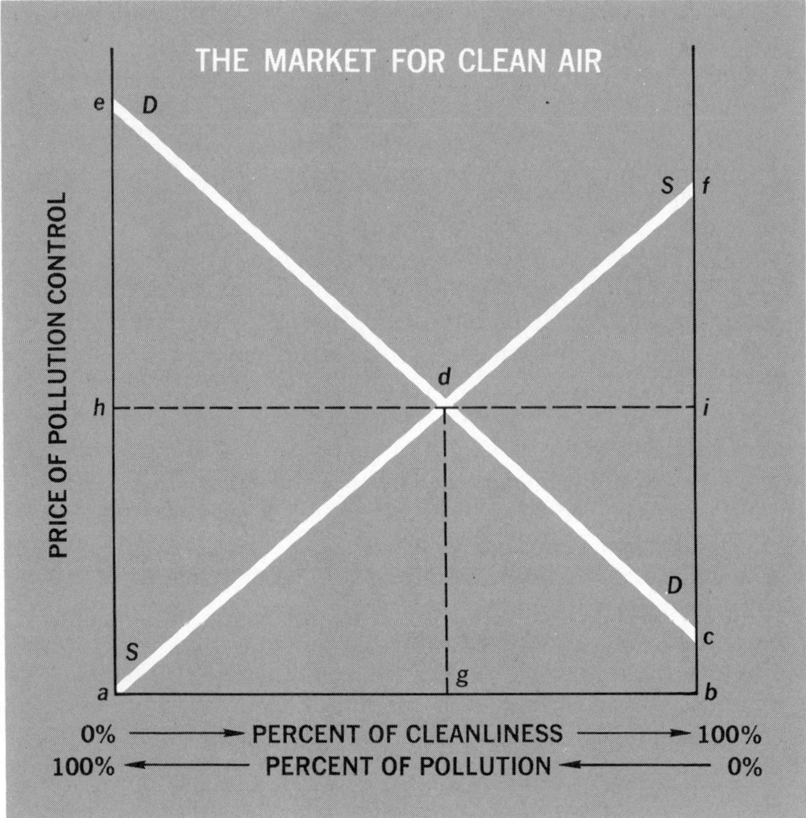

Figure 7-15

increase the level of control to *ag*. At that point, it will be costing them *ah* per unit of control, and this is just the price we are willing and able to pay for that level of control. For cleaner air, we are not prepared to pay a sufficiently high price to cover the cost of the increased cleanliness. The supply curve representing costs of control is greater than the demand curve representing our willingness and ability to pay for cleaner air. However, even if there is some pollution left, the market has reduced it from the point where the air was being treated as a free good by U.S.S.

Now we assume that the air rights are assigned to us, the sufferers. At first, we might demand that U.S.S. clean it up altogether—that they provide 100 percent control. To provide that level of control will cost U.S.S. a price of *bf*. But to us, that level of control is only worth a price of *bc*, which is much lower than U.S.S.'s cost. Therefore, they can and will purchase our pristine air as long as their costs exceed our valuation of the level of control concerned. The solution will move from right to left until again, the equilibrium level of *bi* price (same as *ah*) and *bg* pollution (same as *ag* control) is reached.

If it is that simple, why does the market not reduce the pollution problem? Why do we have municipalities and industries dumping into the air and streams as though there were no tomorrow? A large part of the answer lies in the problems associated with defining, assigning, and enforcing the property rights to flowing air and flowing water. To control the *space* over a factory or area is simple. But to control the *air* over the same factory or area is another problem. Unless you seal it in, the air over one spot becomes the air over another spot in a brief period. The same applies to flowing waters. It is almost impossible to establish and enforce meaningful property rights over such resources. Hence, they are often treated as free goods, and because they are *not*, the people who use them as free goods impose costs *on other people* who are not necessarily reaping any offsetting benefits.

The answers? There is no single answer to pollution problems. If potential polluters can be made to bear the full cost of their polluting activities, the problem will be improved. But doing this will require combinations of sanctions and incentives that will vary from situation to situation. The worst thing that could happen is for someone to come up with *the* solution to the entire range of problems that make up the pollution situation. There is no single answer. One major answer is to raise the demand for pollution control—to shift the demand curve in Figure 7-15 upward to the right. Another is to advance pollution control technology which will allow greater control for less resources expended. We can stop *all* pollution tomorrow morning at 8:00 A.M. if we all really want to. But are we prepared to pay the price?

SUBSIDIES AND PRICE SUPPORTS

Another example of the impact of minimum prices set above the market equilibrium prices is found in the case of government subsidies or government-set floors on the prices of various commodities. One of the best known of these cases is government support of agricultural prices for some of the major crops. Figure 7-16 gives a hypothetical example for wheat. Assume a free market equilibrium price of $1.50 per bushel. At this price, many farmers start complaining that they are going to be forced out of business if something does not happen to the price. Small and inefficient farmers in particular are going to scream long and loud. Assume that their screams are heard in Washington, and the federal government decides to guarantee wheat farmers a price of $1.75. At this higher price, the quantity

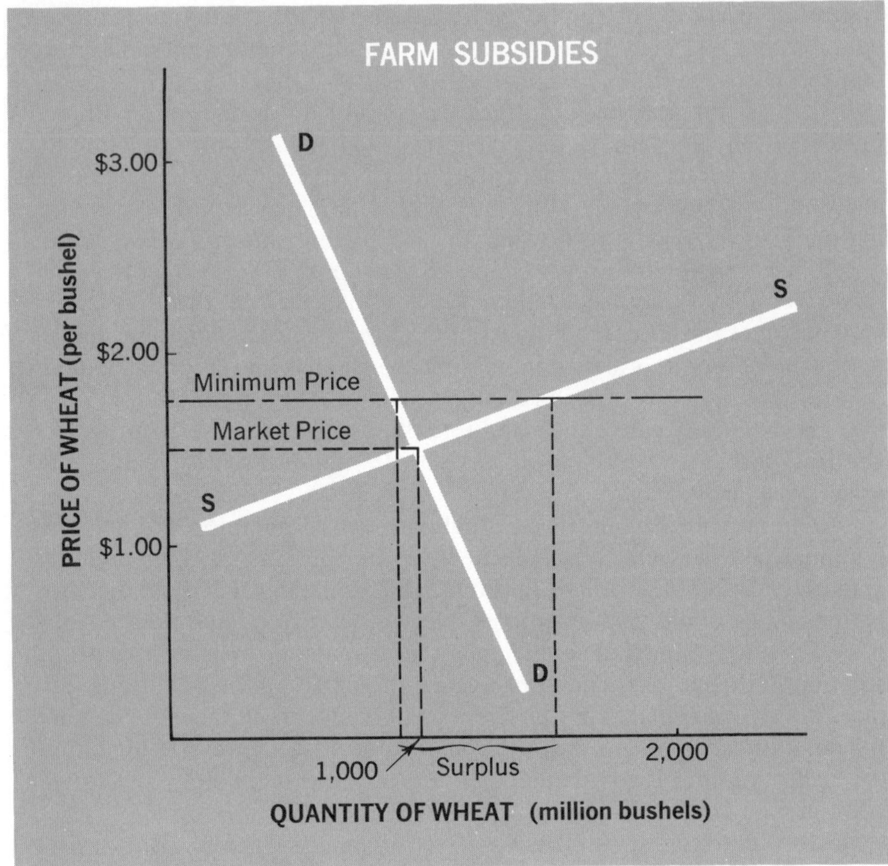

Figure 7-16

of wheat demanded is going to be lowered from 1 billion bushels to 900 million bushels, but at the same time, the higher price is going to stimulate wheat production. Farmers will now be willing and able to produce a total of 1½ billion bushels instead of only 1 billion. We have, therefore, a surplus of wheat in the amount of 600 million bushels. The market will not handle it—not at the $1.75 price, at least. So to support the guaranteed price, the government gets into the wheat business by purchasing the surplus and putting it in storage throughout the country. In fact, renting storages to the government in which to keep wheat becomes a good business.

In the decade of the 1950s, this is precisely what happened. The United States government purchased surplus wheat and stored it in every available space that could be found in the wheat-producing areas of the country. Today, the problem is less serious, because the U. S. has used

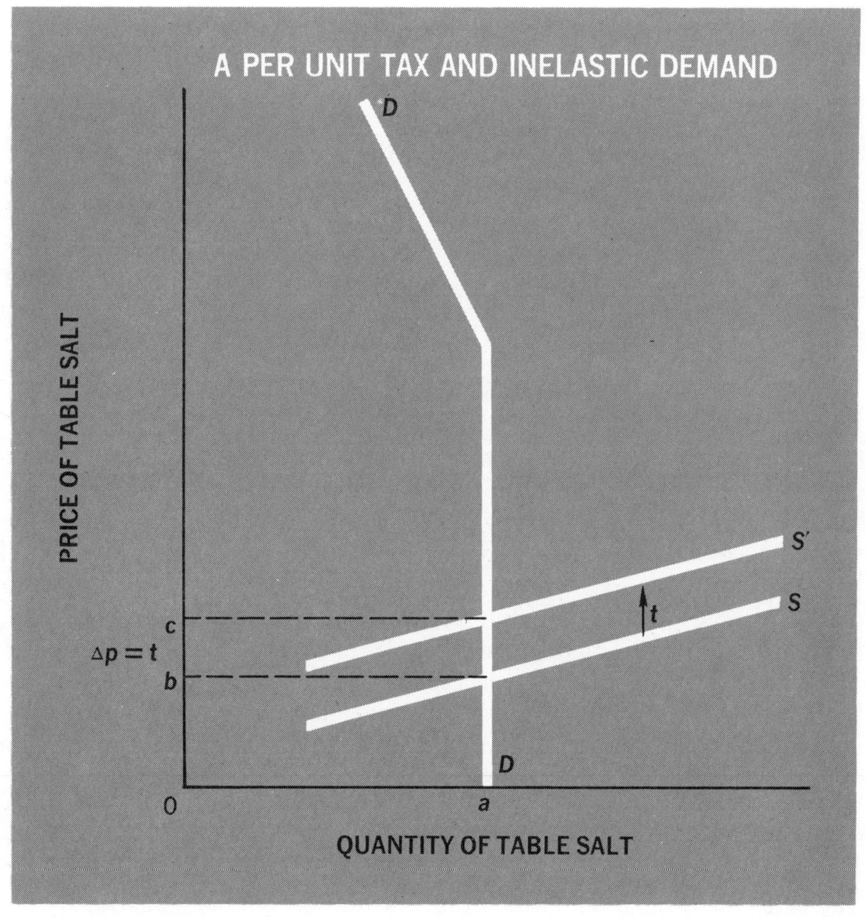

Figure 7-17

foreign aid programs of various types to give away much of our agricultural surpluses. Spoilage, too, did its share to reduce the problem. Of course, tremendous quantities of resources were wasted, but the backbone of America, the family farmer, was protected and that seemed to be the main point of the exercise. Those same farmers could have been millionaires several times over if the resources had just been given to them instead of handled through surplus and its disposal.

One other thing the government did when the surpluses got overwhelming was to decide that if they were going to support the price, then people would have to cut back their production. But at the higher prices, people did not *want* to cut back their production—they wanted to *increase* it. So the government decided to impose *production quotas*. One of the first forms of this was an acreage allotment in which farmers were allowed to plant fewer acres of crops than they had previously done. This idea did not work very well. They took their least productive acres out of production and poured the fertilizer on those that were left. Production did not fall much. In fact, in some instances it even rose. Finally, the government made allotments based on output rather than acreage. The farmer was allowed to sell only so much in order to qualify for government support. Of course, the very efficient farmers did very well on these programs. They would have made money without any programs at all and were the ones who ended up with the lion's share of the benefits anyway.

TAXES AND WHO PAYS WHAT

Several times we have made the statement that sooner or later increased costs of producing any particular good would have to be paid for by the consumers. This is generally true, but there are some ramifications that need to be looked at to see how and when this statement is true. We can kill two birds with one example by illustrating what happens when a *per unit* tax is imposed on the manufacturer of some particular good. In Figure 7-17, we show the supply and demand for table salt. It assumes that table salt is the kind of a product that has a *very* inelastic demand. Its use amounts to an infinitesimally small part of most family budgets. A certain amount of salt is essential for human life, and there are no decent substitutes. The demand curve is drawn perfectly inelastic. The quantity demanded is shown as completely independent of the price of salt *until* a very high price is reached. At that point, price would begin to make a difference in the quantity demanded. A supply curve of normal shape is hypothesized that indicates the usual assumption of increasing costs in the industry. Before the imposition of the tax, there is an equilibrium output of *0a* and an equilibrium price of *0b*. Now, a per unit tax equal to *t* is placed on the output of the industry. The supply curve shifts *up* by an amount equal to the tax. Each unit of output now costs more to produce. If you prefer, costs have increased by *t* for each unit of output. Because demand is completely inelastic in the relevant range, the new equilibrium quantity will be the same, and the entire increase in cost, the amount of the tax, will be passed on to the demanders of table salt. Actually, this makes perfectly good sense. If the demand is inelastic, this says that people are going to demand that particular quantity regardless of the price. If costs go up, they will pay to get the same quantity they were demanding before the cost increase.

Now, assume that some substitute is found for table salt as shown in Figure 7-18. Supply conditions have not changed, and the impact of the tax

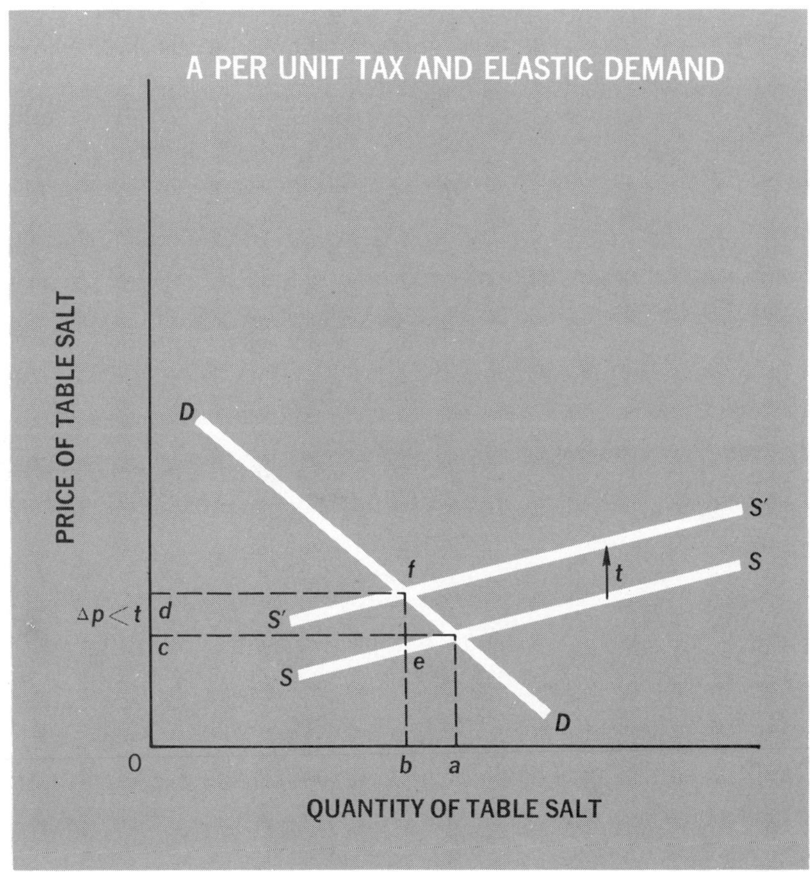

Figure 7-18

increase on costs and supply stays the same. But, there is a change in the result. Now, the increase in taxes and costs results in an increase in the equilibrium price, but the price does *not* rise by the full amount of the cost increase (the tax). Now, people cut down on their purchases of salt because of the higher price and a decrease in the quantity marketed takes up part of the adjustment process. Higher cost suppliers are forced out of the market or output is reduced by firms in an attempt to use only the most efficient production resources. In this case, both consumers and producers bear the burden of the tax (cost) increase. In this case, assuming someone besides the producer or consumers get the tax collected, then the tax raises the price of the good to the consumer, but by less than the total amount of the tax. It raises the price from *0c* to *0d*, but this difference (*cd*) is less than the tax (t). It also lowers the price received by the supplier. He is now receiving a price of eb compared to the $0c$ he originally got. Again, this price received is lower, but by less than the full amount of the tax. Who is going to bear the tax? It will depend upon the *relative* elasticities of supply and demand.

QUESTIONS

1. Under what conditions would workers *currently working* in an occupation *not* suffer unemployment from the imposition of an effective minimum wage?
2. Explain how a black marketeer can actually improve economic efficiency when price ceilings are imposed below the market equilibrium.
3. Assume supply and demand functions that are neither perfectly elastic nor inelastic. Explain, *without* using graphs, how the long-run housing market will be affected by imposing an effective ceiling price on housing now.
4. In what way is income redistributed by imposed ceilings and floors in markets?
5. Using consumer and producer surplus, list some ways that welfare can be described differently than the way it is in the text.
6. What are the *economic* arguments in favor of stiffer drug prohibition laws and better enforcement of them?
7. Who pays for pollution? Make sure you define pollution in your answer.

8

Introduction to Macroeconomics

OBJECTIVES

Macroeconomics consists of putting all the pieces in the economy together into one big system. This aggregation *process has its problems, but it can give important insights into some basic principles. Economies consist of flows of goods, services, and factors of production. In most economies, these flows are matched by an opposite flow of a good called* money. *A look at these flows can demonstrate a most important idea–that all units in a production economy are intimately tied with other units, all of which interact together. Attempts to measure the magnitude of these flows are made through* National Income Accounting *which, although imperfect, does give some idea of how the economy as a whole is performing.*

INTRODUCTION

This chapter may fit into one of three different categories. First of all, many of you will be starting your course in economics with Chapter 1 and this chapter. There is a lot of discussion among teachers of economics as to which is the best starting point. One option is to use the method that starts with the study of bits and pieces of the economy (microeconomics) and then builds into a study of the whole (macroeconomics). A second option is to proceed in the opposite direction: take a look at the forest first, and then study the trees that make it up. Personally, I like a modified version of the first approach, where the strict micro approach is combined with the study of such things as trade, circular flows, and similar items. It really isn't all that important, however; for the instructors that prefer macro first, this will be your starting point after covering the material in Chapter 1.

This chapter will take a look at circular flows and the operation of markets in order to give you enough information to handle the macroeconomics of the following six chapters. Those of you who really understand the material up to this point in the book can easily skip this section. Some of you can use it as a review, and for those of you who are beginning at this point, welcome aboard!

Before I got into this business of teaching and writing textbooks, I used to be "in business for myself." I ran two or three small businesses over a period of years and gloried in the fact that although I was broke much of the time, I was "independent." I was "my own boss." Looking back at those years, I really have to smile a bit. In our market economy, particularly when an enterprise is small and "independent," the independence can be psychologically important but is in fact illusory. It is true that I was independent when it came to the price of my products. Whatever the price was, I had to take it. The market didn't care whether I produced or not. I depended on all kinds of factors, many of which were completely beyond my control.

One such enterprise that I was involved with was the old family cherry and apple orchards. At that time, I assure you, the market approached a perfectly competitive model with many small buyers of both fresh fruit and the fruit that was destined for processed markets. Our enterprise was large, and yet whether we had a good production year or a disaster, the market prices for cherries and apples didn't react one cent per ton. But whereas we were miniscule in the production end, our actions had some noticeable local impacts. The hiring or firing of fifteen to twenty full-time men in a community of only a few hundred meant not only jobs for the men, but also buying power for the community and its supporting establishments. With the influx of several hundred migrant harvest workers in the summer and fall, the impact on the community was even greater.

This small community would not have any impact on the outside world, however. The increase in the purchasing power generated from such farms might mean two or three more new automobiles purchased from the local dealers. This is significant to them, but of little importance to Chrysler, GM, and Ford. Nevertheless, it is the impact of tens of thousands of miniscule elements like this that keep Chrysler, GM, and Ford in business.

No one can claim true independence any longer. A few hermits may achieve virtual independence, but most are doomed to interdependence, whether we like it or not. In microeconomics, one can talk about individual markets as though they existed in isolation. Analytically, this may be correct, and useful insights may be gained from handling single markets in this way. But, it must always be remembered that we are all part of a *system*, a general system in which the bits and pieces interact and are interdependent even though the degree of that interdependency may be small.

CIRCULAR FLOWS

Monies received from the sale of the fruit of those cherry and apple orchards became purchasing power for the farmers and those who worked for them. This purchasing power became income to the shopkeepers in the village. In turn, this income became the basis for their purchases of everything, from foodstuffs to TV sets. Some of these spenders probably even bought an apple pie, the money for which paid the piemaker, who paid the apple processor, who maybe even paid us. Here, the circular flow that goes on throughout the economy closed itself in a relatively few steps, such as illustrated in Figure 8-1. Labor is supplied by the farm worker who assists in the production of apples. These apples go to a freezing plant where they are processed and made ready for use in frozen pie production. The pie manufacturer gets the apples, makes pies, and sells them (through a distribution system) to a retailer in the village. The retailer sells the pie to the farm worker, thus completing the circle. This is called the *real* flow. Material goods and the services of factors of production flow around the pattern. But, making that flow practical is another flow in the opposite direction—the flow of *money*. Money is paid by the orchard owner to the farm worker. This money becomes the purchasing power with which he pays the storekeeper, and so on. Notice that the *income* of any element in the flow becomes the *purchasing power* with which purchases are made from the next element. *Money flows* and the *value of real product,* are nothing but mirror images of each other.

In a market economy, each step of this circular flow pattern involves the operation of at least one *market*. Markets themselves consist of forces that roughly can be broken into two parts—forces affecting the quantity people are willing and able to purchase (demand) and forces affecting the quantity of the goods people are willing and able to supply. Elsewhere in the book, this whole business is gone into in some detail, but, for now, it is enough to say that we assume that the quantity of goods people are willing and able to purchase will vary inversely as the price of the good, everything else being equal. Conversely, we assume that, in most cases, the quantity of goods that people are willing and able to supply will vary directly as the price, again, everything else being held constant. In an aggregated and highly simplified way, we can see how these markets fit into a generalized circular flow within an economy.

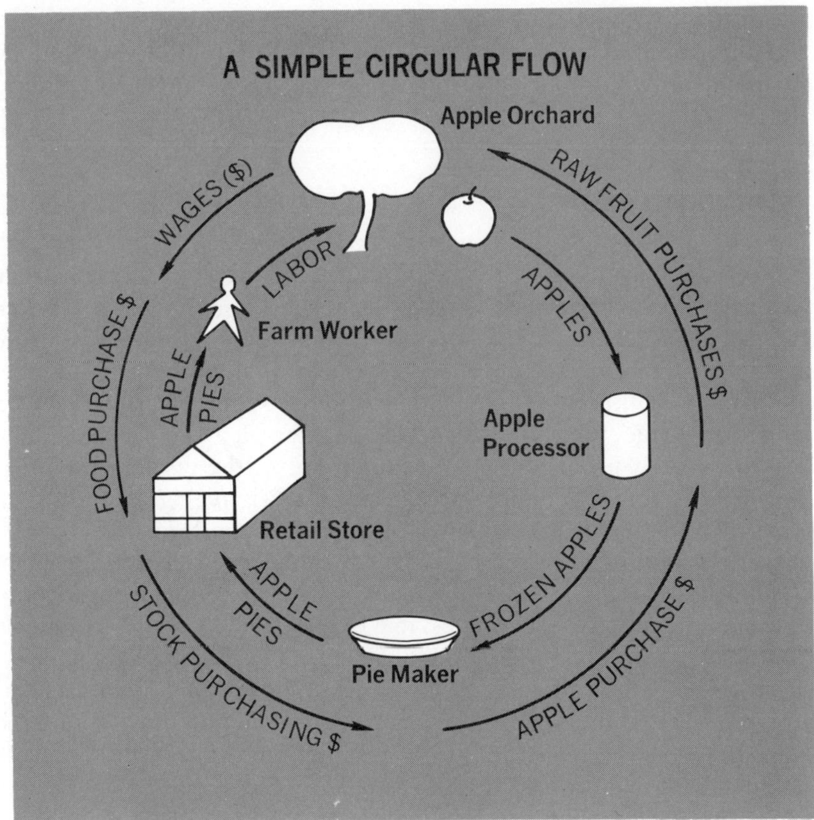

Figure 8-1

First, we separate everything in an economy into either a *household* or a *firm*. We will further separate all factors of production into just *labor* and *capital*. To simplify one step further, we assume that all factors (labor and capital) are supplied by households and demanded by firms. Conversely, we will assume that all goods are supplied by firms and demanded by households. In a general way, these assumptions are not too far from the way things work. In Figure 8-2, the flows are illustrated. The demands of households for goods are reflected in the goods market, and the demand tells us that the cheaper the goods, the greater will be the quantity demanded. Firms are supplying goods to the marketplace, and the supply curve tells us that the higher the price of goods, the greater will be the quantities that firms will be willing and able to supply (*ceteris paribus*).

On the other side of the flow, capital goods and labor are supplied to the market by households. Higher wages and interest (both *prices*) imply

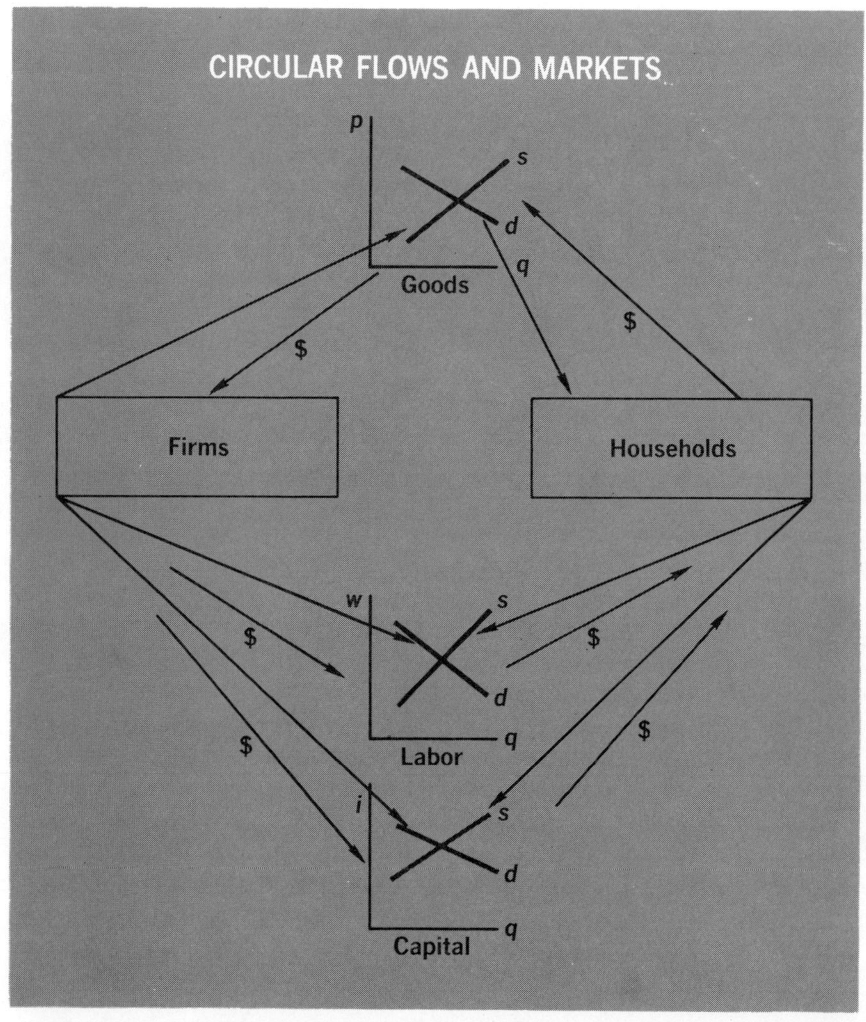

Figure 8-2

greater quantities supplied of both factors, again, *ceteris paribus*. Firms demand the factors and exhibit the usual cheaper/more-hired assumption. Notice that each *real* flow has a *money* flow counterpart.

NATIONAL INCOME ACCOUNTS

Amazingly enough, we actually *try* to measure some of these flows in the "real" economy. Every year, and throughout each year, departments of government estimate the volume of economic activity in the country through *National Income Accounts*. This may be more familiar under the title of *Gross National Product* or GNP accounting. National Income Accounts measure various segments of the flows within the complex structure of the whole economy. The process is highly inexact and leaves much to be desired both conceptually and in practice. Figure 8-3 shows the major breakdowns in the National Income Accounts along with the estimated values for calendar 1970.

Gross National Product (GNP) is the money value of all goods and services produced in the country in a given year for final use. For example,

NATIONAL INCOME ACCOUNTS – 1970

	(billions of dollars)
Gross National Product (GNP)	$976.5
Less: Capital Consumption Allowance	84.3
Equals: Net National Product	$892.2
Less: Indirect Business Taxes	92.0
Business Transfer Payments	3.6
Statistical Discrepancies	– (2.5)
Plus: Net Subsidies of Gov't. Enterprises	1.8
Equals: National Income	$800.8
Less: Undistributed Corp. Profits	77.2
Social Security Payments	57.1
Plus: Gov't. Transfer Payments	73.9
Interest Paid (Gov't. & Indiv.)	31.8
Dividends	25.2
Business Transfer Payments	3.6
Equals: Personal Income	$801.0
Less: Personal Taxes	116.3
Equals: Disposable Personal Income	$684.8
Less: Personal Outlays	634.6
Equals: Personal Saving	$50.2

Figure 8-3

if one ton of iron ore is mined, it is sold to the steelmakers for a particular price. The steelmaker manufactures steel and sells the steel to an automobile manufacturer for use in making cars. The car manufacturer includes the cost of the steel in pricing his product to dealers. The dealer takes the cost of the cars including the steel and including the original input of iron ore and adds on the value of his distributing services. Finally, the customer ends up buying the car at a price that includes the value of the dealer's services, the cost of the car manufacture, the cost of the steel, and the cost of the iron ore. A problem called *double counting* now becomes apparent.

If the value of each transaction were taken as part of GNP, the actual value of product added to the economy would be grossly overstated. In our simple example, the original value of the iron ore would have been counted four times; the steel, three times; the car, twice; and the retailer's services, once. So, estimates of GNP try to eliminate such multiple counting of goods and services. The attempt is not completely successful, but the grossest categories are eliminated. This is not just the final value of goods destined for consumption purposes, but includes the value of capital goods produced as well. However, there is no deduction at this stage for capital equipment used up in the production processes—no deduction for *depreciation*. At this stage, so-called transfer payments also are not included. Transfer payments are transfers of purchasing power from one economic unit to another for which there is no corresponding offset in either production or trading something of like value. Obviously, the biggest portion of transfer payments comes from welfare payments from various governments as well as gifts from businesses and individuals. But, by definition, nothing of value was produced in return for the transfer payment and therefore it is excluded from Gross National *Product*.

As just stated, GNP does not deduct any allowance for the economy's capital stocks used up or depreciated in the production processes, so this is the first adjustment we make. Deducting an allowance for depreciation or capital consumption allowance, give us Net National Product. Notice, we are still on the *product* side of the circular flow—the dollar value of *goods*. Supposedly, this is the figure that represents the economy's ability to produce year after year without depleting its productive capacity.

From now on, we want to round the corner in the flow pattern and talk about the *income of factors* rather than the *value of product*. To do this, the value of business taxes is deducted from NNP because these are resources that are never paid to any of the factors, at least not directly. Any payments by businesses that do not represent return for productive services also are deducted (business transfer payments). After an adjustment for statistical error and the profits or losses (generally the latter) of government-run enterprises, we come up with the value of product as viewed by the factors that produced that product. We arrive now at *National Income*. The next job is to see how much purchasing power actually gets into the hands of the public, so we have to adjust the National Income figure with both pluses and minuses.

First of all, if corporations retain their earnings, then they are not available for spending by either stockholders or factors of production working for the corporations. Therefore, undistributed corporation profits are deducted from NI. Payments for social security both by workers and employers also come out of the NI because these, too, are not available for expenditure. But now, we add government transfers into the equation for the first time because these payments are very much a part of the population's spending capabilities. Interest payments from governments and individuals, and dividends from business are also added into the mix at this stage. Finally, the business transfers that were deducted from NNP are now added back; they, too, are part of the purchasing power available to buyers in the economy. The net result of this operation produces something called Personal Income (PI). It represents the gross amount of money in the public's hands during the year.

Personal taxes are now deducted and the resulting figure is called *Disposable Personal Income*. This is the net buying power of individuals. When their expenditures are taken away from this figure, the remainder is the amount that individuals saved—*Personal Saving*.

PROBLEMS WITH GNP ACCOUNTS

Starting at the top, there are many problems with GNP as it is currently constituted and measured. Some of these problems can be adjusted, but others are basic faults with the methods used.

To begin with, GNP is used by many as a measure of how well the country is doing and roughly whether the welfare of the people is increasing and by what degree. But GNP is measured in terms of the *current* prices of things. If the general price level is increasing by, say, 6 percent, and GNP is rising at an annual rate of 6 percent, then the net overall change in output is zero. This is a particular problem during periods of substantial inflation or when comparing performances of widely separated time periods. This particular problem can be resolved through the correction of the *current dollar* GNP by a price index that brings the dollar value of different time periods down to a comparable figure based on some given base year.

Another criticism of GNP is that it does not allow for changes in population. This criticism is particularly important when National Income Accounting is used in countries experiencing rapid rates of population increase. For example, if the population of an economy is increasing at the rate of 3 percent per year, and the GNP is increasing at a rate of 2 percent per year, then the *GNP per capita* is actually decreasing. Here again, however, this calculation can be made and the figures used accordingly.

Still another criticism of using GNP as a measure of welfare is tougher to allow for. There is nothing in the GNP figures that indicates anything about the *distribution* of either the product or the income flowing from the product. It would be possible (and actually happens in some Middle Eastern oil countries) for *real* GNP *per capita* to be increasing at a prodigious rate, and yet the incomes of the bulk of the people could actually be going down. A few at the top get the whole increase, but through the magic of simple averages, it looks as though the prosperity of the entire country is increasing rapidly.

GNP figures only reflect transactions that go through the marketplace. This is a major problem when one considers something like the imputed value of housewives' services in the home as well as the value of all volunteer services performed to increasing degrees as our leisure increases. And, speaking of leisure, there is no allowance for the value of leisure in the accounts. As an example, assume that productivity increased to the point where a thirty-hour week could produce what a forty-hour week does now. With stable prices, the value of GNP would remain the same, and yet people would have over one day per week of additional leisure—something that hopefully makes people "better off." Of course, again, in economies where a substantial portion of total production takes place outside organized markets, this omission can and does grossly understate the value of the production in such economies.

GNP assumes that a dollar's worth of product in one endeavor is precisely the same value as a dollar's worth of product in something else. Given free markets and all products going through those free markets, this assumption is not too bad, but given an economy in which many purchases are made through governmental agencies whose demands are only indirectly responsive to the general populace, this assumption may be less than correct. A dollar spent on a missile may or may not be as "important" as a dollar spent on literacy training.

Finally, there has been increasing criticism of the depreciation used in GNP, or rather, NNP figures. These values contain no allowance for possible depreciation of environmental quality. There is no consideration of the damage being done to clean air, clean water, or the human costs attributable to such environmental problems. Also, there is some question as to whether the market is allowing sufficient value for natural resources that are being consumed at very rapid rates.

With all of these problems, does it mean that GNP accounting should be scrapped or ignored? Hardly. What it does mean is that GNP figures should be understood with all of their shortcomings and omissions. In our contemporary and complex society, the public must have some understanding of the conditions around them. Like all other aggregate numbers, the problems and limitations involved in data collection, taking averages, and trying to get a static picture of something that is changing at a fantastic rate must be understood by those using the numbers *and* those who are paying the wages of those who are using the numbers. It is part of the larger problem of an informed and responsible citizenry.

QUESTIONS

1. List three or four examples of a circular flow within an economy. How do these influence the total circular flow described in this chapter?
2. This is the only "busy-work" question in the book but it may be useful. List the main categories in the National Income Accounts and compare their dollar values for 1930, 1940, 1950, 1960, and 1970. Now do the same thing for the value of National Income Accounts in terms of *constant dollars*. It isn't important at this stage which year is used as the base for the constant dollars. It is important that you learn what constant dollars are. All of this information can be obtained from any major economics principles text. It will help you in the next few chapters.
3. Can you think of any problems of the National Income Accounts other than those mentioned in the chapter?

9

Money

OBJECTIVES

Money developed as both a way to store the value of human effort *and facilitate the process of* exchange. *It is also used to compare the different values of dissimilar goods as a* unit of account. *In performing these functions, money can either act in a moment in time or perform the functions over longer periods of time. To work efficiently, money must have the characteristics of durability, divisibility, and uniformity. Unlike other goods, too much money can ruin its usefulness–it must be limited in relation to the available goods and services. The* price *of money is what money will buy–it is the* purchasing power *of money. This price is the* inverse *of the* General Price Level *since the General Price Level measures how much money can buy. As it goes up, the price of money goes down. As it goes down, the price of money goes up. The supply and demand for money are comparable to the supply and demand for any other good which yields services. However, in this market, we are talking about producing something that has much greater value than its cost, consequently governments generally control money production. Among other factors, the quantity of money demanded will depend on its price (the inverse of the General Price Level), the amount of goods in the economy, and people's expectations about the future movement of prices.*

INTRODUCTION

The first thing we are going to look at in our study of the aggregate economy is probably *the* most important good that people use—*money*. As you must know by now, there are many economic terms and concepts that are loosely used and little understood in the day-to-day world. *Money* is one of them. For most of us as individuals, there is never enough of it. Many times, government *monetary policy* seems to be aimed at making us suffer even more. All in all, the function of money seems to be confusing, at best. In this chapter, an attempt will be made to lay out some of the basic principles that concern money—its creation and use.

Return for a moment to our heroes of Chapter 1. When we left Charlie and Clyde, they were merrily working and bargaining. Charlie was producing all the carcasses in their two-man, two-product economy, and Clyde was producing all the coats. Because we assumed that each man wanted some of each good, they were trading carcasses for coats and vice versa.

One day, Charlie was walking along a stream, thinking about nothing in particular, when he noticed a shiny rock in the water. He was sufficiently intrigued to get his feet wet. Retrieving the rock, he took it home and put it on the fireplace mantel. The following Friday, as was his usual habit, Clyde came over to pick up his weekly supply of meat and deliver a new coat for Charlie's wife. The minute Clyde saw the rock on the mantel, it occurred to him that the rock would look more attractive hanging around his wife's neck than it did over Charlie's fireplace. You guessed it! Charlie got the coat for the rock, and he didn't have to give up any of his carcasses for it. Now, so far, all that had happened was the introduction of a new good into the economy—*shiny rocks*. The rocks *at this stage* were *not* money.

As Charlie and Clyde expanded their scope of operations to include more people and more goods, they (and everyone else) noticed that this trading business was taking more and more of their collective time. As long as there were only coats and carcasses, the two people had few problems (except that carcasses didn't store very well and began giving off strange odors after a few days in the cave). However, a character by the name of Melvin came along who had invented a very useful little gadget called a spear. Richard came on the scene with some crazy pads he called shoes, and life became more difficult. For example, Melvin refused to own a pair of shoes or wear a skunkskin coat, but he did like brontosaurus steak. Charlie had no problem in getting a spear because Melvin was perfectly willing to exchange spears for carcasses. Clyde did have a problem, however. If he wanted to get a spear, he had to trade some extra coats to Charlie, get a few more carcasses than he wanted for himself, and then trade the extra carcasses to Melvin for a spear. This process became increasingly cumbersome as trading expanded until, finally, people found they were spending about half their time *producing*, and the other half trying to arrange multiple trades that would finally give each of them the goods they wanted for their own use.

One day Boris, a traveling man, appeared in the community. Boris had noticed a few of those shiny rocks, which had developed into a kind of prestige symbol for those who held them, in the various caves he had visited. Boris, a wise man by nature, came to the marketplace the following Monday with an ingenious idea. "Why not," he suggested, "agree among yourselves that these prestige-yielding rocks be used in trading?" Almost everyone wanted them, but Charlie had been very cagey about the location of the source and had stubbornly refused to supply more than just a few every year. Everyone was willing to accept at least a few of these rocks in return for whatever good he was producing. Boris's idea was merely to expand this process. Because all the goods being produced had a *price* in terms of so many rocks of a certain size per unit of the good they were producing, why bother with other prices such as spears/carcasses, hides/shoes, or shoes/spears? If each of these goods already had a price in terms of rocks/good, wouldn't this be sufficient to express all trading values? Of course it was sufficient, and people found that not only was pricing much simpler, but also it was much easier to pass rocks from hand to hand than to drag dead brontosauri around. Another advantage became apparent when people realized that they could "store" the fruits of their labor by producing, selling all their products for rocks, and trading to others *only* enough rocks to get their minimum consumption requirements. The rest could be stored for a rainy day when it was more pleasant to sit around the cave than to work. *Money was born.*

Of course, being born and being accepted are two different things. It is one thing for a group of traders to agree that they are going to accept rocks for goods, but, unless these transactions come off with a minimum of problems, the agreements are not worth much. On the other hand, as more traders began to see the advantages of using "money," the money itself became more useful. *Money became valuable for what money could buy.* The people's acceptance of these rocks as a medium of exchange was *critical* to the whole system.

The system almost collapsed on one occasion when Charlie's son, John Maynard, decided to go into the business of carrying rocks from the secret place to the marketplace. This seemed to him a much better way of life than following in his father's footsteps, hunting animals. The problem was that suddenly there was an increase in the number of rocks everyone had to give up for the other things in the market. Everyone, including John Maynard, started complaining about the high cost of living. Fortunately, Charlie, who had aged in both stature and wisdom, found out about his son's antics and he and Boris put a stop to the unrestricted sale of rocks. Prices stopped increasing and everyone forgot about the whole affair after a short period of time.

Again, we leave the wonderful world of Charlie and Clyde and see what their progeny hath wrought in today's world. *Money* is a *good*. It is an *economic good* because it *yields services* and is *scarce*. The services it yields fall into two basic categories and one subcategory. First of all, money *has to be* a store of value. It has to be able to do this before it can do either of the other functions. Think how important this is, particularly for people who provide services for others, services that themselves cannot be stored. For example, a teacher of economics works for nine months a year. It is conceivable that each student might "pay in kind." That is to say, some might pay in food, others might trade the use of an apartment, still others might bring their old clothing, and someone might even trade an old automobile for the instructor's services. Even if this system worked out during the school year, the instructor would still have a problem in the summertime. The students actually pay via the university and pay in *money*. Therefore the instructor could hold part of this command over goods and services (money) to tide him over the lean summer months. Money allows him to "store" his buying power until such time as he requires it. As we will see, if the value of money goes down, then its usefulness as money decreases. As a store of value, money is like a great many other goods. People store value by holding land, stocks, jewels, even cars and houses. So, as a store of value, money is not *unique*.

The next function of money is the one that *does* make it unique among goods. Money serves as a *medium of exchange*. In fact, this function is precisely what makes something *money*. In other words, money must be accepted in exchange for the goods that need to be traded. If money does *not* perform this function, it is no longer money. It is money's ability to make trade and exchange less time-consuming and more efficient that leads man to use it in *every* production economy that exists. As soon as any community gets more complicated than simple subsistence do-it-yourself, money always comes into being.

Finally, money gives us a way of comparing the values of different goods in a simple and uniform way. By having the value of all goods *except* money expressed in terms of money, the complex system of barter prices can be eliminated. We no longer have to talk about coats per carcass, carcasses per spear, and back to spears per coat. Now we can talk about, for example, *dollars* per coat, *dollars* per spear, and *dollars* per carcass. By comparing the money value of each item, the relative values of the items to each other can be compared. Figure 9-1 summarizes the functions of money.

If money is to yield the mentioned services, what characteristics should it possess? Basically, there are five.

> Money should be *physically durable*. As it passes from hand to hand in the trading process, it should maintain its physical quality and quantity. This has been a problem with many monies used throughout

MONEY is a Good.

Its VALUE AS MONEY results from the SERVICES it performs and its SCARCITY

The SERVICES performed by money result from its use as a:

1. STORE OF VALUE
2. MEDIUM OF EXCHANGE
3. UNIT OF ACCOUNT

Figure 9-1

history. For example, if fine gold is made into coins, the coins will soon become smoother, thinner, and lighter because gold does not resist the erosion that comes with handling.

Money should be *divisible* into small enough units to make low-valued transactions practical. It would be difficult to use the Hope diamond to buy the daily coffee. True, it could be splintered, but the sum of the values of these small pieces would never approach the value of the jewel as a whole.

Money must be *easily transferable*. Wheat has been used at various times as money. We cannot picture anyone carrying a bushel of wheat to pay for lunch.

A point that will be mentioned only in passing at this stage is that money must be *limited in quantity* relative to the available goods in the economy and number of needed transactions. This characteristic is the subject of the next few pages.

Finally, money must be *uniform in quality*. In order for one trading partner to know what the other is talking about, the common denominator—money—must be the same for both. Figure 9-2 recaps these points.

If money is an economic good, one might suspect that people will *demand* it. If they demand money, then they must be willing and able to pay a *price*. What is the *price* of money? If I go to the bank and borrow a few

To perform these functions efficiently, money should be:

1. PHYSICALLY DURABLE

2. EASILY DIVISIBLE

3. EASILY TRANSFERABLE

4. LIMITED IN QUANTITY relative to available goods and services

5. UNIFORM IN QUALITY

Figure 9-2

dollars, the price I will have to pay for *borrowing* money is called interest. But this is a different thing and we'll cover it shortly. The price we're talking about here is the price to *hold* a dollar of current purchasing power.

When going to the store and purchasing a good, a money price is paid for that good. It is usually expressed as so many dollars and cents per unit of the good. This is a common experience. We talked about the relative prices when discussing trade and comparative advantage. By definition of price, it is possible to express the price of one good, x, in terms of what must be given up of an alternative, say y. But, once this relationship is established, it is also possible to talk about the price of y in terms of the x

that must be given up to get one unit of y. This is just another way of saying that the price of one good in terms of another is the same as the *reciprocal* of the other in terms of the first. So what!

The "so what" in this case has tremendous implications, as we shall soon see. If the price of *goods* is the number of dollars that must be given up to obtain a unit of *goods*, then the *price of dollars is the number of units of goods that must be given up to obtain or hold one dollar.* Even this idea is not difficult if we are talking about the dollar price of *one* good (singular) or the *good* price of *dollars*. If the only good in a man's life is coffee, and he has to pay ten cents per cup, it is easy to see that it will cost him ten cups of coffee for the privilege of keeping one dollar. In this case, the price of dollars is ten cups of coffee per unit. When talking about the price of dollars in terms of the whole economy, we run into some problems. Not everyone purchases the same goods, and therefore, when we talk about the price of dollars, the foregone purchases will vary greatly among different members of the community. There is a technique that is used, imperfect though it is. We have already alluded to it in the introductory macro chapter. It is possible to estimate a "market basket" of goods that an average buyer purchases. By determining the value (in dollars) of this market basket, a basis for the General Price Level can be established. In other words, we can determine the number of dollars that must be paid per *market basket* for the average consumer of *all* goods and services, or for consumers of specific kinds of goods—all automobiles, household appliances, consumer goods, and so on, as in Figure 9-3.

It will be useful here to construct an example of a price index calculation. This example is highly simplified but demonstrates the methods used as well as some of the shortcomings of averages and aggregations.

In Figure 9-4, the value of a simple market basket is calculated for the year 1973. In this case, we assume the average consumer will purchase one Chevrolet automobile (some standard combination of available options), 500 pounds of beef (again, some standard of quality and cuts), and one house. Remember that the use of averages means that some individuals and some products are going to be very different from the averages.

In our simple example, the total money our average consumer would have to spend for these products in 1973 is $20,000. The price of the market basket is $20,000. One year later, we will assume that the items purchased at 1973 prices have been completely used. The car collapses into a pile of junk, the beef has been eaten, and the house disintegrates into a pile of wood and plaster dust. So Mr. Average has to start all over again and we further assume that he buys the same package of goods. But in 1974, the prices have changed. They Chevy now costs $3,000 instead of $2,500 (is a 1974 Chevy the same good as a 1973 Chevy?). Beef has gone from $1.00 to $1.20 per pound, and the standard house has increased in price from

The price of "GOODS" is
$/good

The price of DOLLARS is
goods/$1

FOR THE WHOLE ECONOMY:

Prices can be aggregated into a
GENERAL PRICE LEVEL
for all goods and services

$/"market basket"

Figure 9-3

$17,000 to $21,400. The total expenditure required to purchase this market basket has risen from $20,000 to $25,000.

Figure 9-4 shows how these figures are translated into what is known as a *price index*. First, we choose one year as a *base* year—in this case, 1973. We say that prices in this base period equal 100 percent, or simply 100. Dividing the price of our market basket in the base year ($20,000) into the price of the same market basket in the other year ($25,000 in 1974), we find that the General Price Level, *as defined by our market basket*, has risen 25 percent, or to an index figure of 125.

PRICE INDEX

Good	Quantity	1973 Price	1974 Value	1973 Price	1974 Value
Chevrolet	1	$2,500	$2,500	$3,000	$3,000
Beef	500 lbs	$1	$500	$1.20	$600
House	1	$17,000	$17,000	$21,400	$21,400
Price of Market Basket			$20,000		$25,000

PRICE INDEX CALCULATIONS

$$\frac{\text{PRICE (1974)}}{\text{PRICE (1973)}} = \frac{\$25{,}000}{\$20{,}000} = \frac{125}{100}$$

1973 = base = 100

The price level has gone up 25%

BUT

Prices of:

CARS are up 20%

MEAT are up 20%

HOUSING is up 26%

NOTE the WEIGHT of housing

Figure 9-4

We have lost some important facts, however, in this averaging process. If each category is looked at separately, we find that the price of cars (as we have defined cars) has risen only 20 percent. The price of meat (as

The PRICE of money equals
"market baskets" per $1

or

$$P_m = \frac{1}{GPL}$$

Figure 9-5

we have defined meat) has risen only 20 percent, too. However, the price of housing (as we have defined housing) has risen 26 percent. But, the *weight* of housing is so large as to more than proportionally influence the price index. The *weighted average* rose by 25 percent.

What about our price of dollars? In 1973, the price of dollars in terms of our market basket would have been 1/20,000 of a market basket per dollar held. In 1974, the price of dollars would have been 1/25,000 of a market basket. *The General Price Level ROSE 25 percent, which is equivalent to saying that the price of dollars FELL by 25 percent.* The price of money equals the market baskets that must be given up to hold one dollar, or

$$p_M = \frac{1}{GPL}$$

where p_M = price of money and GPL = General Price Level.

We now have the economic good, money, and a concept of the price of that money—the inverse of the GPL. It is now time to look at the market for this good.

DEMAND FOR MONEY

Figure 9-6 depicts a demand curve. The quantity of money or stock of money (M) is plotted on the horizontal axis and the price of money is plotted on the vertical axis. But there are two ways of looking at or interpreting the values on the vertical axis. True, the price of money is what we are after to develop a demand-for-money curve. But, because the price of money is identical to the inverse of the GPL, then we also could put in

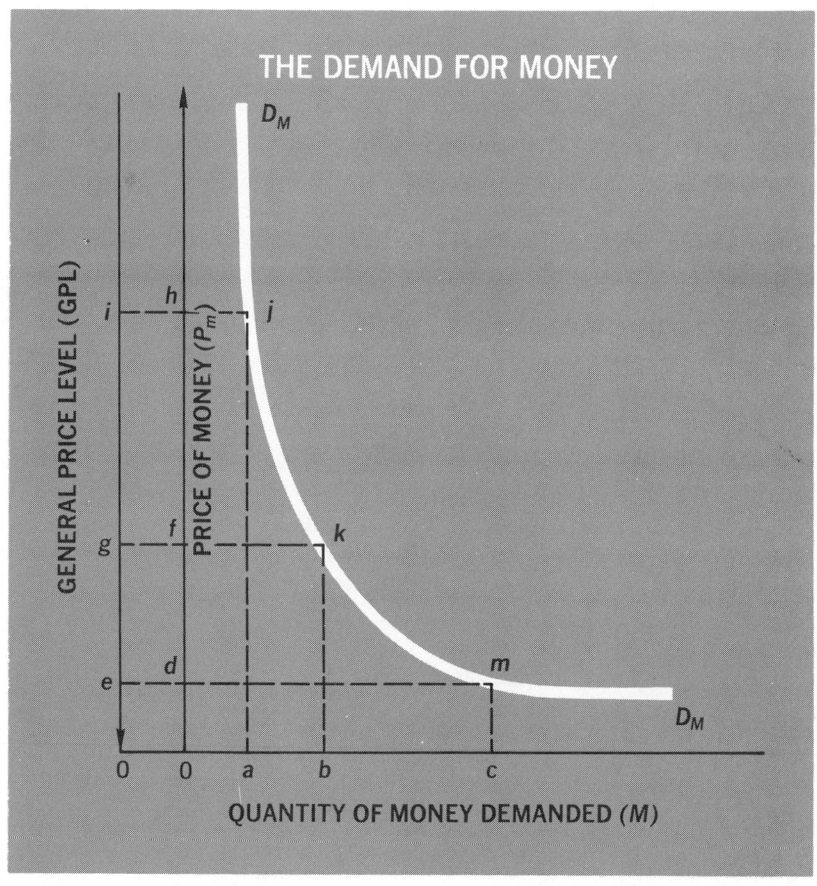

Figure 9-6

another vertical axis pointing down instead of up, and use General Price Level figures instead of price of money figures. For example, the price of money *Od* is exactly the same thing as General Price Level *eO* (you can assume that *O* is the same point on both axes). Price of money level *Of* (a higher price of money) is the same thing as *gO* (lower) General Price Level. *Oh* price of money (again, higher price of money) is the same thing as *iO* General Price Level (again, lower price level).

What about the strange shape of this demand curve? Now you know why we spent time talking about a unitary elasticity demand curve in Chapter 4. That is what we have here, and a few thoughts on the matter will show why. A unitary elasticity demand curve says that any price multiplied by its corresponding quantity demanded will always yield the same value.

When talking about the demand for most goods, that constant total would equal the total revenue spent on the good. Price goes up but quantity demanded always goes down in such a way that the product of the two stays constant. In our graph, the area of any box, such as *Ohja*, always equals the area of any other box so constructed, such as *Ofkb* or *Odmc*. In the case of money, the idea of total revenue changes a bit. Here the area of those boxes equals

$$p_M \times M = m$$

where p_M = Price of Money, M = Stock of Money, and m = Some Constant. This constant is the total purchasing power of money. The *price* of anything is really the ability of that item to purchase something else as well. Therefore, the *price* of money is just another way of saying the *purchasing power* of one unit of money. If we take the *per unit* purchasing power of money (again, price of money) and multiply it by the number of units of money (M), we end up with the total purchasing power of the stock of money concerned (m), and this demand curve says that m will remain constant. Total purchasing power demanded will remain constant regardless of the price of money.

There is another way that this can be approached. Because the price (purchasing power) of money also equals the reciprocal of the GPL, then our constant, m, also equals

$$\mathrm{p_M} \times \mathrm{M} = \frac{1}{\mathrm{GPL}} \times \mathrm{M} = \frac{\mathrm{M}}{\mathrm{GPL}} = \mathrm{m}$$

This shows us that as the General Price Level falls, the stock of money needed to carry out any given level of transactions also falls. Conversely, as the General Price Level rises, the quantity of money needed to perform any given level of transactions will rise. This arithmetic and the graphs make it seem more complicated than it should. If you are buying a book that costs eight dollars, you are going to need (in this case, demand) eight dollars in your pocket to pay for the book. If the price of that book goes to sixteen dollars, then for the same level of transactions (buying one book), you are going to need twice as many dollars. A doubling of the General Price Level will cause the number of dollars demanded to double. We can say the same thing in a second way. A doubling of the General Price Level is the same thing as a *halving* of the purchasing power of money, and therefore, a need of twice as much money to get the same item. A halving of the *purchasing power* of money is the same thing as a halving of the *price* of money, and, therefore, the quantity demanded of money will double.

Like other demands for other goods, this demand is calculated holding everything else constant. The level of transactions (remember the circular flow?), which is one thing the GNP is supposed to represent, is held constant. The price of substitutes for money is held constant. As we will see, bonds or IOUs are partial substitutes for money as stores of value, so the curve is drawn with *interest rates* constant. The speed with which a dollar goes around the circular flow is also going to affect the total number of dollars demanded so, therefore, the *velocity* of money is held constant along the demand curve.

SUPPLY OF MONEY

Now it is time to look at the other side of the money market. As with any demand curve, the demand for money only shows a series of prices and quantities demanded. In order to see what the price of money is actually going to be, it is necessary to come up with a *supply* of money. As with demand, our interest is in knowing what kind of relationship exists between the price of money and the quantity supplied. The answer to this is simple: there *is no* necessary relationship for the reason that the *government* controls the supply of money and can do as it pleases, regardless of prices. That does not mean that the government is going to be capricious in its control of the money supply, but merely that there is no necessary relationship between price and quantity. Just how the government controls the money supply is another question to be answered in a few pages, but for now we need to say only that the price of money and the quantity supplied of money are *independent.* The supply of money is perfectly *in*elastic, as shown in Figure 9-7.

But now, we have a demand for money, $D_M D_M$, and a supply of money, S_M, that intersect at an equilibrium price of money equal to *Ob.* Because the supply is completely inelastic, once the quantity of money in the economy is set, such as at *Oa*, then the price of money will be determined, *ceteris paribus*. This means that, again, *ceteris paribus*: once the quantity of money is set in the economy, the General Level of Prices is also set. Could this possibly be that simple? Can the government literally determine the price level by controlling the money supply? Yes, it is that simple *if* all prices and wages are completely and instantly flexible, and if nothing else changes in the meantime. It is those two assumptions that are going to take up a great deal of space over the next couple of chapters.

Even though it should be fairly obvious, this is important enough so that several possible actions and reactions should be looked at explicitly. First of all, in Figure 9-8, we will assume that the government sets up the printing presses and puts the bills in B-52 bombers. They then bomb the

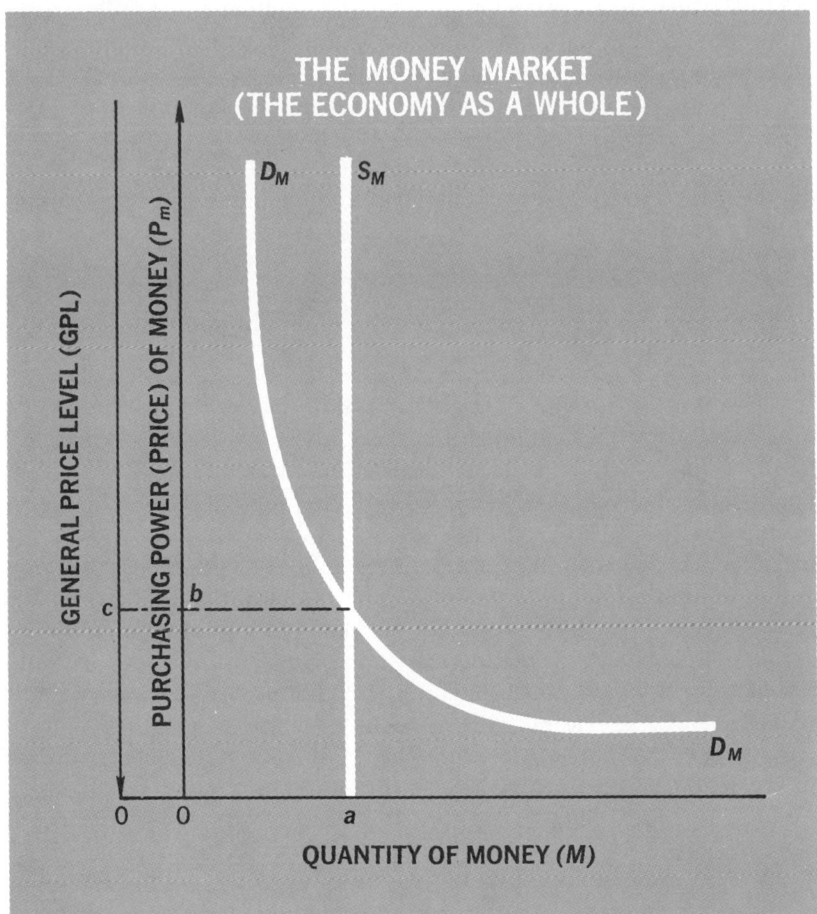

Figure 9-7

entire country with dollar bills so that everyone gets proportionally the same increase in *nominal* money. (Nominal money is our M, which is nothing more than the face value of all bills, coins, and checking accounts. *Real* money, on the other hand, is what we are calling m, or purchasing power money.) The supply function shifts from S_M to S_M' and quantity supplied rises from $0a$ to $0b$. But, assuming nothing else has changed in the economy, the demand for money *function* stays the same, so that quantity demanded at the given price level stays at $0a$ but quantity supplied has risen. What happens now is just like any other market reaction. Quantity supplied is greater than quantity demanded. We have a *surplus* of money at the given level of prices in the economy. In other words, with the quantity

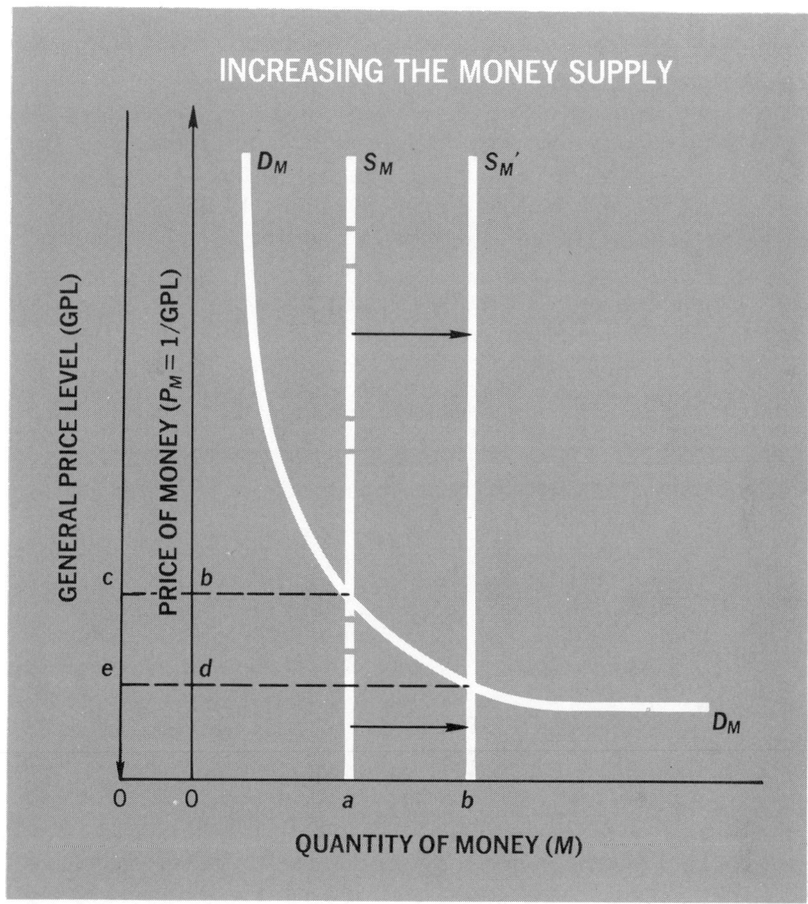

Figure 9-8

of goods being exchanged in the economy and at the prices those goods have, there is more money around than goods to purchase. Each dollar starts bidding for more goods, but there are no more goods, and the price of *goods* starts going up. This is the same as saying that the price of money (purchasing power of money) starts going down. As this happens, the surplus of money begins to be absorbed by the higher General Price Level. The quantity of money demanded starts to rise following the demand curve for money until a new equilibrium is reached at price of money *0d* (GPL of *e0*). The new equilibrium quantity demanded has risen to the quantity supplied by the government, quantity *0b*. We have just experienced *inflation* in the economy—a rise in the General Price Level with no corresponding increase in the goods produced.

In Figure 9-9, the opposite situation is illustrated. In this case, the government reduces the supply of money from *0a* to *0f*. At the initial price level, the quantity of money demanded stays the same (*0a*) but the quantity of money supplied has dropped to *0f*. We have a *shortage* of money. Again, at the existing structure of prices in the economy, there just are not enough dollars to make all of the needed transactions. As a result, goods are left unpurchased. The shortage of dollars translates itself into a *surplus* of goods. This generates downward pressures on the price of goods which is the same as an upward pressure on the price (purchasing power) of money. The price of money starts rising along the demand curve which reduces the quantity of money demanded from the initial level of *0a* back to the new quantity supplied of *0f*. Equilibrium is reestablished at a higher price of money (lower General Level of Prices). There has been a deflation in the economy. Again, it is important to remember that we have been assuming

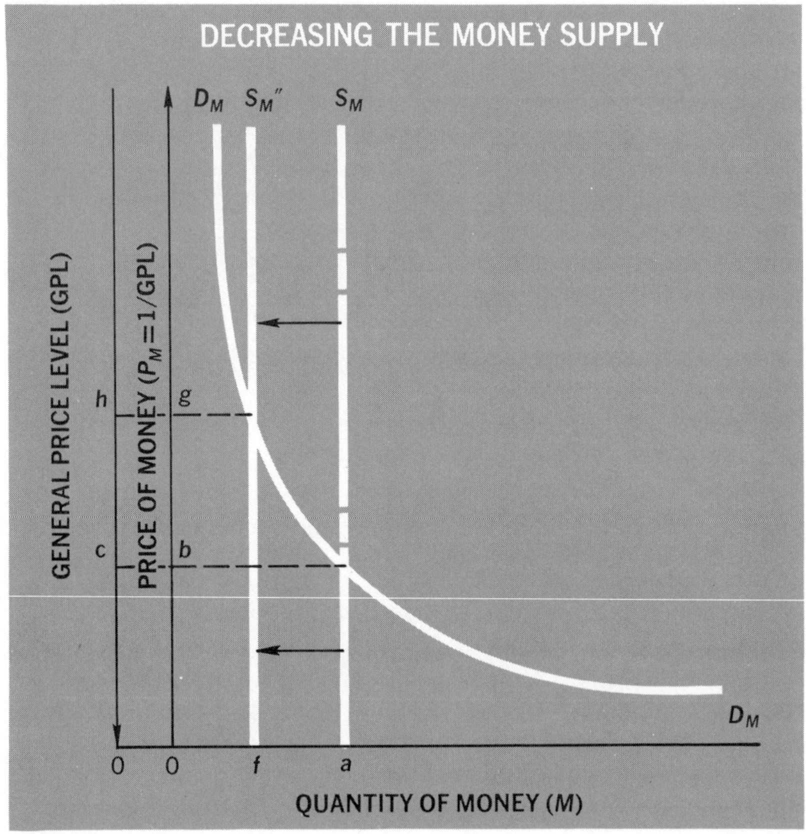

Figure 9-9

both flexible wages and prices and no changes whatsoever in the demand for money function.

Now, let us see what happens when the supply of money is held constant and something happens to demand. In the first instance, assume that the demand for money decreases, as in figure 9-10. This could occur for many reasons, most of which will be gone into in greater detail in the upcoming chapters. But, briefly, if the output in the economy goes down, then there will be fewer transactions, which will require less money to support the lower level of output. If, for some reason, the velocity of efficiency with which a dollar makes the rounds in the economy goes up, then, again, less cash would be required to support a given level of transac-

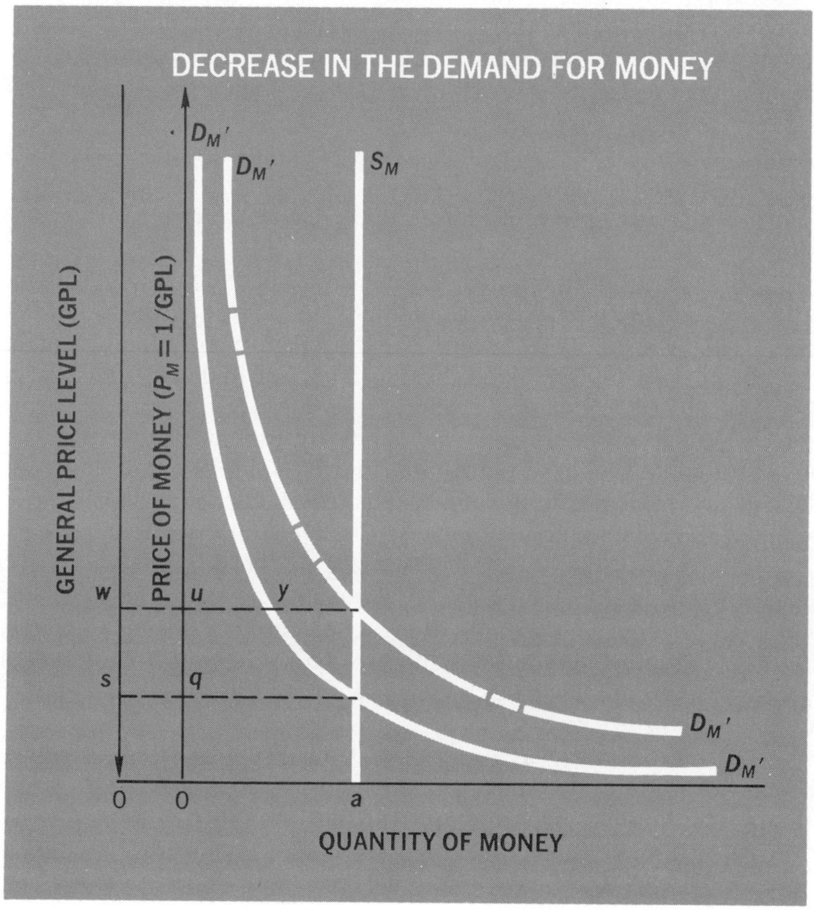

Figure 9-10

tions. If the opportunity cost of using money as a store of value increases, then one would expect the demand for cash used as a store of value to decrease. If the interest rate in the economy goes up, then to hold cash *instead* of an interest-bearing asset becomes more expensive, and, thus, the demand for cash decreases. Also, if people get the idea (right or wrong) that the price of goods is going to rise, this means that the value of their cash holdings (purchasing power of money, again) is going to fall. As a result, they will tend to get rid of the asset whose value they expect to fall. The spending of funds goes up, and the demand for money will fall.

When any of these things happens to decrease the demand function for money, demand will shift down to the left as from D_MD_M to $D_M'D_M'$ in Figure 9-10. Given the supply function S_M, the quantity of money demanded at the initial price of money will fall back to point *y*. Quantity supplied is now greater than quantity demanded. We have a surplus of money, which means a shortage of goods, which means upward pressure on the prices of goods. This is the same as a downward pressure on the price of money. Goods prices rise, the purchasing power of money goes down, and quantity of money demanded rises along the new demand curve until a new equilibrium is established at quantity *0a* (the same quantity as before) and money price *0q* indicating the General Price Level has risen from *w0* to *s0*.

When the opposite of any of these things happens, then the demand for money will increase as shown in Figure 9-11. Here, the shift in demand from D_MD_M to $D_M''D_M''$ means that the quantity of money demanded exceeds the quantity supplied. There is a shortage of money that translates into a surplus of goods *at the initial price level*. Downward pressure is exerted on the prices of goods that is upward pressure on the purchasing power of money. The quantity demanded of money falls back along the new demand curve until equilibrium is reestablished at the old quantity supplied and a higher price of money. The General Price Level has risen.

Notice that, in all of these cases, the market for money is a mirror image of the market for goods. A surplus of money translates into a *shortage* for goods. A *shortage* of money becomes a *surplus* of goods. A *high* price of money is the same thing as a *low* General Price Level, and vice versa. This point will be coming up again and again, so it is a good idea to understand it.

There is another way of looking at this proposition by using a tool developed in the trade chapter of the book. In Figure 2-1, for example, Charlie's alternatives in production were illustrated. In that case, he could produce *either* five coats *or* ten carcasses *or* any linear combination in between. However, for each additional coat he produced *up to five coats*, he had to give up the production of two carcasses. In other words, the price of coats was two carcasses per coat. In that simple two-good, two-man

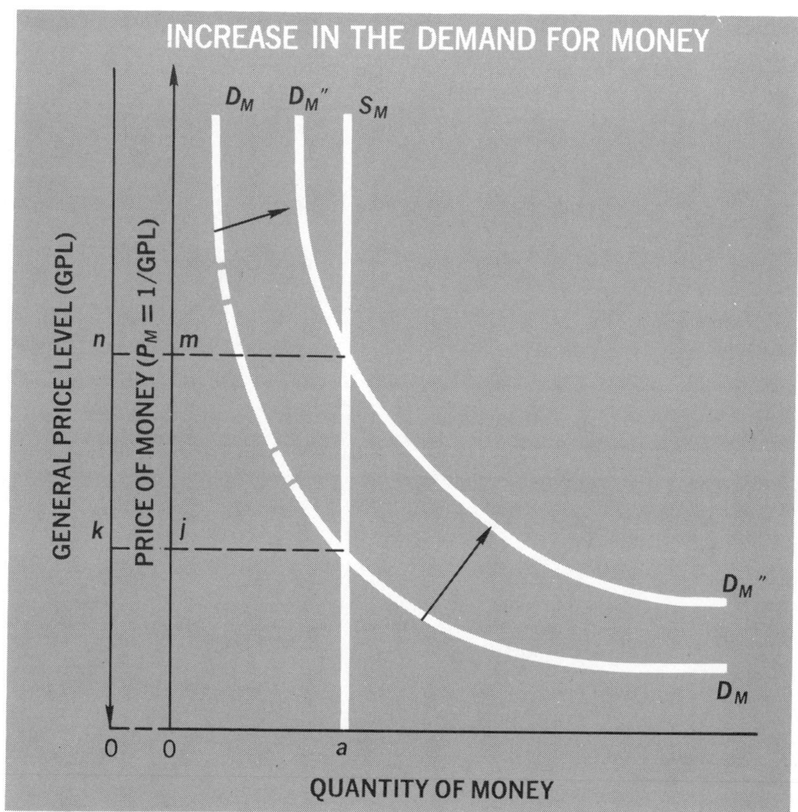

Figure 9-11

world, the price of coats was expressed in terms of carcasses *foregone* to produce one coat. Of course, the price of carcasses was shown to be the reciprocal of the price of coats. With just a few changes, this same *production possibilities curve* can be used to illustrate another set of possibilities—the possibilities of holding *money* or *market baskets*, and the relative prices of the two goods.

Figure 9-12 presents two options facing a consumer. He can either hold *money* or he can hold *market baskets* or he can hold some of each. Again, what is a market basket? It is an *average* combination of goods purchased by an *average* consumer in the economy. As you can see, even with their problems, averages can give us some useful insights.

In the example at hand, our average buyer has the choice of holding either four dollars of the good called money, or two market baskets consisting of all other goods. The line connecting the four dollars and two market baskets represents the *maximum* combinations of money and market baskets in between the two possible extremes. Notice that for every additional

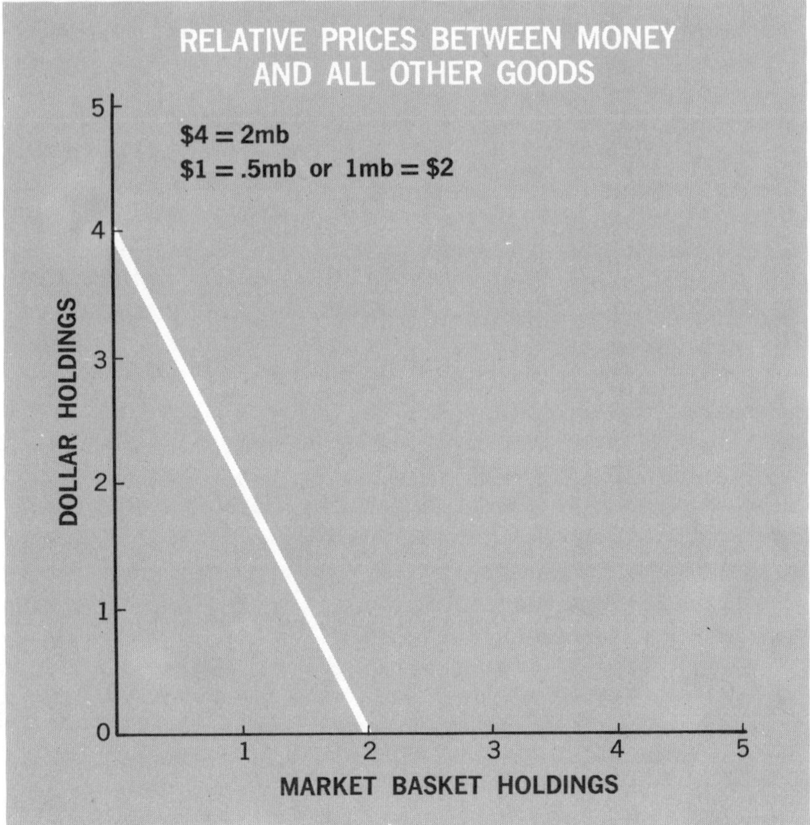

Figure 9-12

dollar he wants to hold, he must give up purchasing half of a market basket. In other words, the *price* of a dollar equals half a market basket. Similarly, to hold an additional market basket up to a possible total of two, two dollars must be given up—the price of market baskets (the General Price Level) is two dollars. As before, the price of dollars is equal to 1/GPL, or the reciprocal of the General Price Level.

Assume that the Internal Revenue Service comes along and takes half of the dollars that potentially would be available to our buyer, but leaves everyone else in the economy alone. All this will mean is that he will only be able to buy half as much as he did before. By himself, he would not affect prices very much. However, if half of the dollars are taken from each and every average person in the economy, then the alternatives available to each and every buyer will be those illustrated in Figure 9-13. On the

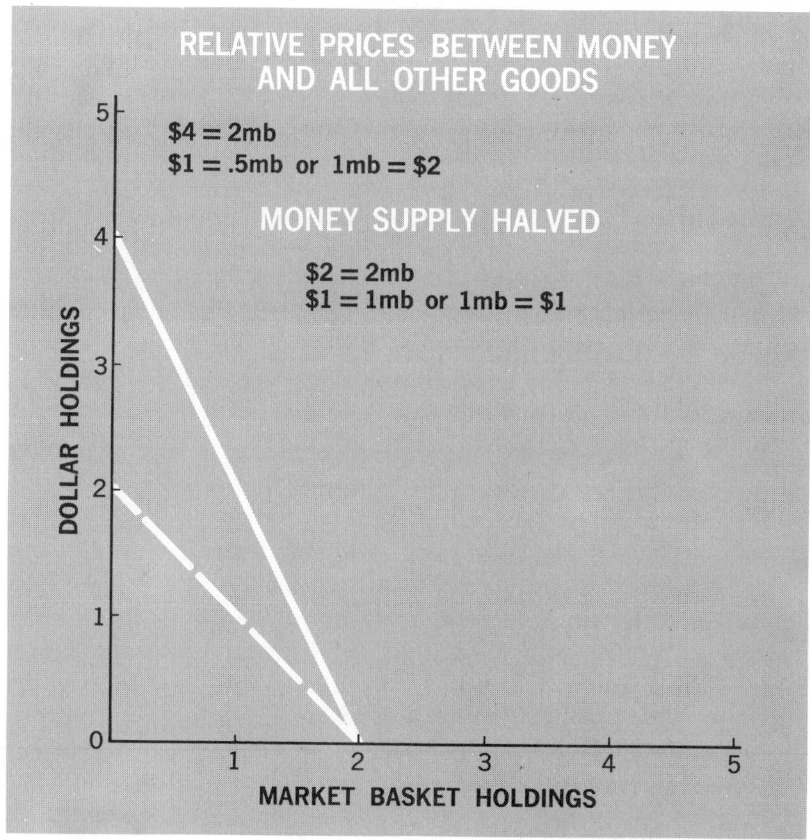

Figure 9-13

average, people can now hold either two dollars or two market baskets. At the old price of two dollars per market basket, a surplus of market baskets will develop (again, a shortage of money). This will put downward pressure on the price of market baskets until the price falls to the new level of one dollar per market basket. The shortage of dollars (or the surplus of market baskets) at the old price forces prices down.

The name of the constraint we are using here is changed somewhat. We are no longer talking about *production possibilities* but rather consumption possibilities. The most common name attached to this idea is *budget constraint.*

Just as with the earlier analysis, the one here assumes that prices and wages are free to move in the economy as market forces direct.

A look around at the economy shows all kinds of problems with inflation, unemployment, shortages and/or surpluses, and other facts of life that should make one question the simple analysis just presented. Does the existence of these problems mean all of this monetary theory is just a bunch of nonsense? No, but what it does suggest is that life is not as perfect as our model. These imperfections will be the whole subject of later chapters.

QUESTIONS

1. In the Charlie and Clyde example, when Charlie traded a rock for a coat, the text states that the rocks were not yet money. Why?
2. Money is unique as a medium of exchange and not unique as a store of value. Explain this statement and its significance.
3. What problems would arise in the economy if money were not physically durable? Does today's money fit that criterion?
4. Describe a system in which coffee beans are used as money. Include a discussion of the purchasing power of coffee beans. Cover the differences between coffee bean money and Federal Reserve Notes.
5. In 1973, the price of food rose at record rates during several months of the year. The cost of living index rose rapidly, primarily as the result of increased food prices. Was this inflation? Discuss the pros and cons of this idea.
6. List some difficulties in constructing a General Price Index that are not mentioned in the text.
7. Assuming that the demand for money is a rectangular hyperbola, what would be the shape of a graph in which the GPL and the quantity of money demanded were on the two axes. Since this function is upward sloping, does that mean that the Law of Demand has been changed? Why or why not?
8. How would the graph for the money market look if government policy varied the money supply directly with changes in the GPL?
9. Describe in your own words what is meant by the statement "The money market and the demand for goods and services are mirror images."
10. What kinds of purchases would be most affected by a shift in people's expectations of future price changes?

10

Borrowed Money

OBJECTIVES

Borrowing money is really borrowing command over goods and services in the present, while loaning money is giving up command over goods and services in the present. When a borrower repays a loan to the lender, the process is reversed. Since lending money involves both some measure of risk and the giving up present purchasing power, lenders generally receive a payment in the form of interest. *Thus there is a market (actually, many markets) in which interaction of supply and demand, as well as various institutional arrangements, determine a structure of interest rates. As people desire present spending to a greater degree, then both demand for loanable funds increases and supply decreases. The converse takes place when all units in the economy become more "thrifty".*

BORROWED MONEY

There is another market that often is called the *money market*. This market consists of demanders who wish to borrow funds and suppliers willing to loan funds. It is very important that we look deeper into this market and see what is really being "borrowed" and "loaned."

Most people who borrow money wish to do so in order to purchase something *now* as opposed to waiting until some *future* time period when they would have accumulated the needed purchase resources. Money, of course, gives the holder command over goods in the present. There is another side to this coin. To borrow something implies that it will be *repaid* at some future date. Therefore, one who borrows command over goods today will lose command over goods at the future time when he repays the loan.

Suppliers of loan funds are in precisely the opposite situation. When money is loaned, its owner (the lender) *gives up* command over goods in the present until such time in the future when repayment again gives him the ability to buy goods. Figure 10-1 summarizes these facts.

WHAT ABOUT BORROWED MONEY?

Borrowing money is borrowing command over *present* goods and services.

Loaning money is giving up command over *present* goods and services.

Borrowers LOSE command over *future* goods and services.

Lenders GAIN command over *future* goods and services.

Figure 10-1

All the alternative choices we have discussed so far have dealt with one particular time period. We could purchase meat now, or a coat now, or some other good now; and the total we could purchase depends on our resources *now*. Being able to borrow *expands* our choices. With credit, it is also possible to choose between consumption and/or investment *now* and consumption and/or investment at some time in the future. With given levels of resources, we may choose a pattern of consumption and/or investment that will just use these resources. With credit, we can also choose an expenditure pattern that *exceeds* our current resources (by borrowing) or that is less than our current resources (by saving or lending).

Everything else being equal, most people would prefer to consume now, or at least to save their money (store of value) under their own control. They would prefer not lending their resources, because to do so involves at least some risk and uncertainty about the future.

Therefore, given free choice, people must be *paid* to forego current command of resources and to make those resources available to someone else. This payment is called *interest*. Interest is the wage paid for not spending in the present and for making those "savings" available to someone else. Interest is also the price people are willing and able to pay in order to spend now rather than in some future time period.

Notice, interest is the price paid for present expenditure—not just for expenditure using *borrowed* funds, but for *all* expenditure. How can this be? If *now* I consume my own resources, how can it be said that I am paying interest? The answer, of course, lies in the ever-present concept of *opportunity cost*. Even though they are my own resources, I have the alternative of lending them at the going interest rate if I do not spend them. Therefore, by consuming, I incur an implied cost consisting of the interest I have *foregone*. The opportunity cost of present spending is the interest lost.

Obviously, we are now confronted with another market situation. The "good" in this case is *present purchasing power* expressed through the market for loanable funds. Never lose sight of the fact that the loan fund market is merely a reflection of the markets for *present* purchasing power versus *future* purchasing power.

INTEREST AND DISCOUNT

Some may not be familiar with the mechanics of interest rates, so let us review some of these mechanics. When interest rates are discussed in this book, the reference is to *simple interest*. Here is an example: Charlie borrowed $1,000 from Clyde on January 1, 1973, for a period of one year at an interest rate of 8 percent per annum (year). Charlie had the use of this money for a full year, and on midnight of December 31, 1973, he repaid

PRESENT SPENDING is generally preferred over FUTURE SPENDING.

RISK and UNCERTAINTY DECREASE the desirability of future spending.

Therefore, given free choice, people must be paid to forego current spending.

This payment is called INTEREST

INTEREST IS THE OPPORTUNITY COST OF PRESENT SPENDING.

INTEREST IS THE WAGE RECEIVED FOR NOT SPENDING (for saving) IN THE PRESENT.

Figure 10-2

Clyde the $1,000 he borrowed *plus* interest of $80 (8 percent of the principal amount), or a total of $1,080.

Clyde could have loaned the money under slightly different conditions. He could have said, "I will loan you $1,000 for one year at 8 percent, but I am going to deduct the interest right now." In this case, Charlie would have borrowed $1,000, but Clyde would have deducted the $80 off the top, and Charlie would have had the use of only $920 for one year. On December 31, 1973, Charlie would have had to repay the full $1,000. This is called *discount interest* or just discount. But 8 percent discount is not 8 percent simple interest. Charlie would have had the use of only $920 for one year. He would have paid back $1,000 at the end of one year. In other words, he would have paid $80 interest on a principal amount of only $920. This would have amounted to *simple interest* of about 8.7 percent. Nice business for Clyde!

A third device used today really makes the credit customer think he is getting a true bargain. Suppose Charlie went instead to the friendly finance company down the street and borrowed $1,000 at only 6 percent for one year. Sounds good. To help Charlie fit the repayment into his budget, the friendly finance man set up an easy payment plan so that Charlie would not have to cough up this staggering debt all at once at the end of the year. Charlie signed a paper saying that he borrowed $1,000, but of course, to keep things simple, the interest was added on to the $1,000 making a total of $1,060. This $1,060 was then split into easy payments of $88.33 per month. The payments may be "easy," but the interest paid is not. To begin with, the interest was prepaid, not paid after it was earned. Second, Charlie had the use of the $1,000 for only *one month*. At the end of the month, he began to repay the *principal* as well as the prepaid interest. Each month, his repayments reduced the amount he actually had borrowed, although the 6 percent interest had been calculated *as though* he had the use of the original $1,000 for the full year. This interesting method of collecting "6 percent interest" actually amounts to paying just over 11 percent simple interest per year.

Don't misunderstand! The 11 percent may be a fair rate—that is, the market rate for the type of loan Charlie has taken out. The only thing that is disturbing is the fact that such a loan was advertised as "6 percent interest" borrowing. Federal law now required lenders to state the simple interest equivalent on loan papers and include all other hidden charges that are actually gimmicks to increase the actual interest paid by the credit customer. Although this law probably imposes additional administrative costs on lenders, it does improve the information on true costs of credit.

Let us now return to *the* market for loanable funds as shown in Figure 10-3. We emphasize "the" because we are really talking about another aggregate market. There is no single market for loan funds. There are

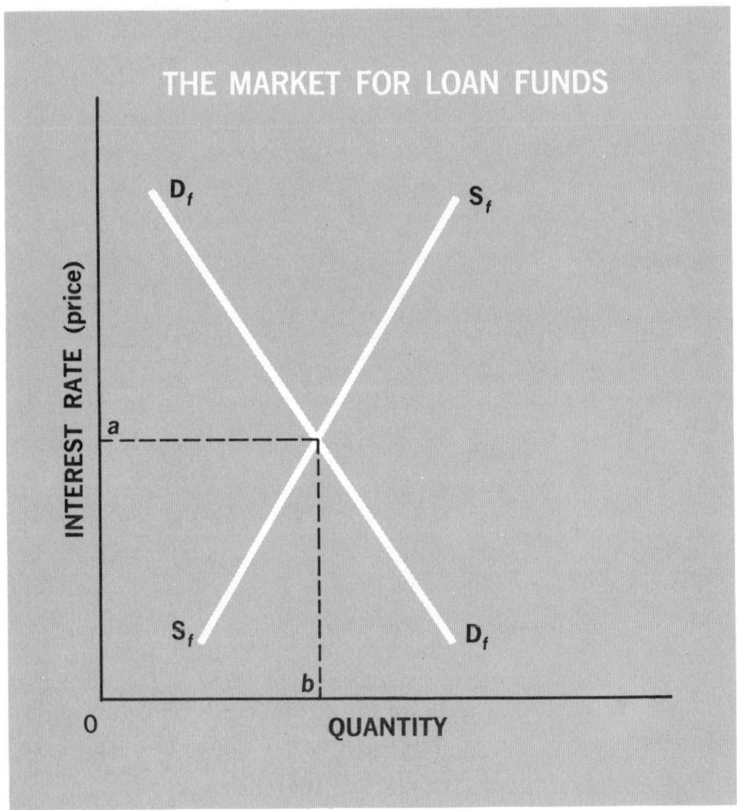

Figure 10-3

many. The prices (interest) in these markets will vary depending on the amount of risk and uncertainty involved in the particular type of credit. Our single market is some type of average derived from aggregating all the separate markets. Although actually constructing such a market would be very difficult, the concept is easy to grasp and using the concept can be very informative in this discussion.

Our demand curve D_fD_f shows the normal shape, that is, downward sloping to the right. As the interest rate gets lower, present spending becomes cheaper in relation to future spending, and more funds for present spending will be demanded. The supply curve for loan funds S_fS_f indicates that as the interest rate increases, people will be more willing to forego present spending and make increasing amounts of loan funds available in the present. The equilibrium interest rate and quantity shows the price people are willing and able to pay (borrowers) and receive (lenders) as well

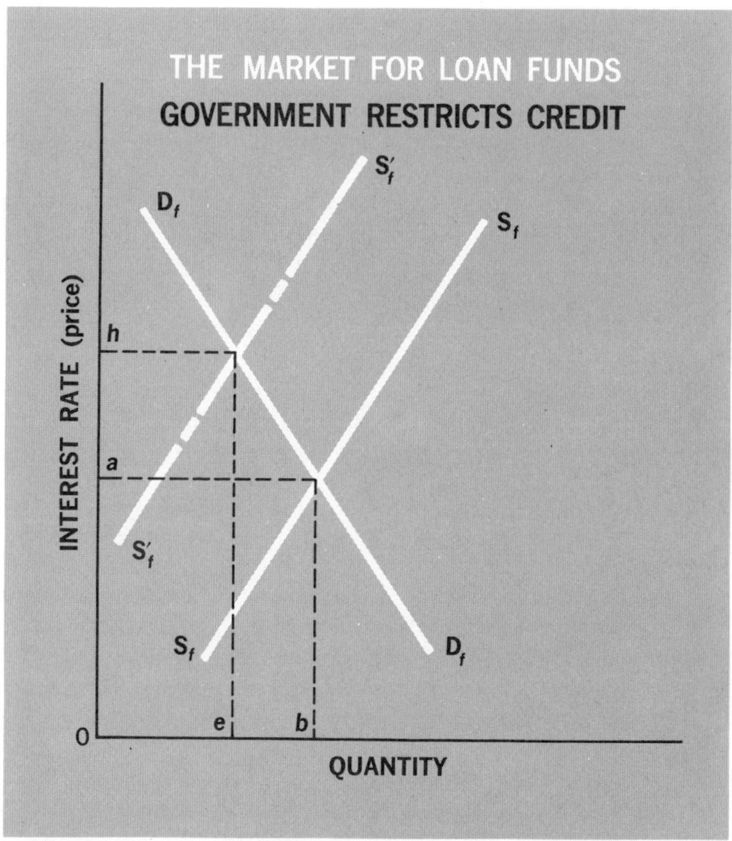

Figure 10-4

as the quantity of goods in money terms that will be purchased on credit now by demanders and foregone by lenders.

There are many things that could affect the shape and positions of these curves, and we will discuss a few. For example, in Figure 10-4, the impact of a government policy that restricts credit is shown. In the pages that follow, we will talk about some of the ways the government can accomplish this, but, for now, assume that the government initiates a "tight" money policy. This will have the effect of shifting the supply curve for loanable funds to the left (a reduction in supply). With no change in demand, a higher equilibrium interest rate and a smaller quantity of loan funds marketed would result. Why would the government want to carry out such a policy? One of the reasons would be to stop or reduce *inflation* in the country—to stop a rise in the General Price Level. Here is the way that would work. Demanders for loan funds demand them for *current* purchases. Inflation occurs when present purchasing power (at the given GPL) exceeds the available goods. By tightening the supply of available loan funds, the quantity demanded for the funds, and, hence, for current goods, goes down because of the increased cost (higher interest rates) of borrowing funds. Raising the interest rate also makes future consumption cheaper relative to present consumption. This means that the people will tend to postpone current purchases even if those purchases were to be made with owned funds. It's the business of *opportunity cost* again. Thus, some of the pressure of current purchasing power on currently available goods is reduced and, therefore, inflationary pressures are reduced.

Look at the other possibility. Assume that the government wants to stimulate the demand for goods *now*. One way to do that is for the government to embark on an "easy" money policy designed to increase the supply of loanable funds. Figure 10-5 illustrates the possibility. By increas-

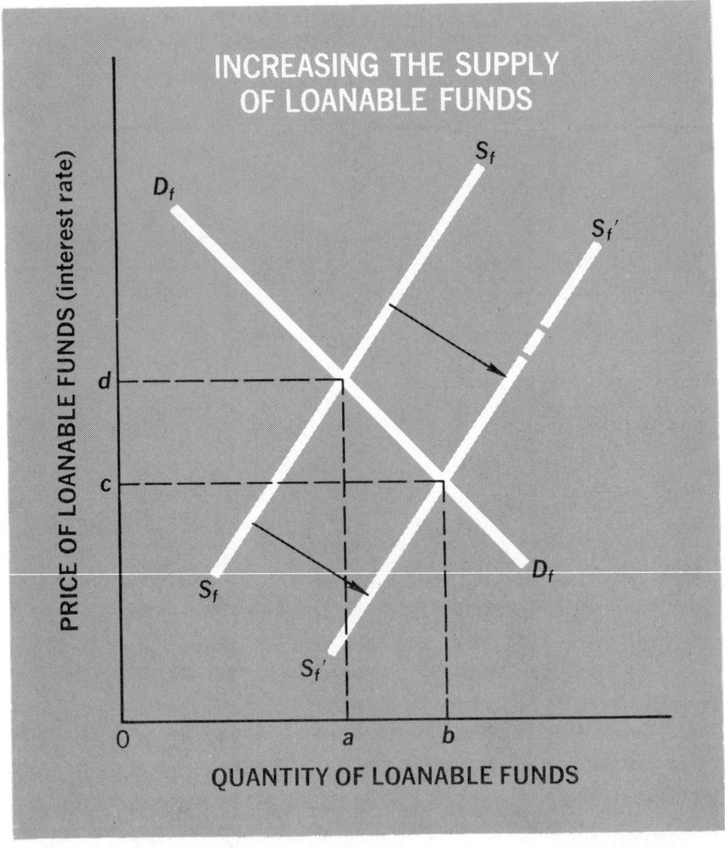

Figure 10-5

ing the supply of loanable funds from S_fS_f to $S_f'S_f'$, the quantity of loanable funds on the market increases from $0a$ to $0b$ and the cost of those funds decreases from interest rate $0d$ to $0c$. Because more funds are available at a cheaper rate, more current consumption is stimulated. In addition, the lower interest rate also means that the opportunity cost of present consumption has decreased. If this happens when the economy is operating below full employment levels, then such a policy can help increase the demand for goods and, hence, the demand for factors producing those goods.

Look at an example of a shift in the *demand* for loanable funds. In fact, in this example, assume that both supply and demand change. Assume that people throughout the economy become spendthrifts. Say everyone is led to believe that the world is going to come to an end next year, so we all decide to live completely now. First of all, the *demand* for loanable funds would obviously increase. People's demands for current goods would increase and be reflected in an increased desire to borrow against a very questionable future. In Figure 10-6, demand would increase from D_fD_f to $D_f'D_f'$. By itself, this movement would tend to raise interest rates (raise the cost of current consumption) and increase the quantity of funds marketed. But, at the same time, this change in expectations about the future probably would *reduce* the supply of loanable funds. Nearly everyone wants to borrow, but few people want to lend. Therefore, supply decreases as from S_fS_f to $S_f'S_f'$. This shift accentuates the increase in the interest rate, but works in the opposite direction on the quantity marketed. As a result, we cannot say what the net result will be on the quantity of loan funds. But surely, the interest rate will rise rapidly, and, given full employment in the economy, the chances are the prices will rise rapidly as well.

Because we are talking about people's expectations, let us see what some other impacts of people's expectations might make on the economy. Suppose, for the moment, that most people become convinced that inflation is here to stay for the foreseeable future, and they expect a continued rise in the General Price Level of about 5 percent per year. Assume that many people in the economy are working either with cost-of-living clauses in their work contracts or in markets where pressure will maintain the purchasing power of wages even if prices rise. In other words, if prices rise by 5 percent, wages will also rise by 5 percent. Would this affect the demand and supply for loanable funds? It certainly *could*. If I borrow \$1,000 today for a period of one year, I borrow command over \$1,000 of goods valued in *today's prices*. If the rise in prices over the next year is 5 percent, and my salary, increases by 5 percent, then at the end of the year, I will be repaying only 95% of the original buying power of the loan. The lender will have lost 5 percent of the *value* of his principal. If I paid the seemingly high rate of interest of 9 percent for borrowing this money, what would be the *effective* rate received by the lender at the end of

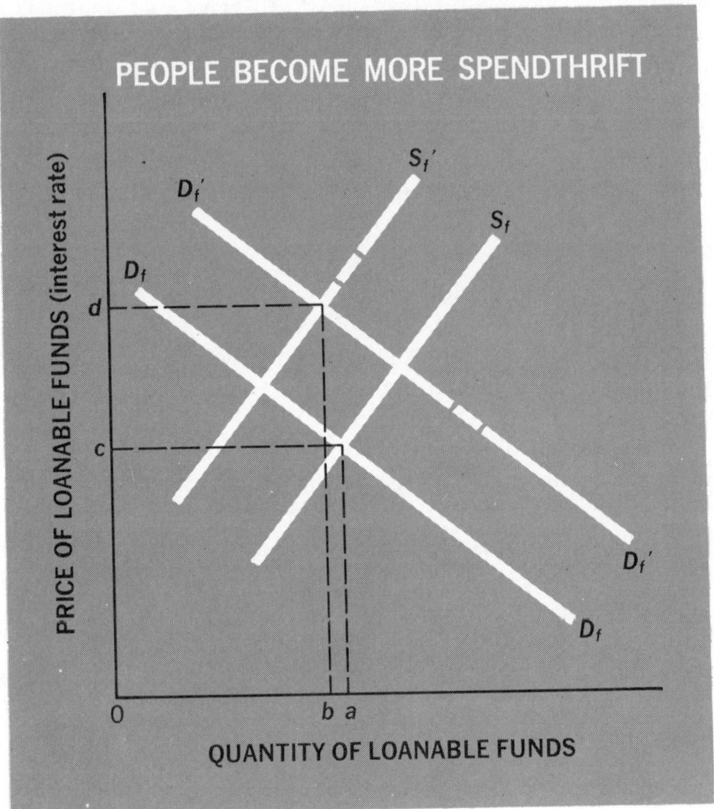

Figure 10-6

the year? He would *receive* 9 percent of the principal amount of the loan as interest, but he would *lose* 5 percent of the value of the principal amount to inflation. Therefore, the *real* or *purchasing power* rate of interest would be only 4 percent. By the same token, with wage increases matching the cost-of-living increases, the nominal rate of interest paid was 9 percent but the *real* cost was only 4 percent in terms of foregone purchasing power.

If people *expect* the price of money to decrease (the General Price Level to increase), they obviously will not want to hold money any more than they would want to hold any asset that they expected to go down in value. Hence, they will try to increase their expenditures of money in favor of holding more goods whose prices and money value will rise with inflation. Thus, the demand for current goods is increased, which by itself will add pressure to increase general prices and feed the inflation. Expectations of inflation can actually increase inflationary pressures.

Obviously, *unexpected* inflation will really foul up the loanable funds market. For example, people fortunate enough to get an FHA home loan at 4½ percent annual simple interest back in the 1950s did well during the inflation of the late 1960s. With a money interest rate of 4.5 percent per year, and an inflation rate of 6 percent per year, lenders were actually *losing* interest at the rate of 1½ percent per year. Unexpected inflation makes borrowers better off and lenders worse off. The market will adjust for inflation, but if it guesses wrong about the future, there can be a transfer of purchasing power between creditors and debtors. This, in turn, can distort the pattern of long-term investment vital to the future productivity of the economy.

QUESTIONS

1. In most microeconomic markets, we assume that *supply* and *demand* are completely independent—that forces changing one would not influence the other. In the market for loanable funds, this is no longer true. Why?
2. Explain why for the total economy, inflation would tend to cancel out effect on borrowers and lenders. Are there any ways in which this "cancelling out" might not be equal?
3. This one is a little complicated, so be careful. If IOU's are a way for lenders to store value, then they also should be a *partial* substitute for money. If this is true, would an increase in the interest rate increase or decrease the demand for money?
4. Explain the difference between add-on, discount, and simple interest.

11

Money Production

OBJECTIVES

Money in our economy consists of currency (coins and paper bills) and checkbook money *or* demand deposits. *Gold is no longer used in domestic circulation but is used, at times, to settle international accounts. Money is created primarily by commercial banks loaning money based on fractional reserves of government money. Checkbook money by far makes up the major portion of the total money supply of the country. It maintains its value by carrying the guarantee of "instant repurchase" by the issuing bank, should the holder wish to have government money instead. The Federal Reserve System is charged with the management of our money supply and does so using three main tools. It can control the reserve requirements of commercial banks and thus influence the amount of loans they can make. The Fed can also change the interest rate of loans made to commercial member banks thus encouraging or discouraging the bank's loans to private customers. Finally, and most importantly, the Fed can buy and sell government securities and can thus increase or decrease the amount of government money in circulation.*

Once more, we return to our cavemen. When last seen, they had made certain basic discoveries, such as fire, trade, and using shiny rocks for something called money. The rocks were a clear improvement over switching goods themselves back and forth. The rocks continued to be popular with the women of the community as decorative items. Thus, they were an economic good in their own right, but their importance, as a medium of exchange, store of value, and unit of account, appeared to have become even greater than their decorative functions. Many generations came and went, each bringing some crazy fad and material development. The young complained that everyone was becoming too concerned with gadgetry and the good old gods and values were being lost to the gods of materialism. Imagine, someone dreamed up a process of beating swamp reeds into flat sheets of something called paper. Another came up with a charcoal stick to make marks on the paper. Soon, everyone seemed to be concentrating on how to make these marks mean the same thing to everyone else so that something called written communication could take place. Who needed it!

It was found that people needed it, even to the extent of being willing to pay something for it. The great-great-etc.-etc.-grandson of Boris, the moneyman, became particularly interested in this new-fangled marks-on-paper game. Since he had inherited the prestige of his forebears (and a good chunk of their assets as well), the people of the community respected both his wisdom and character. One day he was watching his fellow countrymen lugging their rocks to the marketplace and then lugging their purchases back home. Since it was less than good sense to leave moneyrocks lying around, everyone had become accustomed to carrying their worldly rock-wealth around with them wherever they went. This practice tended to keep cave burglaries to a minimum, but the practice also made everyone very tired at the end of the day and was hard on pants pockets as well.

One day the latter-day Boris had an idea. He rushed down to the town square to make an announcement. "I am going to become a *banker*!" he shouted. Well, as I said, most people in town respected Boris the 125th very much, so when he made this announcement, they allowed as how that was just fine. They figured if Boris wanted to be a banker, they certainly weren't going to stop him. No one had the faintest idea what a banker was anyway. As luck would have it, there was one character in the group who popped up with the impertinent question, "Hey, Boris! What's a banker?" With the patience of Job, Boris explained.

Clearly, there were more rocks around than people actually used in their day-to-day transactions. Boris agreed to take on the function of safeguarding extra rocks until people needed them. The method was simple. People would bring him their extra rocks and he would give them a piece of paper that told the world that Charlie, Clyde, Melvin, et al., had on deposit with Boris so many rocks of such and such weight and quality. Boris would collect a small fee for this service. Everyone agreed that the service was cheap at twice the price. (What was their consumer surplus for this service?) Boris became a money warehouseman. The service proved to be immensely popular and even generated some side effects that no one had envisioned.

First, everyone had faith in the pieces of paper that the banker had issued as receipts. If Boris said there were ten one-pound rocks belonging to Clyde, then for sure, there were ten one-pound rocks in the pile. The next step was simple. After Clyde learned how to write, he found it was much simpler to pay for something by writing a note to Boris on the back of his receipt, saying that he transferred ownership of the rocks to the seller, old whats-his-name. If old whats-his-name wanted to collect the actual rocks, he could take the endorsed receipt back to Boris and collect the rocks out of the pile. If he did not want to bother, he could transfer the receipt to someone else with another small written endorsement. After watching this performance for some time, Boris had another idea. Instead of issuing receipts to someone in particular, he would issue a piece of paper saying that "the bearer" of the paper was entitled to so many rocks from the warehouse. This saved on both paper and charcoal sticks and also made it possible to issue paper for different quantities of rocks—a one-rock bill, five-rock bill, ten-rock bill, and so on. Paper money had hit the market.

Some other things started happening about this time. People in the economy were beginning to use some of their goods to produce other goods. In other words, they were beginning to use *capital* in the production processes. This presented a problem. Resources were being used to produce capital goods, and, therefore, resources to produce consumption goods were reduced. It is true that at some later time period, the capital goods themselves would produce higher levels of all goods. At any particular moment, however, the accumulation of capital goods required *someone* to give up *consumption now*. Fortunately, there were people who were willing to make this temporary sacrifice *if* they could be reasonably sure of getting their resources back at some future time *and* if someone would pay them for giving up this present consumption. The moneyrocks provided a way of performing this function. People would take their "extra" rocks to Boris. Boris, who was well known in the business world, would act as a broker by checking various requests for loans from businessmen (checking their credit references) and then loaning out the rocks that had been brought to him by *savers*. An important point in this operation is that money was brought to Boris, who gave the lenders interest-bearing receipts for the money. The *lenders* no longer held the money. The *borrowers* held and spent the money loaned by the savers. *No new money was created in the process.*

Aside from being an intermediary between lenders and borrowers, Boris continued his original function of storing rocks and issuing paper receipts for these rocks (paper currency). One further development took place in these paper receipts. Instead of issuing one-rock, five-rock, or ten-rock bills, the banker started issuing books of blank bills in return for rock deposits that people were still using for money (not savings deposits). As people spent their money, they merely made out one of these blank bills to the seller in the exact amount of the purchase. The seller could then either deposit this paper in his own account in the bank or collect actual rocks from the bank. Now we have *checkbook money* or *demand deposits* in the system. This system laid the groundwork for establishing a money production industry through which the private banks could actually *create money*. We will look into the mechanics of this process in the following pages.

Again, it is time to leave our fantasy world of the past and talk about the fantastic world of the present. What makes up our money supply today? In the United States, there are three basic forms of money. We still have *commodity money* in the form of gold. The only place this money is used is in international transactions. The government guarantees to pay legitimate foreign interests in gold in exchange for U.S. dollars. It is, however, *illegal* to use gold in domestic transactions. In fact, it is illegal to hold gold at all unless it is in the form of jewelry or some industrial product, such as certain complex electronic gear. Contrary to some popular thinking, there is *no* legal requirement for the government or banks to "back" our money with gold. In other words, *gold is no longer money*, as far as the domestic economy is concerned.

A second kind of money that we still use is currency—that is, paper bills (now primarily Federal Reserve Notes) and coins. Not so long ago, if one read the printing on United States government bills, he would have found a promise from the government to pay so many dollars in gold (or silver) *on demand*. Later, some of the notes promised to pay the holder so many dollars, without saying in what form the dollars would be (presumably, another piece of paper saying that dollars would be paid on demand!) Finally, it was decided that we did not need that myth anymore, and now our Federal Reserve Notes merely say, "This note is legal tender for all debts, public and private." It is worth what the general economy thinks it's worth. *It is worth what it will buy*, and this is precisely what money really has been worth throughout history. We know now that the value will depend on how badly people wish to use money (demand) and the amount the government allows to be supplied. Modern money's value depends on its *usefulness*, not its value as a commodity. In this country today, cash (currency) makes up only a small portion of our total money supply. Most money is in the form of *demand deposits* or *checkbook money*.

Checkbook money is a form of money that is produced by banks. It has several advantages over either commodity money or currency. It is reasonably safe from theft (except for forgeries) and can be issued by the owner (the depositor) in exactly the amount he desires. (Can you imagine a $1.02 bill, or a $1.03 bill?) The checking account also simplifies the accounting of receipts and disbursements for the holder. When one buys a demand deposit, he pays either in cash or with another demand deposit

WHAT MAKES UP OUR MONEY SUPPLY?

1. **COMMODITY MONEY**
gold (not circulated domestically)

2. **CURRENCY**
coin and paper

3. **DEMAND DEPOSITS**
checkbook money

Figure 11-1

on a dollar-for-dollar basis for this new kind of money. Notice that "making a deposit" is really buying checkbook money from the issuing bank. The buyer may pay a small service charge to the bank in return for the bank's performance of the clearing and accounting services for the customer. In no sense, however, is the depositor (buyer) *loaning* money to the bank. If I deposit $100 in a checking account, I still have $100. If I deposit *cash*, I have changed the form of the money from cash into checkbook money but I haven't given up one single cent of my money *as money*. A saver making a *time deposit* or *savings deposit* loans his money to the savings institution. He no longer holds money but rather a promise from the bank to repay his money within some specified time period. That time period might be very short, but, nevertheless, as long as the money is in the savings account, the holder cannot use it as money anymore. You can't pay the supermarket with a "golden passbook." This basic difference between a time deposit and a demand deposit is very important when it comes to the money creation process.

The way commercial banks produce money is quite simple. At any moment in time, the amount of government money (cash or currency) required to meet the desires of the demand depositors is comparatively small. This is particularly true as demand deposits are more widely used. A withdrawal of a demand deposit is generally offset by a deposit into another demand deposit. This offset may or may not take place in the same bank, but for the banking system as a whole, these offsetting withdrawals and deposits result in the banking system's having a stock of government money well in excess of that required by customers wishing to repurchase government money with their checkbook money. This fact gives the banks the *potential* of creating new demand deposits by the simple medium of making loans—not loaning out any specific depositor's money, but the money that is excess to their estimated requirements.

Figures 11-3 through 11-5 illustrate the process with very simple *balance sheets*. Balance sheets show the summation of assets, liabilities, and net worth of each of the economic units involved. Assets, of course, are goods that are "owned" or controlled by the holder. These could be physical goods, such as buildings and equipment, or they could be pieces of paper that represent resources owed to the holder. Liabilities are resources owed to someone else. Net worth is the difference between assets and liabilities. In other words, by definition and calculation, assets always equal liabilities plus net worth. In the *T*-accounts used in Figures 11-3 to 11-5, the value of assets is always shown on the left-hand side of the *T* and liabilities and net worths are shown on the right-hand side of the *T*. Because of the accounting identity, the total value of the left-hand side must always equal the total value of the right-hand side.

We will now assume that one day Charlie dug up an old sock containing ten $10 bills that were old enough so that the economy had forgotten about them, but still not old enough to be collectors' items. Whatever his initial financial position, he now had $100 of assets more than he had before, and, because his debts had not increased, his net worth was also increased by $100. The total money in the system is now increased by $100, and the form of the money is government $10 bills.

The second stage of the process is the purchase of a $100 demand deposit by Charlie at Boris's bank. As shown in Figure 11-3, the total money in the system does not change with this purchase. The bank has Charlie's cash, which it received in return for the demand deposit. This cash is now resting safely in the vault. Charlie still has $100, but it is now in the form of a demand deposit. *The cash is no longer Charlie's.* However, as part of its deal, the bank has agreed to repurchase Charlie's demand

HOW IS MONEY CREATED?

1. By COMMERCIAL BANKS creating demand deposits in return for money-earning PROMISES TO PAY

2. By the FEDERAL RESERVE BANKS creating demand deposits in return for government PROMISES TO PAY (BONDS)

Figure 11-2

deposit at any time he wishes on a dollar-for-dollar basis using government money.

The third step of the process occurs when Clyde comes into the bank for a loan. Assuming that history has shown that the total amount of government money demanded by the bank's deposit customers will never exceed 20 percent of the bank's demand deposits, Boris can loan 80 percent of the cash reserves he has available. He can either loan the actual cash (80 percent of the $100 cash received from Charlie), or he can create another demand deposit for $80 in return for a promise-to-pay from Clyde. Either way, the money in the system has been increased from $100 to $180. Of

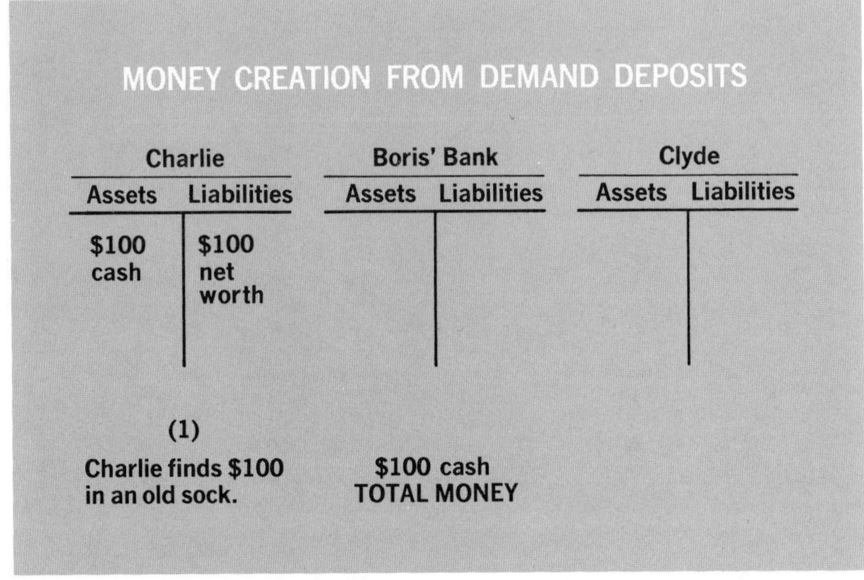

Figure 11-3

course, Clyde may take this new $80 and deposit it in another bank in the system. Now the whole process starts over again except with $80 instead of the original $100. The other bank can create 80 percent of $80 or $64 of new money. This process could conceivably continue in ever decreasing amounts until, finally, the original injection of $100 could cause an expansion to $500 of new money. The expansion possible is expressed as *1/reserve requirement.* Thus a 20 percent reserve requirement could expand the money supply by 1/.2, or five times the initial injection of "new" money.

As you may have guessed, by setting the reserve requirements for commercial banks, the government can exercise a measure of control over the amount of money that banks will be permitted to create. Raising the reserve requirements will tend to reduce the potential money expansion and lowering the required reserves can increase the expansion potential.

The unit of government that sets minimum reserve requirements for the commercial banks of the country is called the *Federal Reserve System.* It consists of twelve banks in different regions (districts) of the country, each of which acts like a "banker's bank." Although each district has its own administration, the system as a whole is controlled by a board of governors. This board controls the overall policies of the regional banks and also sets some of the conditions under which the commercial banks that belong to the system must operate. All *national banks,* that is, banks

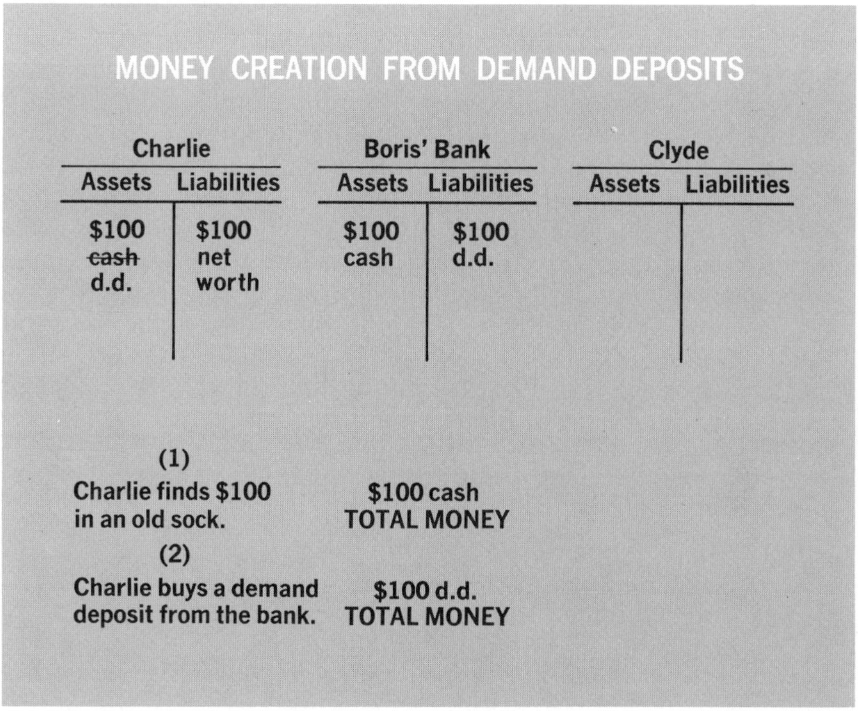

MONEY CREATION FROM DEMAND DEPOSITS

Charlie

Assets	Liabilities
$100 ~~cash~~ d.d.	$100 net worth

Boris' Bank

Assets	Liabilities
$100 cash	$100 d.d.

Clyde

Assets	Liabilities

(1) Charlie finds $100 in an old sock.	$100 cash TOTAL MONEY
(2) Charlie buys a demand deposit from the bank.	$100 d.d. TOTAL MONEY

Figure 11-4

operating under a federal charter *must* belong to the Federal Reserve System. In addition, a *state bank*, a bank chartered by a state, *may* belong if it meets certain requirements. Members of the board of governors are appointed by the president, on a staggered basis, for fourteen-year terms. These appointments then are confirmed by the U.S. Senate. The basic purpose of the *Fed* (as the system is usually called) is to manage the money supply of the country. As you can see, an attempt has been made to divorce this control from *direct* interference either by the legislative or the executive branches of the federal government. With regard to our money, the board of governors is supposed to act independently in the best interests of the country as a whole. Setting reserve requirements for monies created by the commercial banks is one of the three ways the Fed carries out this assignment.

There are two other tools that the Fed may use to control the money supply of the country. One of these is fairly simple. Some of you may have seen a potential problem in the way money creation was demonstrated in the preceding pages. What happens if, suddenly, everyone in a certain bank decides to hold government money instead of checkbook money? Clearly, a single bank that was *loaned up* to its minimum reserve requirements could be in trouble very quickly. It simply would not have the *cash* to pay off (buy back) all its demand deposits. Of course, it could call in all its loans (pay up *now*), but, generally, this would be difficult, if not impossible, in any given short period. The Fed provides a method by which banks can cover themselves in the event of a "bank panic." Member banks would be able to borrow funds from the Fed to cover the *instant repurchase* agreements they have guaranteed to their demand depositors. There are other circumstances under which member banks can borrow money from the Fed. The interest that banks pay for these funds is called the *rediscount rate*. It is *rediscount* in that the banks give as a guarantee to the Fed certain types of earning assets (promises to pay) against which the bank itself has

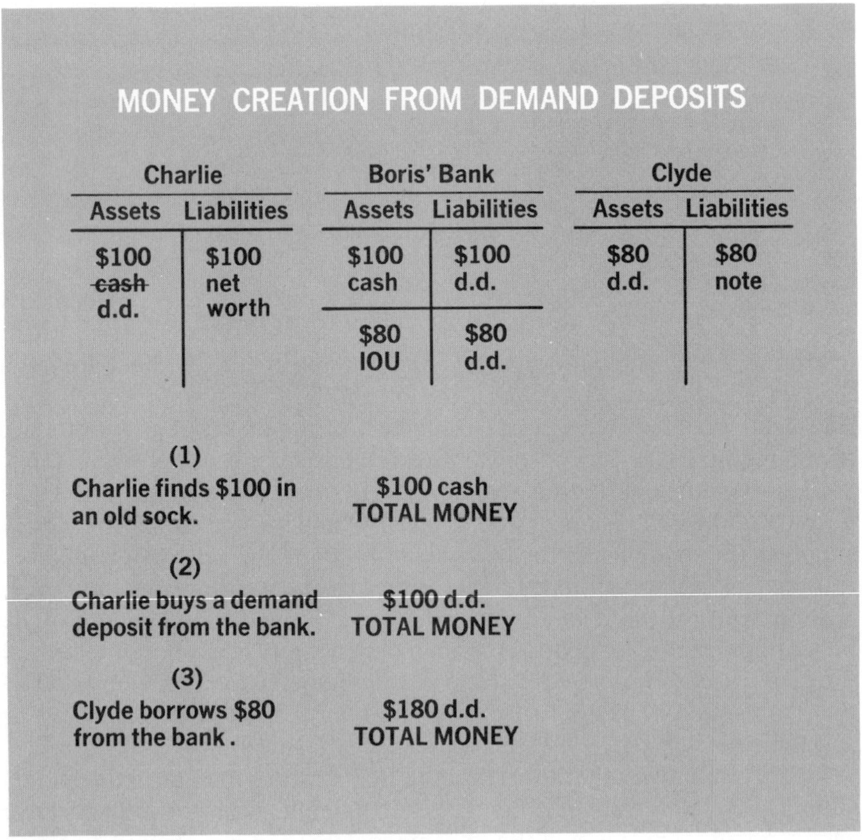

MONEY CREATION FROM DEMAND DEPOSITS

Charlie

Assets	Liabilities
$100 ~~cash~~ d.d.	$100 net worth

Boris' Bank

Assets	Liabilities
$100 cash	$100 d.d.
$80 IOU	$80 d.d.

Clyde

Assets	Liabilities
$80 d.d.	$80 note

(1) Charlie finds $100 in an old sock.	$100 cash TOTAL MONEY
(2) Charlie buys a demand deposit from the bank.	$100 d.d. TOTAL MONEY
(3) Clyde borrows $80 from the bank.	$180 d.d. TOTAL MONEY

Figure 11-5

made loans. Clearly, making it more expensive for banks themselves to borrow money (raising the rediscount rate) will discourage further lending and thus tend to reduce banks' potential creation of new loan money. The converse is equally true as far as *potential* expansion is concerned. Lowering the rediscount rate could make it more profitable for banks to create new loan monies. A note of caution should be introduced at this point. Although lowering reserve requirements and/or lowering rediscount rates will *encourage* expansion of the money supply, such an expansion *will not take place* unless borrowers in the economy take advantage of the new (and presumably cheaper) loan funds available. Again, borrowers' expectations of the future will influence the actual impact of either of these two policies on the supply of money.

Another way in which the Fed can influence the money supply is through its position as a major holder of federal government debt. The Fed buys and sells government promises-to-pay in the *open market* that exists to buy and sell these securities. The impact of such transactions is easy to see. If the Fed *buys* government bonds, for example, it must pay the previous holder. If it is a new issue, then the Fed would have to pay the U.S. Treasury. Usually, this payment is made by the simple expedient of *creating* a demand deposit on itself. The Fed writes a check to the bond seller, who then deposits it in a commercial bank. In this way, new money is introduced into the system in much the same way that new money was created when commercial banks made loans based on private individuals' or companies' promises-to-pay. Again, money created in this manner does not stop with the original deposit. The new government money (which it is) forms the base on which a multiple expansion can and does take place. *Selling* government securities has precisely the opposite effect. If the Fed sells government bonds, the money paid for those bonds goes back to the Fed, which can sterilize (destroy) it. Thus, comparatively minor sales and purchases by the Fed can have a much-magnified effect on the money supply because of the fractional reserve expansion and contraction system.

Lastly, the Fed can and does *print* money. Take a look at a dollar bill. The title printed on this piece of paper says, "Federal Reserve Note." If it says anything different, such as "Silver Certificate," see a rare money collector. If the Fed wished to do so, rather than create new demand deposits, it could merely pay in cash that it printed. Obviously, in this country, the demand deposit is more convenient and generally involves a more efficient way of doing business.

As with each of the subjects on which we touch, this discussion of money is not comprehensive. A study in depth is to be found in a "Money and Banking" course.

THE FEDERAL RESERVE SYSTEM CAN INFLUENCE THE MONEY SUPPLY BY:

1. **Buying and selling government securities**
2. **Changing RESERVE REQUIREMENTS for member banks**
3. **Charging more or less for loans to member banks**

Figure 11-6

QUESTIONS

1. List things that would tend to prevent the money multiplier from expanding the money supply to its full potential.
2. What would happen if the Federal Reserve used General Motors Corporation bonds instead of U.S. government bonds in its open market operations?
3. Discuss the importance of a commercial bank's implicit "instant re-purchase" clause when you purchase checkbook money.

12

Aggregate Demand

OBJECTIVES

*In aggregate demand, the idea of circular flows again becomes important. Purchasing power flowing in the economy can "leak away" if people hoard resources (*save*) without these savings finding their way back into the stream in the form of* investment *or other demand for goods and services. Other things can also act as leakages, such as imported goods replacing domestic goods and government taxation which is not spent. On the other hand, injections can take place which can stimulate the circular flow. These include increased demand for consumption goods, increased demand for investment goods, increased government expenditures, and increased demand for export goods. These leakages and injections can have a* multiplied *impact on the economy, so that under some circumstances, a small change in the injection or leakage results in a relatively large change in the magnitude of the total flow.*

INTRODUCTION

In the microeconomics portion of this book, it was easy to separate the two types of forces operating in the market into those affecting supply or quantity supplied and those affecting demand or quantity demanded. The assumption was that these forces operating on supply and demand were *independent* of each other. None of the variables in the demand function were in the supply function (except, of course, price), and vice versa. Now we will be adding up all demand and all supply into aggregate concepts. We will be talking about *aggregate* demand and *aggregate* supply. As already was seen, when the economy is viewed as a whole, we are looking at a circular flow. On one side of the circle, goods flow from producers to users. On the other side, factors flow from users to producers. It is obvious that the idea of independence between supply and demand disappears. If factors do not produce, then goods are not available. If factors are not paid, then there can be no demand for the goods. In other words, when talking about the aggregate economy, the supply of goods and the demand for goods are closely related to each other. But, conceptually, a separation of aggregate supply and aggregate demand is still possible and useful.

Before the Great Depression of the 1930s, market economists held that if there were any kind of economic slowdown, the market price mechanism would right everything. If the quantity of goods demanded in the economy fell, then inventories of goods would build up, businessmen would cut prices, at lower prices people would begin buying more, and quantity demanded again would rise. As prices went down, money wages also would go down, but buying power would remain the same. In other words, with flexible prices and wages, the system was (and probably would be today) completely self-correcting.

Some of the so-called Keynesians argued that even with completely flexible wages and prices, if people's expectations about the future state of the economy were bad enough, then hoarding of money and resource control could leak purchasing power out of the circular flow to the point that each round in that flow could become smaller. There would be a vicious circle of downward economic activity that could only be cured by massive injections into the system of outside buying power. Naturally, this outside force would have to come from "the government," and, hence, massive government spending programs were suggested.

Even though the analogy is trite and perhaps overused today, let us talk about the economy as though it were a simple plumbing system. An old-fashioned country well with a hand pitcher pump can give us the elements needed to illustrate the points. Figure 12-1 pictures this operation. Water is pumped out of an underground pool of finite volume. If none of the water is taken away, then it drains back down through the soil into the pool again. The flow up through the pump equals the flow back down through the soil. Even if the water is "used" right in the same area, the waste water still will percolate back down through the ground into the pool. The level in the water pool will remain constant. The demand for water from the pool will just equal the supply of water for the pool. The *flows* out of and back into the pool are equal and therefore the *stock* of water in the pool stays the same.

The analogy is quite obvious when applied to the whole economy.

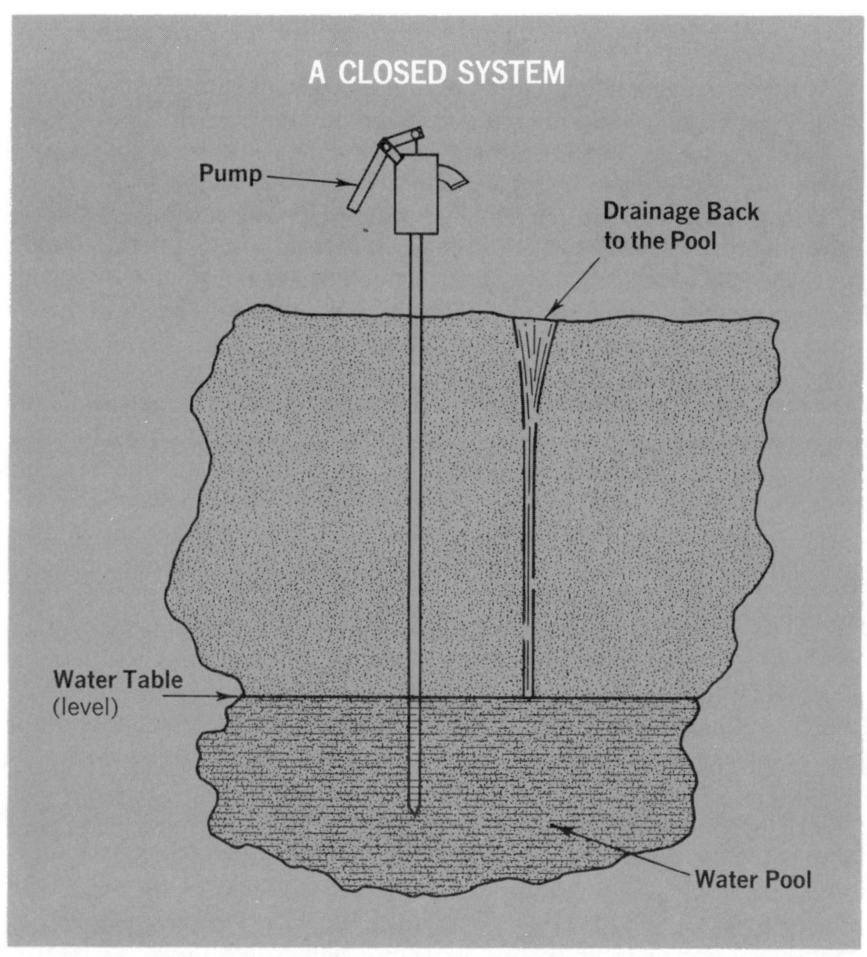

Figure 12-1

There are *stocks* of goods in the form of inventories and capital equipment. For that matter, even human capital is a stock. From these stocks, goods *flow* to users who, in turn, provide the factors of production to replenish the stocks through productive effort. As long as nothing interferes with the flows, then everything stays the same—the level of output, level of consumption, level of stocks.

In the pump example, let us now assume that one of the neighbors starts taking water out of the system and not replacing it. Now, the flow out of the well will be larger than the flow back into the well, and the stock of water in the pool will get lower and lower until finally the flow dries up as does the stock. If the neighbor takes a little water out of each cycle that is being pumped for home use, then the flow back will be continually less than the flow out.

In the economic system, there are "leakages" very much like this. Suppose that people start drawing money out of the system. They draw it out and do not spend it. They hoard it in their mattresses, or financial institutions store money without loaning it out, or businesses hoard money. This will be a leakage just like one out of the well. Similarly, if the government taxes people and then does not spend the money, a leakage has occurred. Finally, if goods are imported into the economy and these goods displace domestic products, the system will suffer as though domestic production potential had leaked out. Stocks in the system will fall, and the flows in the system will diminish.

The other possibility with our pump arrangement is for the neighbors to come in and start dumping water from an outside source into the drainage area to this well. The flow back into the well would increase and be larger than the flow out of the well. The stock of water in the pool would increase. Of course, with this increased source of water (if it could be made to last), it would be possible to increase the flow back up through the pump without reducing the pool level.

The analogy still holds. If the government starts spending funds, then this will inject more buying power into the economy and increase the demand for total goods—aggregate demand. If exports are demanded from the system, then aggregate demand will increase. If people use purchasing power to increase purchases of investment goods, then total demand in the economy will rise.

There are several ways this whole idea can be expressed in graphic and mathematical terms. Let us start with the simplest of all assumptions and build from there. In Figure 12-2, the two axes represent the dollar value of both sides of our circular flow. On the horizontal axis, the Gross National Product is plotted. This is the same thing (more or less) as income. On the vertical axis, spending is plotted. In the first instance, we will assume that every nickel that is paid out by factors of production from their earnings goes to consumption. In this case, consumption supplied will always equal consumption demanded. The resources paid for production are turned around and spent on goods that are consumed. The supply into the system equals the demand from the system, or

$$\begin{aligned} \text{Supply} &= \text{Demand} \\ \text{Consumption} &= \text{Consumption} \end{aligned}$$

On our graph, the 45° line represents points of possible equilibrium between consumption goods supplied and consumption goods demanded.

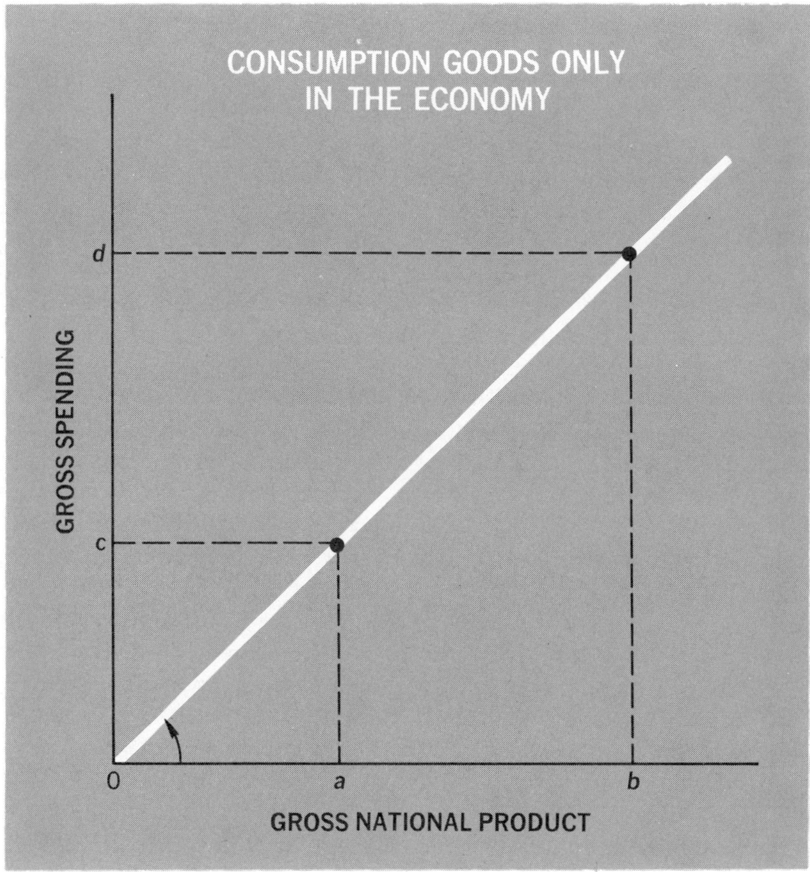

Figure 12-2

The economy would be in equilibrium at any point on the line. Where would the economy actually operate? It would depend strictly on the conditions of aggregate supply—on the capacity of the economy to produce. As we will see in the next chapter, this capacity is limited by factor availability, factor productivity, and the effectiveness of incentives. But, whatever that capacity turned out to be, the economy would produce that level, and the production would find a home as consumption. In this case, supply is creating its own demand. If *0c* is spent, *0a* will be produced, and the value of the goods produced is paid to the factors that produced it. This becomes the buying power for another round of purchases. If capacity is somehow raised from *0a* to *0b*, then, again, factors will have the resources to purchase the product they produced in the aggregate.

But now we get a bit more realistic. Let us talk about both a possible set of injections to demand and leakages from demand. Assume that as incomes rise, the people will *not* spend all of their incomes on domestically produced consumption goods. For example, we can say that out of current income, people will only spend seventy-five cents from each dollar they earn. For the moment, we will also assume that they *save* the other twenty-five cents. But now we reach an important point in discussing individual behavior versus that of the economy as a whole. For an individual, the idea of saving *anything* when his personal income is very low is unlikely. For the individual, saving will not even start until the basic requirements of life are met. In other words, for individuals, saving will not take place until some minimum level of income, and, beyond that level, saving will increase as income increases. If the individual has any accumulated wealth, then, not only will saving not start until some minimum level of income, but the opposite will take place. He will spend more than he is earning. In Figure 12-3, such a pattern is illustrated. At income level *0b*, our individual spends every cent he makes—no more, no less. *0f* and *0b* are identical and equilibrium exists. If his income drops to *0a*, then he will have *0d* (again, the same as *0a*) to spend from current earnings. But he will want to spend *0e*, which is *de* greater than current earnings. This gap will have to come from previously accumulated wealth, or from some kind of transfer payment (such as welfare), or from borrowing against his future earning power. On the other side of the coin, if his income is greater than *0b*, then he will tend to save a portion of that income. With income *0c*, he will spend *0h* but save *hg*.

If we assume that every individual in the economy is precisely the same, each with exactly the same income level and spending patterns, then the consumption function for the economy (*C* in Figure 12-3) would look very much like the one in Figure 12-3. Of course, we would be assuming that there were *stocks* of some kind of accumulated wealth from which *negative saving* could take place when income levels got low. But the assumptions we will be using are a little different and probably more realistic and useful. We will, first of all, include, on both the income and expenditure axis, income and expenditures *only* from current operations. We will talk only about *flows* and not mix in the idea of changing *stocks* of wealth until later. We will also assume that there is a cross section of people with different levels of earnings and expenditure patterns. We will assume (correctly, by most empirical data) that at zero national income, saving would be zero, and that the percentage of additional income saved as national income rises will remain constant. It is obvious that dissaving (spending more than is earned) out of current income cannot happen for the economy as a whole. There is no way to spend more than is being produced *from that current production*.

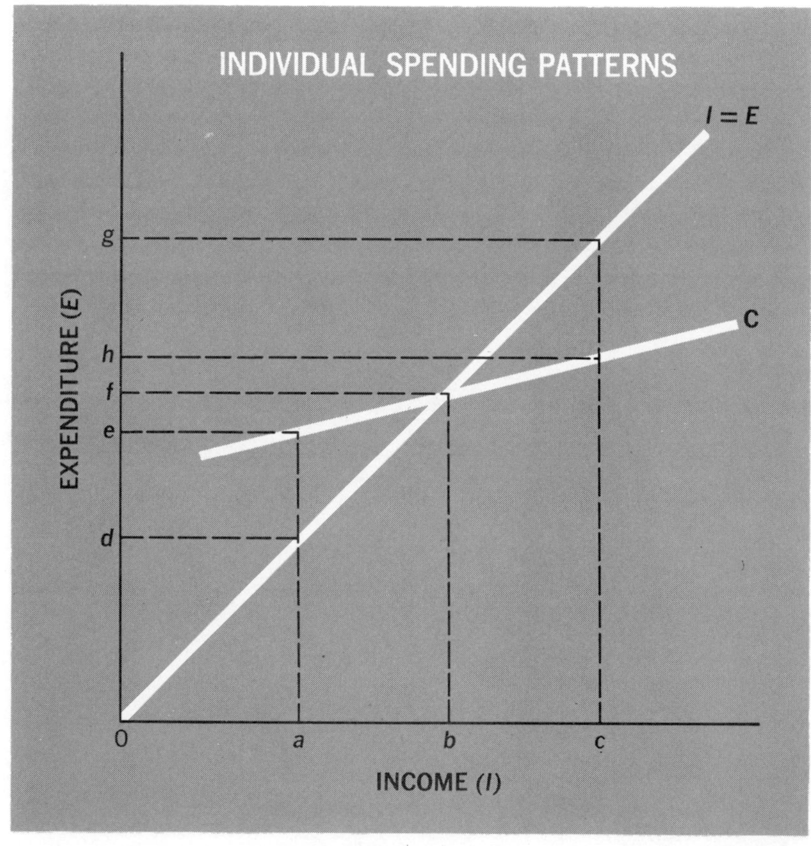

Figure 12-3

Given these assumptions, the consumption function for the economy as a whole looks like the one in Figure 12-4. Even at very low levels of national income, there will be some people who will still be saving. As incomes rise for the nation as a whole, saving rises, too, and at a constant rate. On the horizontal axis, we now plot current output, and on the vertical axis, we plot the use to which that output (income) is put. Initially, we will assume that the economy is operating well below capacity so that there are unemployed resources available if only the output is demanded. Prices are constant and can neither rise nor fall for the moment. The only expenditure we have is for consumption and the only leakage we have is in the form of hoarded saving.

For ease of reading the graph, we have identified only points rather than the coordinates of those points. Assume that in time period zero (any given time), output in the country stands at *0a*. With the consumption

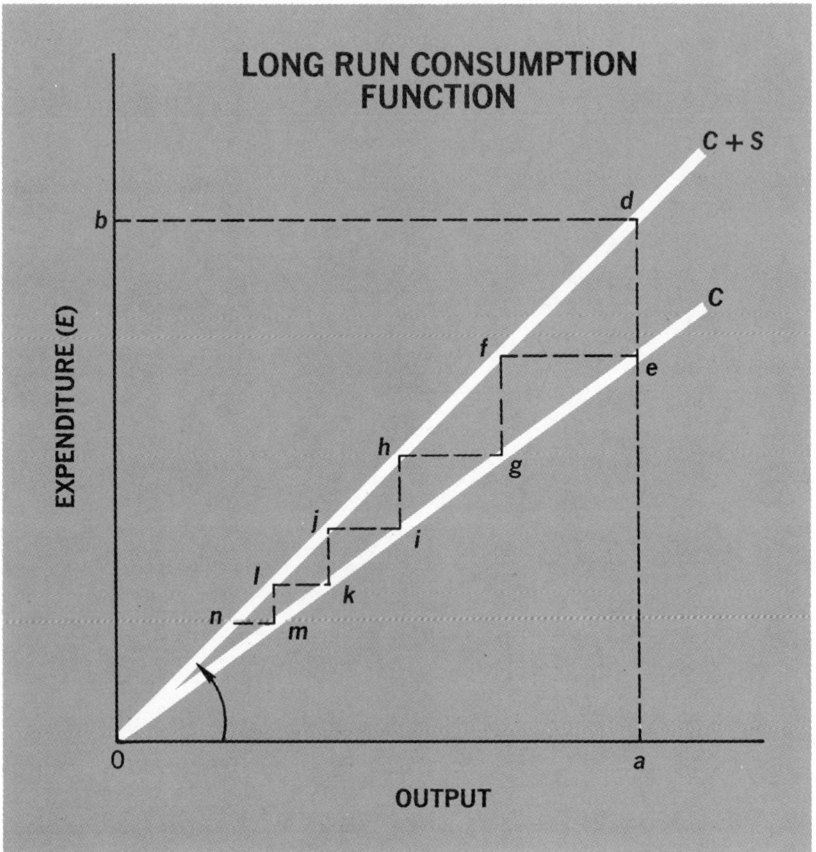

Figure 12-4

function C, then level e will be consumed but de will be *saved*. By our assumption, the saving is hoarded and not returned to the circular flow of the economy. As a result, these funds are not available as purchasing power for the next round. So, in time period one, output will fall from e to f. At output level f, fg will again be saved, thus reducing the output of the next round to h. Given the consumption function that we have shown, unless something were done, the economy would grind to a halt after some series of time periods. Remember, this would be possible only under the *most* important assumptions of unused capacity and fixed prices and wages.

Now, put one of several possible injections into the system to supplement the consumption expenditures. Assume that the demand for investment goods exactly equals the funds saved at output $0a$. In other words, assume that the demand for investment goods equals de and that it

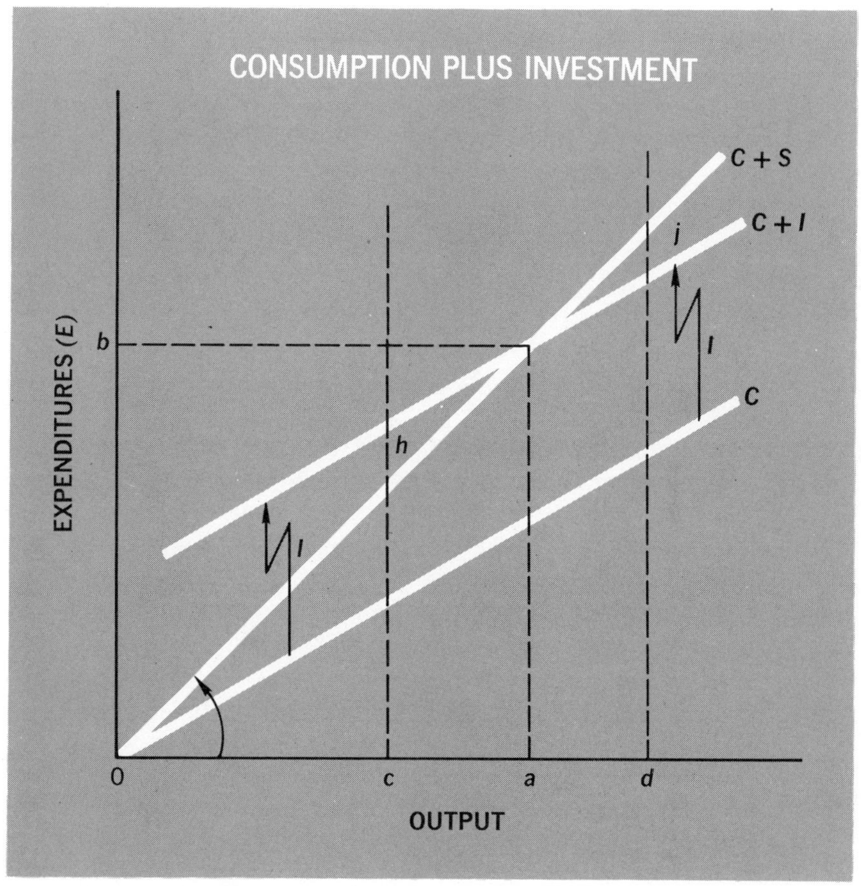

Figure 12-5

will equal *de* regardless of the level of national income. Now, we have an equilibrium at output *0a* that will be stable, as we will demonstrate using Figure 12-5.

Assume that for some reason, output drops below the equilibrium level of *0a*, say to *0c*. At this output, the output demanded $(C+I)$ is greater than output supplied $(C+S)$, and with the falling stocks of inventory that will result, producers will have incentive to increase production. Notice that this incentive will exist *without* any price change, because, by assumption, we are holding prices constant. In this case, it is the impact on inventories that gives the signals for either increased or decreased production. Remember, several times in this book there has been reference to the fact that, in the market system, there are two ways of reaching a solution. If the prices of the goods under consideration are rigid, and supply or demand conditions change, then output—quantity—will have to change to bring about a sort of equilibrium.

Finishing our example here, should the output stray above the equilibrium level of $0a$, then the quantity of output supplied $(C+S)$ will exceed the output demanded $(C+I)$. Inventories of finished goods will rise, and producers will cut back output until the equilibrium level is again reached.

A MULTIPLIER

One of the most difficult things to keep in mind during all of these discussions is the fact that we are talking about *flows*. If we place another dollar into the system, it may make the rounds several times in, say, a year. The dollar spent becomes demand for the product bought plus the products that the seller buys plus the products that his supplier buys, and so on. If the process of investment is a flow (which it is, by definition) then this constant rate of demand will have a *multiplied* impact on the level of output demanded in the future. If no one leaked any of this increase in purchasing power out of the economy through increased saving, taxes, or imports, then the long-term multiplied effect on output demanded would be infinite. One dollar of extra consumption, investment, government expenditure, or exports could produce an infinitely large increase in national output over the long run. But, in fact, each time the increased injection goes around, a portion of it is pulled out through saving, taxes, or imports. Assuming that the only leakage is saving, then the multiplied effect of any injection into the system will depend upon the amount of leakage that happens during each go-around of the dollar. From our earliest example, if the country is spending seventy-five cents of every dollar earned, and saving twenty-five cents, then *each* go-around will reduce the impact of any injection by 25 percent. In the same way that the money expansion multiplier depended on the value of required reserves, so the investment multiplier depends on how much saving comes out each time around. Everything else being equal, the maximum impact of the multiplier is equal to the reciprocal of the percentage people are saving. In our example, the marginal propensity to save equals .25 or 25 percent. Therefore, one dollar of increased investment could increase national income by four dollars. If the rate of saving *increased*, then the potential value of the multiplier would *fall*.

In Figure 12-6, this multiplied effect is shown graphically. Starting from an initial level of output $0a$ and equilibrium level of spending $0c$, investment is raised by ΔI, to I'. After this has had a chance to work through the economy, output will have been stimulated four-fold and the

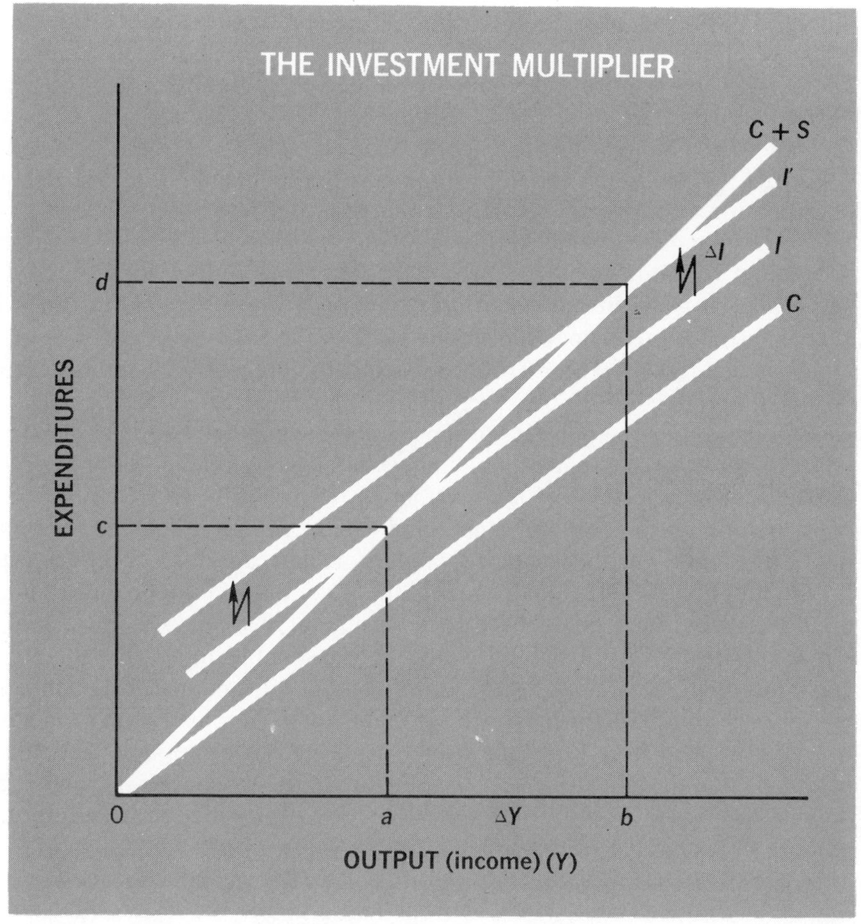

Figure 12-6

increased investment will now be at *0b* with equilibrium level of spending *0d*. The change in output (income), ΔY, will equal the change in investment, ΔI, times the reciprocal of the marginal propensity to save. You can see that the closer the consumption function is to the 45° $C+S$ line, the greater will be the impact of an increase in the rate of investment. This is graphically saying the same thing. The greater the marginal propensity to consume, the smaller is the marginal propensity to save, the less will be leaked on each round through the economy, and the greater will be the impact of *any* autonomous injection into the system. In our simple model, this could be an increase in investment, an increase in exports, or an increase in government spending.

We will be coming back to the policy implications of all of this in Chapter 13, but, for now, look at aggregate demand from a slightly different (and more familiar) view. Throughout this course, we have talked about *demand* as the quantity of goods demanded at different prices, *ceteris paribus*. In the last few pages, demand has seemed to take on another meaning, but it did not need to do so. We can still talk about a demand for all goods aggregated in the economy and make that demand relate *price level* and quantities of output (income) demanded at different price levels.

A demand function, like the one we are going to talk about, can be developed rigorously, but, for our purposes, an intuitive approach will serve just as well. Because we already have been talking about certain categories of goods demanded, let us stick to the same ones. First of all, imagine a giant market for all of the goods that people normally consider to be consumption goods. Now, we can come up with a *demand* for consumer goods that relates the quantity of those goods demanded (some kind of an index of quantity or a *real* value number) with different levels of prices *for those goods* (a price index for consumer goods only). Next, we could take investment goods and do the same thing. There would be some kind of an index of quantity with which we would correlate an index of prices for investment goods. With export goods, the same thing could be done, and, finally, a demand for goods used by government also could be estimated. On a *ceteris paribus* basis, it would be reasonable to expect that for consumption, investment, and export goods, the quantities demanded would rise with falling price levels and vice versa. Remember that one of the things being held constant would be the stock of money. For this reason, if no other, as price levels fell in any of the categories, purchasing power would rise with a given *nominal* stock of money, and, therefore, quantities demanded of the several groups would rise.

The possible exception to this would be the quantity of goods demanded by government. Here, there would probably be less responsiveness of quantity demanded to changes in prices. In fact, we will assume that the demand for government goods is completely inelastic with respect to price.

In the case of investment goods, there is another reason to expect the prices of these goods to be inversely related to their prices. Although we will not prove it here, there is a definite relationship between the General Price Level and the rate of interest. They tend to move together, and the aggregate demand curve that we will come up with assumes that interest rates are increasing at high price levels and decreasing with low price levels. If this is the case, then the quantity of investment goods demanded will be accentuated by a combination of low price for the investment goods and low costs of making investments. The savings that provide the funds for investment can be obtained at a comparatively low cost.

In Figure 12-7, we conceptualize the adding up of each of these

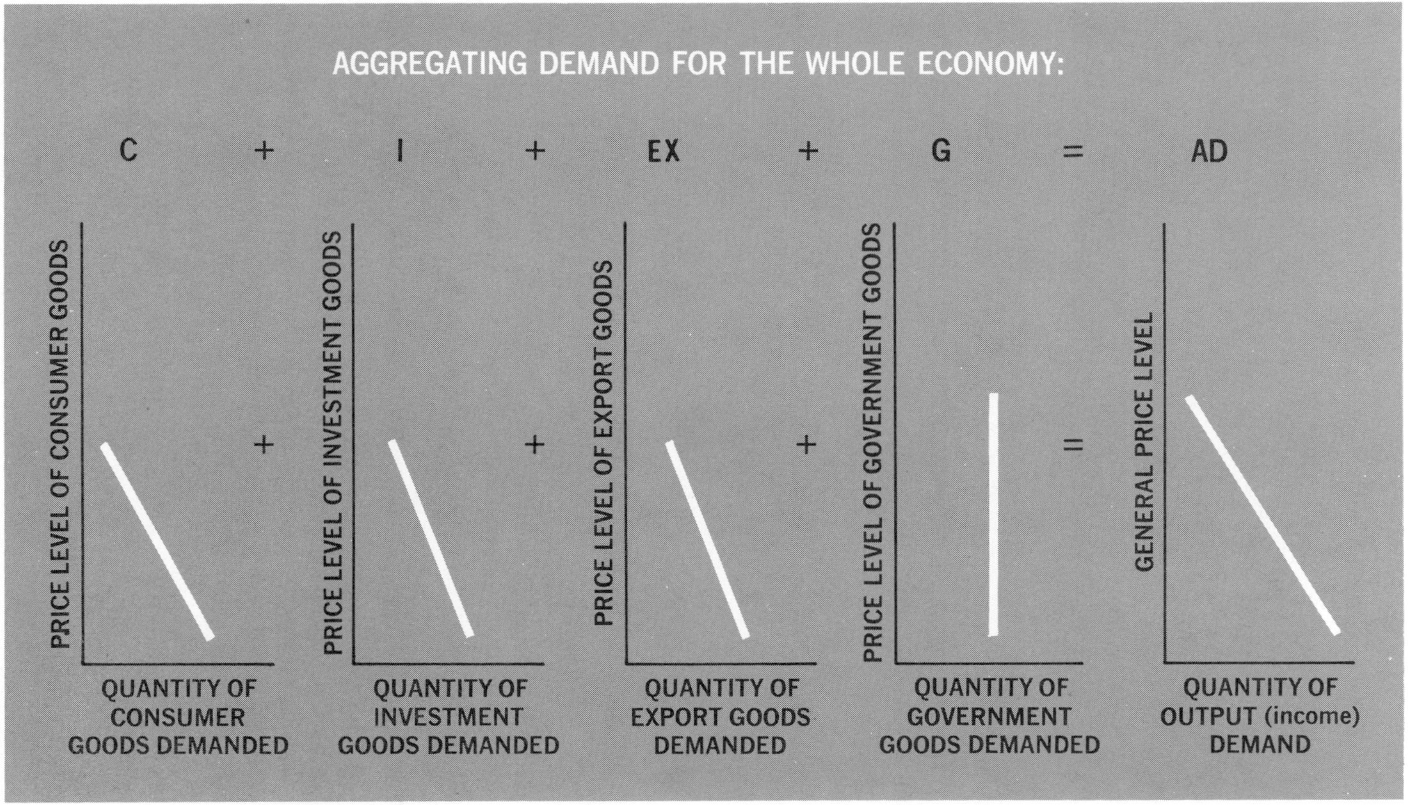

AGGREGATING DEMAND FOR THE WHOLE ECONOMY:
C + I + EX + G = AD
PRICE LEVEL OF CONSUMER GOODS
QUANTITY OF CONSUMER GOODS DEMANDED
PRICE LEVEL OF INVESTMENT GOODS
QUANTITY OF INVESTMENT GOODS DEMANDED
PRICE LEVEL OF EXPORT GOODS
QUANTITY OF EXPORT GOODS DEMANDED
PRICE LEVEL OF GOVERNMENT GOODS
QUANTITY OF GOVERNMENT GOODS DEMANDED
GENERAL PRICE LEVEL
QUANTITY OF OUTPUT (income) DEMAND

Figure 12-7

sectors into one massive and all-inclusive demand curve. Along that demand curve, the stock of money (M) will be held constant, the *demand* (the whole series of prices and quantities demanded) for consumer goods is constant, the demand for investment goods constant, the demand for export goods constant, and the demand (albeit completely inelastic) for government goods constant. Remember, however, that a change in the price of *any* good in the economy will be reflected by a slight change in the General Price Level, which is merely the aggregation of *all* prices in the economy. Similarly, a change in the output of any given item will have an impact, large or small, on the total quantity of output in the economy. Our aggregate demand function now looks like this:

$$y_d = f(\text{GPL}, \overline{\text{M}}, \overline{\text{C} + \text{I} + \text{EX} + \text{G}}, \hat{\text{r}})$$

Just as any demand function discussed previously, the aggregate demand curve such as the one shown in Figure 12-8 assumes that all things are constant except price (in this case, the GPL) and quantity demanded (in this case, output demanded). Here, we have a slight exception because, with all of the things we are holding constant, the interest rate will vary in a specified way with change in the price level. Therefore, we put a hat over the interest rate variable indicating that it is changing along the aggregate demand curve in a specified way.

Raising the stock of money in the economy will increase aggregate demand, such as from AD to AD' in Figure 12-8. Increasing any of the sector demands will increase total demand. Conversely, decreasing the money supply will cut purchasing power *at any given price level*, which means a decrease in aggregate demand. Decreasing the demand in any of the sectors will obviously decrease total demand.

The leakages we talked about in the previous section also enter here. There are three of them and they have to be included in the total demand function. One way would be to look at the net result of *pairs* of variables. We could take saving (a leakage) and subtract investment (an injection) and take the net result in our demand function. Of course, the net could be a net injection or a net leakage depending on which figure was the larger. The same thing could be done with imports minus exports and taxes minus government expenditures. But, the problem with this approach is that, in real life, injections and leakages do not pair off so neatly, and forcing the pairs can hide more than it reveals. For example, there is absolutely no reason to think that an increase in government expenditures necessarily will be offset by an increase in taxes. Instead, the government expenditure increase might completely displace (therefore reduce) consumption expenditures in the private sector. In other words, an increased G might be met by a decreased C rather than an increased T.

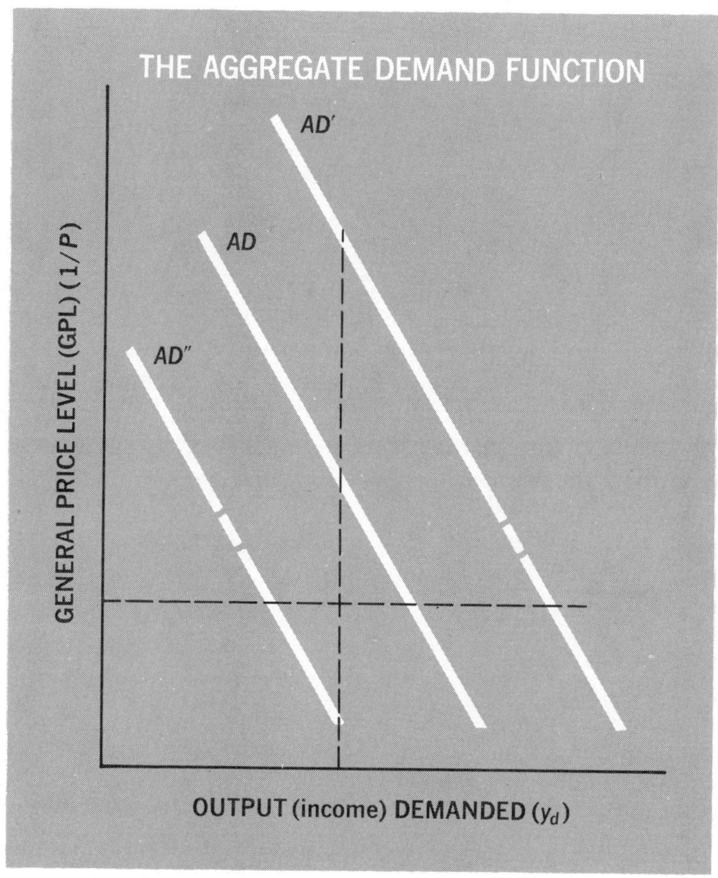

Figure 12-8

Summing up the determinants of the aggregate demand function, the following grouping makes some sense:

$$y_d = f(GPL, \overline{M}, [\overline{C + I + EX + G}], [\overline{S + IM + T}], \hat{r})$$

where:

y_d = output demanded		G = government spending	
GPL = General Price Level		S = saving	
M = stock of money		IM = imports	
C = consumption		T = taxes	
I = investment		r = interest rate	
EX = exports			

This looks complicated but it really is not and when we start using it in Chapter 14 it will become very simple, indeed. All it says is that the relationship between the output demanded in the economy and the General Price Level will depend on the stock of money in the economy, the level of consumption in the economy, injections into the economy (investment, exports, and government spending), leakages from the economy (saving, imports, and taxes), with a varying interest rate. Increasing the stock of money, consumption function, or injections will increase (shift) aggregate demand. Decreasing leakages will also increase aggregate demand. Decreasing the stock of money, the consumption function, or injections will decrease aggregate demand as well as would an increase in the leakages.

What we have developed up to this point are two ways of looking at the quantity of output of goods demanded in the economy. In the first instance, we assumed that supply would naturally follow the quantity demanded—that there were plenty of unemployed resources that would fill the gap at the going prices and wages. In the second instance, we have not said a thing about supply.

The next chapter will be devoted to aggregate supply and what influences it. Finally, in Chapter 14, we will put it all together and try to make some sense out of the complex world in which we live.

QUESTIONS

1. Does an increase in the amount of money people deposit in savings accounts necessarily mean that leakages in the economy will increase? Explain.
2. What would you expect to be some of the long run differences in the economy produced by an expenditure on investment goods as opposed to consumption goods?
3. Would increased government expenditures have any different impact on aggregate demand other than increased consumption expenditures of the same amount? Explain.
4. Comment on the following: "Since imports tend to replace domestically-produced goods, we should raise the tariffs or other trade restrictions in times of unemployment."
5. What things might reduce the effectiveness of an investment multiplier?
6. Under what conditions would increasing the money supply not increase aggregate demand.

13

Aggregate Supply

OBJECTIVES

The level of output that an economy can potentially *generate depends upon the level of resources available, the potential productivity of those resources, and the incentives operating upon those resources. None of these conditions by themselves are* sufficient *to bring forth production. All of these conditions are* necessary, *operating together, to bring about output. Rigidities in prices either of finished goods or in the markets for factors of production can cause surpluses and shortages in the economy. These can bring about unemployment of factors on the one hand or shortages impossible to resolve by the operation of the price system on the other. If prices and wages are perfectly flexible and factors of production are perfectly mobile, then the General Price Level will have no influence on the level of output in the economy. Aggregate supply can be increased by an increase in people's willingness to work at any given real wage, an increase in the productivity of any factors of production, and an increase in the availability of productive factors.*

INTRODUCTION

The last chapter raised important questions about what determines the level of output that an economy is going to produce. One model we developed indicated that demand would actually govern the quantity supplied: demand created its own supply and vice versa. But, there was an interesting assumption in that particular model about the level at which the economy was operating. It was assumed that there was *excess capacity* in the system and, therefore, any increase in demand would automatically call forth extra production. We look at this proposition in more detail a few pages from now, but first, let us look more closely at the thing that sets the limits of output in an economy—the capacity of the economy to produce. If this sounds like the microeconomic discussion of supply, it is because we are talking about the same general variables.

There are three simple limits to the potential productivity of any economy. For an outfit—be it company, individual, or country—to produce anything, it must have *factors of production*. It must have *labor*, both production and entrepreneurial. It must have *capital*, and the three types of capital we identified earlier were producible, depletable, and energy. So, having factors of production is a *necessary* but not a sufficient condition for an economy to be productive.

In addition to having factors of production, the factors must be *potentially productive*. In the case of labor, individuals must have sufficient amounts of human capital investment so that they can perform the skilled tasks needed in the production processes of the community. Capital must be able to utilize modern technology in an efficient way. Natural resources or depletable capital must be of sufficiently high quality as to allow exploitation without requiring unduly heavy expenditures of other resources. Energy sources must be available to utilize the energy itself, again, without having to expend too much in other resources. Here, once more, we are looking at a necessary, but not a sufficient condition, for production to take place.

The third requirement in any supply function is the business of *incentives*. The factors can be there, they can be potentially productive, but something has to happen to make these factors actually produce. There are many ways to accomplish this, ranging from a generous paycheck to threats of capital punishment. In other words, there can be *sanctions* as well as incentives used to call forth productive activity both from *labor* and the holders of *capital*.

We can recap these requirements and put some symbols on them as in Figure 13-1. So, what we arrive at is a supply function that says:

$$y_s + f(n, T, x)$$

But, we have a problem. So far, at least, there is nothing in the supply function that relates the quantity of output supplied with the General Price Level. Look at the variables, one by one. Does the quantity of resources available have anything to do with the price level? No. A changing price level that had some "stickiness" in it might cause some changes in availability. If the price of coal did not rise when all other prices and wages were

WHAT DETERMINES AGGREGATE SUPPLY?

1. QUANTITY OF RESOURCES AVAILABLE (n)

- *a.* **Labor**
  - (1) Production
  - (2) Entrepreuneurial
- *b.* **Capital**
  - (1) Producible
  - (2) Depletable
  - (3) Energy

2. PRODUCTIVITY OF FACTORS (T)

- *a.* **Quality**
- *b.* **Technology**

3. INCENTIVES (x)

- *a.* **Benefits**
- *b.* **Sanctions** (costs)

SO THE AGGREGATE SUPPLY FUNCTION LOOKS LIKE THIS:

$$y_s = f(n, T, x)$$

Figure 13-1

rising, then one could expect a shortage of coal. But our assumption has been that changes in the price level were across the board, and that assumption will hold until the next chapter. Therefore, it is safe to say at this stage that the quantity of resources is *independent* of the General Price Level.

How about the quality of factors or the technology that might be used in the system? Does this have anything to do with the level of prices in the economy? Again, the answer has to be "no." The kinds of things we are talking about in this category are such items as the quality of iron ore deposits or whether the crude oil contains hard-to-remove impurities. We also are talking about the level of health and the physical condition of the labor force. Many things affect this factor, including diet, quality of housing, and the obvious human capital investments of schools and training facilities. But, again, there is nothing that is tied to the General Price Level in the economy or changes of that price level.

In the next variable of the supply function, we begin to encounter differences between economic systems. Any economic system must have resources. Any economic system must have some measure of quality in those resources. But, how a system gets its productive resources to produce is a very different thing and it leans heavily upon differing values. For example, if maximizing the per capita output of the economy is one of the goals, and if human life is viewed as very cheap and highly expendable, then the way to go about producing things will be very different from the situation in which human life is put above output maximization. If human life is expendable, then the incentive and sanction system can be very different from an alternative based on highly valued human life. Most slave and prisoner systems tend to use sanctions for *not* producing instead of incentives *for* producing. This makes some good sense under many circumstances. In general, imposing sanctions is a cheaper alternative than giving some kind of benefit. It is probably cheaper to whip someone than it is to give him an extra meal. If the extra meal means extra strength to do the job, then the potential cost/benefits may change.

Some of the most amazing feats of human effort throughout history have been accomplished using systems based more on sanctions than on positive incentives. The pyramids of Egypt, the Great Wall of China, the industrial transformation of Soviet Russia, and, lately, the capital development within Mainland China all have had large measures of *negative* incentives or sanctions built into their ways of doing things.

The market system with its money wages is still a combination of positive and negative incentives. On the plus side, it is true that either harder or smarter work can increase wages that in turn, give a greater range of choices for the wage earner. For most people, this is a positive incentive to produce. But, on the other side of the coin, not working can mean poverty, vastly reduced choices within one's environment, and, in the extreme, physical pain or discomforts like hunger and cold. So, both positive and negative elements are involved in the market system of incentives.

As far as aggregate supply is concerned, we will assume that people prefer higher money wages to lower money wages. This is certainly reasonable, at least for the working force as a whole. We also will assume that higher *real* wages will increase the quantity of labor people are willing and able to provide in the market. The demand for all labor will be assumed to have a normal shape so that higher real wages will be consistent with smaller quantities demanded.

Do we now have something that will relate the *quantity of output supplied* in the economy with the *General Price Level?* Not if we assume flexible wages and prices. Remember that *real* anything is the money value of that thing divided by some index of the GPL. Real wages (*w*) would, therefore, equal money wages (*W*) divided by an index of the GPL. So, we come up with the formula

$$w = \frac{W}{GPL}$$

With this formulation of real wages, it is easy to see that if the GPL rises, by definition, money wages will rise proportionally, meaning that real wages will stay the same. On the downward side, the same thing applies. If the GPL falls, then money wages, being one of the components of general prices, will fall proportionately, and real wages again will remain constant. Here again, there is nothing in the changing GPL that would affect the level of *labor* output.

The payment to holders of capital takes the form of the interest rate that is a percentage of the money value of the item. We already have seen how the market rate of interest will tend to adjust for changes in the General Price Level, so, even the wages to capital are insulated from price level changes in a free market.

The last item in the incentive department is the aggregate *wealth* of individuals in the economy. Will price level changes affect this one? First of all, wealth can be held in the form of *real* assets. Land, buildings, furnishings, equipment, and other real property come under this heading. Because all of these things have prices, if prices all move together, as we have been assuming, price changes will not affect the *real* value of this kind of asset. Money values will change, but in direct proportion to the changes in the GPL.

A major portion of wealth in this country is based upon *debt*. The money owed as a liability by a borrower is offset by the IOU (bond, note, mortgage, and so on) held by the lender. In the money chapter, we already saw how a change in the General Price Level affects the well-being of borrowers and lenders. If prices *rise,* then the borrower will have to pay back *cheaper* (less purchasing power) dollars than he borrowed. Borrowers do well with a rising price level, assuming that the market has not already forecast such a price rise by increasing interest rates. At the same time, lenders become worse off by increasing price levels. But, when we add the *net* affects on the total economy, the losses of the lenders are exactly offset by the gains to the borrowers. It obviously makes a great deal of difference to the individual, but, in the aggregate, the two effects exactly offset each other. The *net change* in total wealth for the economy as a whole does not change.

There is one kind of wealth that changes in the price level *do* affect. Anyone holding *money* as a store of value, cash money or a noninterest paying checking account, is going to have his wealth increased or decreased by changes in the General Price Level. If prices go up, obviously, the value of money goes down. If prices go down, the value of money holdings goes up. This *wealth effect* could affect the amount people would be willing and able to work, and, hence, affect the level of output in the economy. It is probable, however, that any significant impacts from this wealth effect on the holders of money would occur only if prices fell very far down the scale. As a result, we will assume that employment and output will not vary from price-induced changes in the value of money.

Look at a graphical presentation of the things just discussed. First of all, output is going to come from the productive use of the capital stocks that exist in the economy at any moment in time. But, the use of those stocks implies the application of labor to the capital plant of the economy. Given fixed capital stocks, it is reasonable to assume that increasing application of labor will increase the level of output, but do so at decreasing rates. In other words, it is reasonable to assume that as more and more bodies are employed more and more hours, output will increase, but that the *additional output* from such increased labor will go down. This is called the *law of diminishing returns.* There are some complicated conceptual problems with the "law" of diminishing returns. But, if we talk about *decreasing additional output* from increased use of labor rather than decreasing additional products *attributable* to labor, some of the problems are, at least, minimized.

In Figure 13-2, we show an *aggregate production function* that illustrates what we just said. As labor is applied to the productive plant of the economy, output goes up. If *0a* of labor works, then output will be *0c*. However, if the level of labor is *doubled* (*0a* to *0b* in the graph), then the level of output will still increase, but by less than double (*cd* is less than *0c*).

We also can use this graph to illustrate the impact of improved technology or improved quality of the factors of production by a shift of the production function upward. In this case, any given quantity of labor will yield a higher level of output than before. For example, *0b* of labor will now result in *0e* of output rather than only *0d*. This same sort of a shift would also be expected if the *level* of capital stocks in the economy is increased.

Now look at the aggregate labor market from which the labor inputs come. In Figure 13-3, such a market is illustrated. The fact that the supply curve sweeps upward at high quantities supplied merely recognizes the fact that people are limited by time and physical endurance to a maximum effort per unit of time. Notice that this market is just like any other. The *price* is the *real wage* of labor, W/GPL in our notation. The *quantity* is man-hours that could increase either by individuals working longer hours or by addi-

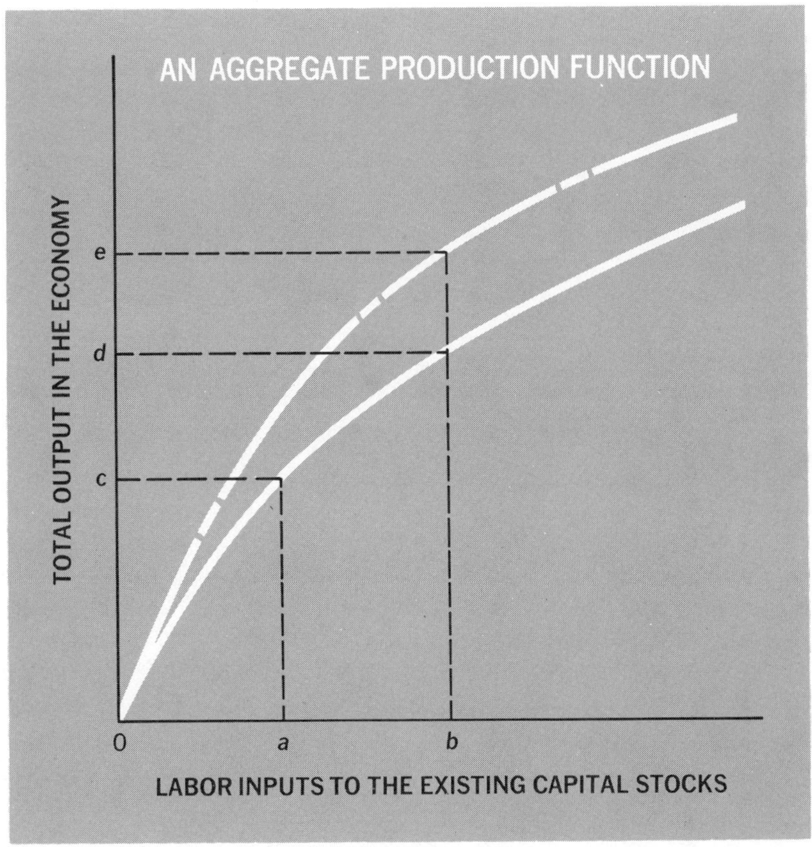

Figure 13-2

tional people working. Given our assumptions of freely moving prices and wages, there will be a unique wage rate (obviously, a unique *structure* of wage rates that aggregates into the single rate described) and a unique quantity of labor marketed at that rate. In the graph, this comes at real wage rate *0d* and quantity *0b*. If this quantity is applied to the aggregate production function, then the level of output in the economy will be *set*. Because changes in the GPL do *not* affect the real wage rate, changes in the GPL will not affect the level of employment. Therefore, *changes in the GPL will not change the level of output in the economy.*

Finally, there it is. Under the assumptions we have at this stage of the game, namely, flexible wages and prices along with no wealth effect, the level of output supplied in the economy is independent of the General Price Level. Figure 13-4 illustrates this situation. At GPL of *0b*, the level of

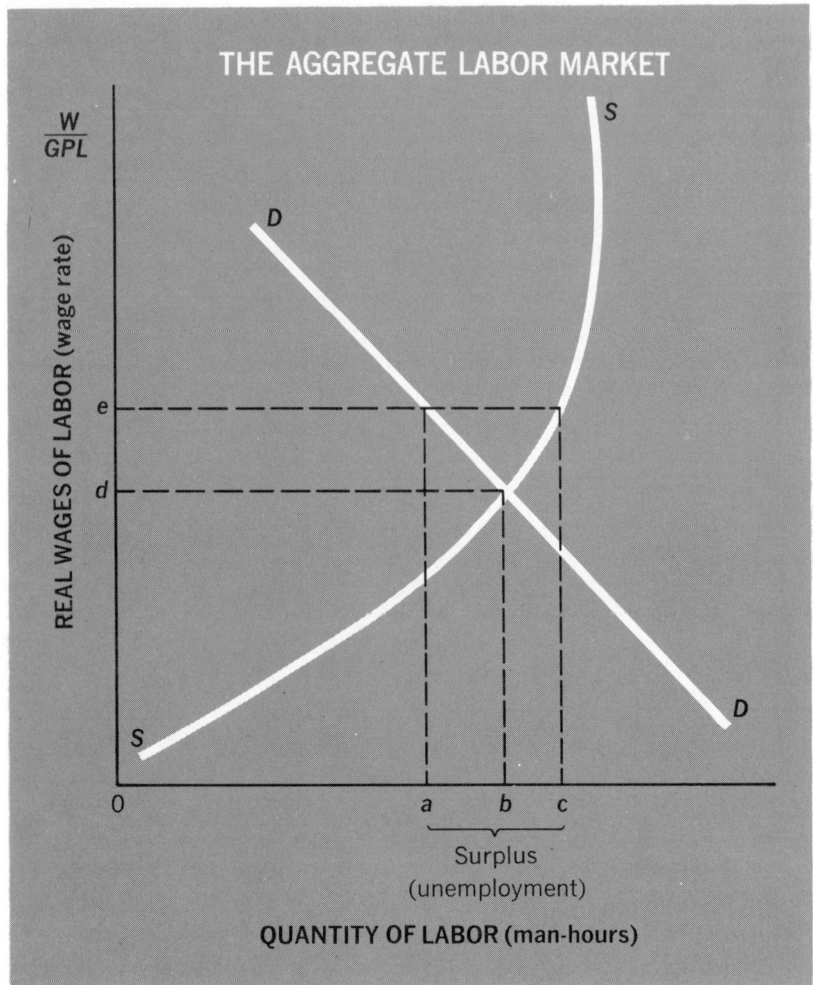

Figure 13-3

output supplied will be *0a*. At GPL of *0c,* the level of output supplied will be *0a*. At *any* price level, the level of output supplied will be *0a*. The aggregate supply curve is completely inelastic with respect to changes in the price level. Again, it is independent of the price level.

If this is the situation, then why did we spend that time looking at demand with the assumption of completely elastic aggregate supply? It may not have been realized at the time, but when we said that output supplied could follow the output demanded even though prices and wages

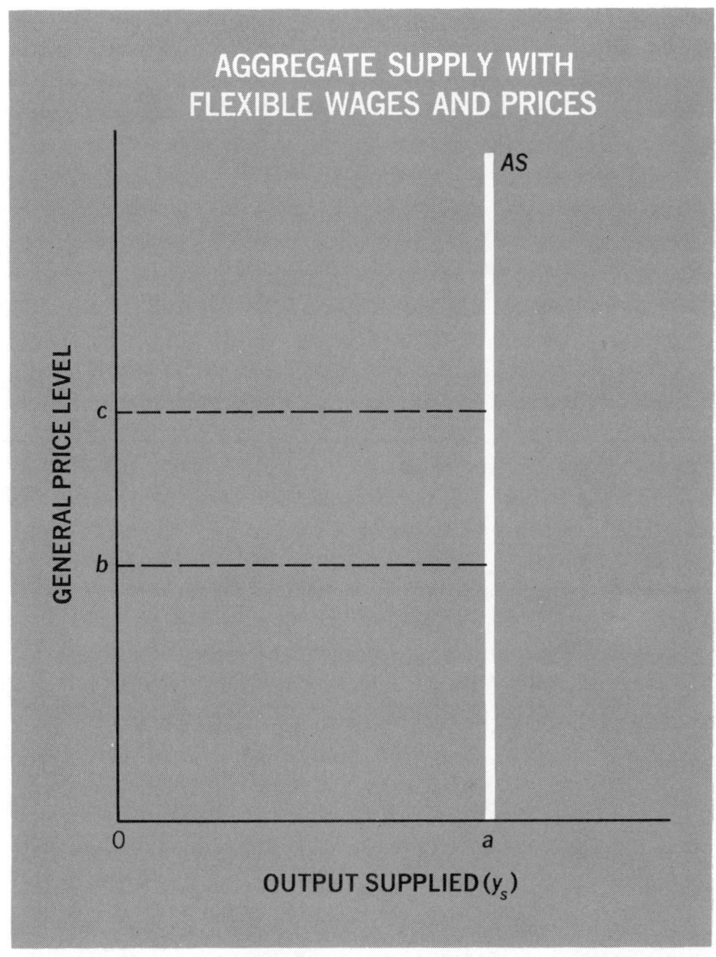

Figure 13-4

were constant, this is just what was implied. In other words, this assumption suggested that the aggregate supply function looked like the segment *bc* in Figure 13-5. In other words, as long as output demanded was between zero and *0a*, there was unlimited capacity in the economy to produce increased output without any increase in prices or wages. Once level *0a* was reached, however, the economy had reached capacity and any further attempts to increase output would only increase the General Price Level. Let us see what kind of conditions would have to exist before that kind of an aggregate supply curve would make sense.

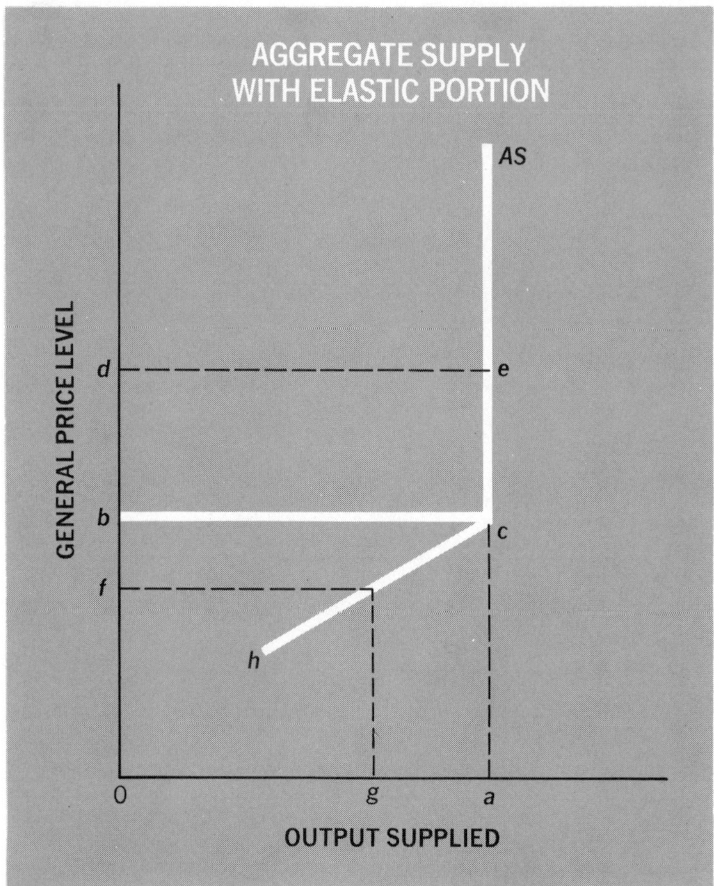

Figure 13-5

Referring to the labor market in Figure 13-3, assume for the moment that *money wages* would not decrease when prices of all other goods did decrease. In other words, money wages were rigid in a downward direction. In this case, if GPL started downhill for any reason, then *real wages* would automatically increase. The value of W/GPL would increase because GPL was getting smaller. But, as the real wages rose above the equilibrium level, *0d*, the quantity of labor supplied would rise and the quantity of labor demanded would fall. The only quantity that makes any difference in this case is the quantity demanded because that is all that is going to be hired. The rest of the workers are not going to find a job but will remain unemployed. Because a smaller quantity of labor now is being applied to the aggregate production function, total output will fall. So, we started with a decrease in prices, and we end up with that decrease causing unemployment and a reduction in output supplied. In Figure 13-5, this will show up as a partially elastic "tail," such as segment *hc*. Starting from an initial price level of *0b*, a movement of prices downward to *0f* with *rigid money wages* caused a lower level of employment and reduced output (from *0a* to *0g*). But, assuming that prices and money wages can move *upward*, then the aggregate supply curve would still be perfectly inelastic for price movements above *0b*.

This still does not get us to the completely elastic segment hypothesized in the earlier example. To get this, we have to assume that prices and wages are absolutely immovable at level *0b*. If this is the case, the only adjustment mechanism available to the economy is in the quantity of output. As long as demand conditions were such as to demand less-than-full-employment levels of output, cheaper prices could not stimulate quantity demanded because the prices are *fixed*. In this case, output supplied would depend strictly upon output demanded, and the price level would stay glued to level *0b* until the full employment level was reached at *0a*. Should demand continue to increase beyond that point, either prices would go up (if they were flexible upward), or, as we shall see, shortages will start to develop.

We are getting ahead of ourselves by talking of aggregate supply and aggregate demand working together. One more thing about aggregate supply should be finished up first. How does aggregate supply change if it is independent of the General Price Level? In Figure 13-6, we have again assumed perfectly flexible prices and money wages, and we illustrate two possible shifts—an increase from *AS* to *AS'* and a decrease from *AS* to *AS"*.

Any of the following *can* increase aggregate supply:

1. An increase in the willingness of people to work for the same real wage
2. An increase in the productivity of labor
3. An increase in the capital stocks of the economy
4. An increase in the labor supply
5. An improvement in technology

But, when prices and/or wages are sticky or inflexible, the General Price Level or changes in the GPL will affect quantity of output supplied.

QUESTIONS

1. List five things that would be incentives for you to work. List five things that would serve to discourage you.

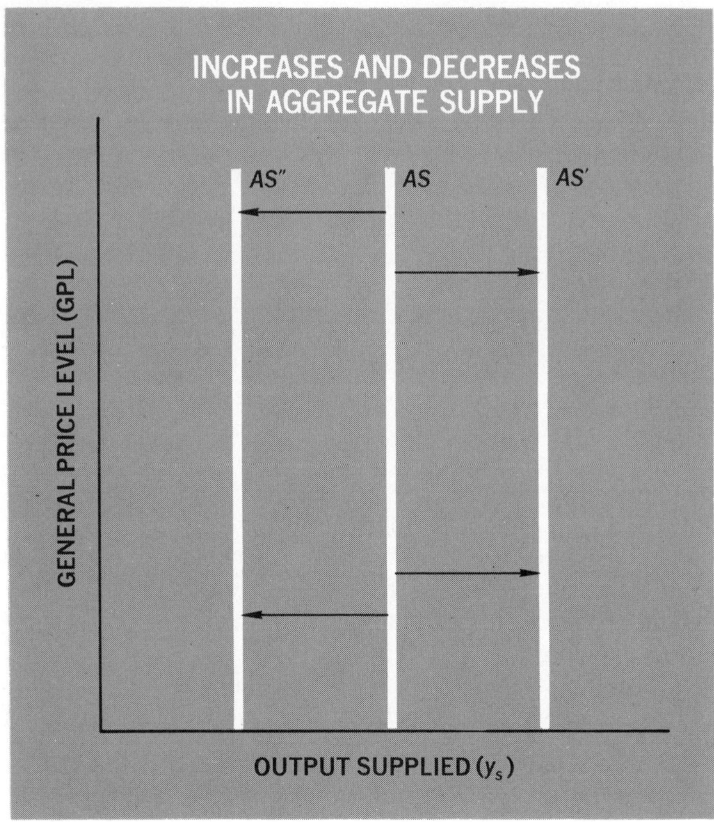

Figure 13-6

2. The wealth effect of changing price levels on the holders of money was mentioned briefly in this chapter and assumed to be unimportant. What would the aggregate supply function on the graph look like if this effect were significant?
3. Would it make any difference in the aggregate supply function if *just* money wages were fixed and not the prices of other goods? Why and how, or why not?
4. Assume that we actually start running out of fossil fuel energy sources and are unable to replace them with such alternatives as nuclear generators. How will this affect aggregate supply? Do you think this will happen? What do you think will happen in the next fifty years to the aggregate supply function? What will change and why?
5. Assume that the wealthier a person is, the less that person will

work for a given real wage. The chapter says that changes in the price level will produce cancelling effects among debtors and creditors. In fact, why might this be untrue?

6. What are the problems in defining "capacity" in an economy? Can you define your own capacity to produce?

14

Operations of an Aggregate Economy

OBJECTIVES

A whole economy using the price system is much like any single market within that system. Basically, if prices are completely flexible, then prices will do the mob of allocating scarce goods. If prices are either "sticky" or inflexible, then quantity *or* level of output *will also change to accomplish the allocation function. In the "real world" of our economy, prices and wages tend to be sticky in a downward direction and relatively mobile in an upward direction. This means that decreases in aggregate demand are liable to cause reductions in output and employment while increases in aggregate demand will result in inflation. The level of aggregate demand can be directly influenced by government policies in both changing the supply of money as well as changing the government's demand for goods and services. One of the most difficult problems in setting the "proper" policy involves timing, because an ill-timed action can accentuate rather than reduce a given problem.*

INTRODUCTION

At this stage of the game, you have quite a mixed bag of tools that can be used to get some insight into the operations of the whole economy. Using the money market, you can get into the problem via one route, or, using the ideas of aggregate supply and demand, get a mirror image of the same operations. As can be seen already, it is important to specify the assumptions under which one is attacking a problem. These assumptions can completely change the result of any analysis being carried out.

This chapter will take the tools thus far developed and use them to analyze some of the events and problems of contemporary interest. There will be quite a few examples, but, nevertheless, they remain examples only. It is up to you to practice using the tools of analysis so that any problem or combination or problems can be attacked with at least some degree of rigor and applied logic.

THE PERFECT SYSTEM

A good way to look at any problem is to start with a model of the world *without* the problem. In this way, one can see the way things are supposed to work and then go from there in finding out why they do not, in fact, work that way. For us, that means starting with an economy in which all prices and wages are freely moving in response to competitive market forces. Using the aggregate supply and demand functions just developed, we can see how changes in supply and demand influence the operation of the economy.

In Figure 14-1, a completely inelastic aggregate supply function and a normal aggregate demand function are combined. Starting with aggregate demand, *AD*, and aggregate supply, *AS*, let us see what happens when aggregate demand is increased. At the initial equilibrium point, output *0a* is both supplied and demanded at a General Price Level of *0c*. The increase in demand can be brought about by any number of things that were discussed in detail in Chapter 11. An increase in the stock of money, an increase in the consumption function, an increase in any of the injections into the economy (government expenditures, exports, or investment demand), all of these could increase aggregate demand. Also, a *decrease* in the leakages from the system (imports, saving, or taxes) would also *increase* aggregate demand.

For whatever reason, assume demand shifts from *AD* to *AD'*. At the initial price level *0c*, the quantity of output demanded has risen from *0a* to *0b*. Quantity demanded is greater than quantity supplied, and, as a result, we have a shortage of goods. With flexible prices and wages, the shortage puts pressures upon prices in the economy. People start a bidding process in an attempt to get the short supply of goods. But the bidding process raises prices. As prices start up, *quantity supplied* does not change. *Supply* is completely insensitive to changes in the GPL. But, as prices start upward, the quantity demanded does change—it goes down. As the prices rise, people's buying power goes down, and the quantity of goods each can control with the given stock of money decreases. Finally, a new equilib-

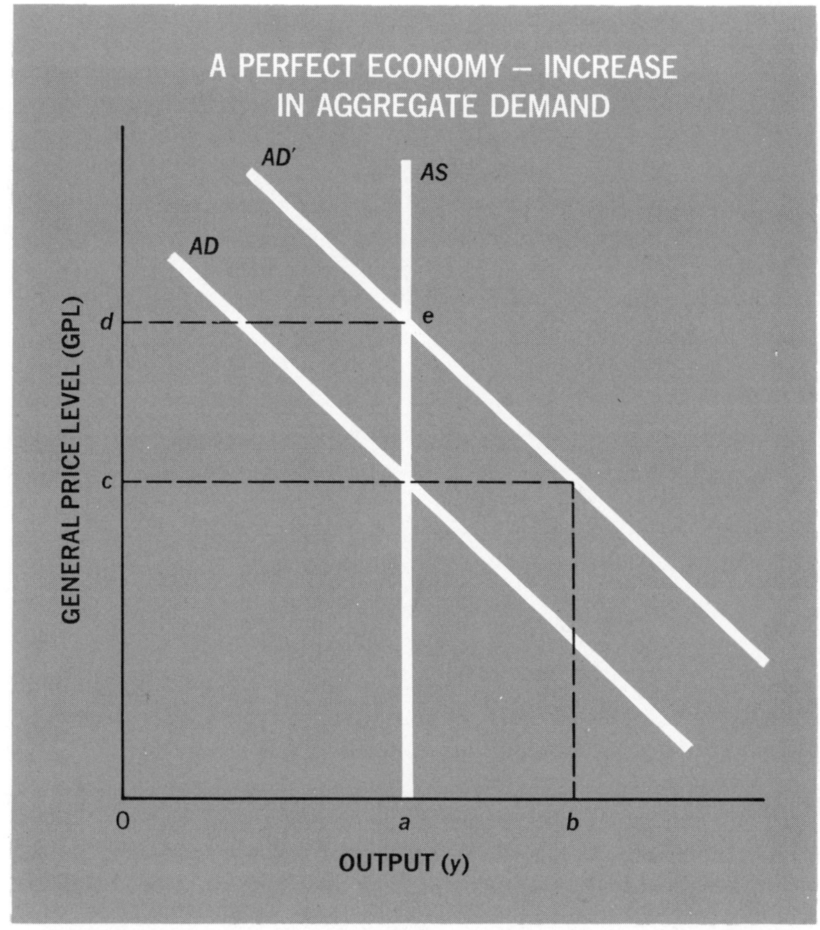

Figure 14-1

rium is established at price level *0d*, and, of course, quantity *0a*. The shortage that existed at the initial lower price level has been eliminated by the increase in prices. The *only* net impact on the economy is for a higher price level.

Now, look at the opposite situation. In Figure 14-2, a decrease in aggregate demand takes place. The reasons can be the converse of any of those mentioned as increasing demand. In the figure, demand shifts from *AD* to *AD′*. Now, output demanded, *0a*, is less than output supplied, *0b*, and there is a surplus of goods. This surplus leads suppliers to cut prices in an attempt to get rid of the goods. As prices fall, the quantity demanded

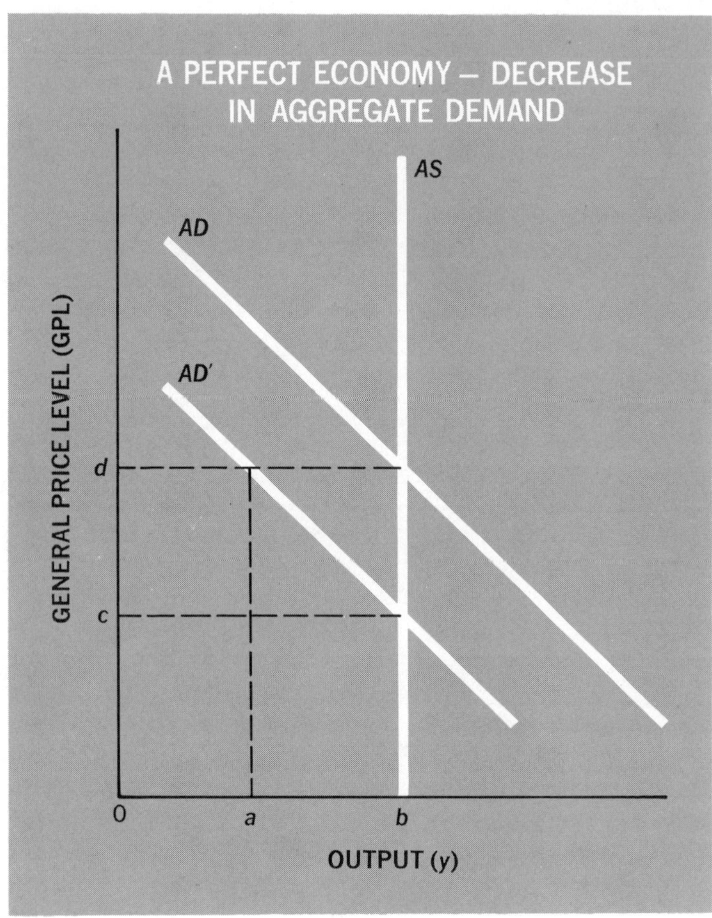

Figure 14-2

rises, output supplied remains the same, and a new equilibrium is reached at the original level of output but lower GPL. The General Price Level falls from *0d* to *0c*, but output remains at *0b*.

The same type of adjustments take place if supply changes. In Figure 14-3, aggregate supply increases from *AS* to *AS′*. The factors that can cause this shift were covered at the end of Chapter 13 and include such examples as improved technology or factor productivity. An increase in supply is the best of all possible worlds because it means that the economy can get more for less. Both the price level and the output change in the "right" direction.

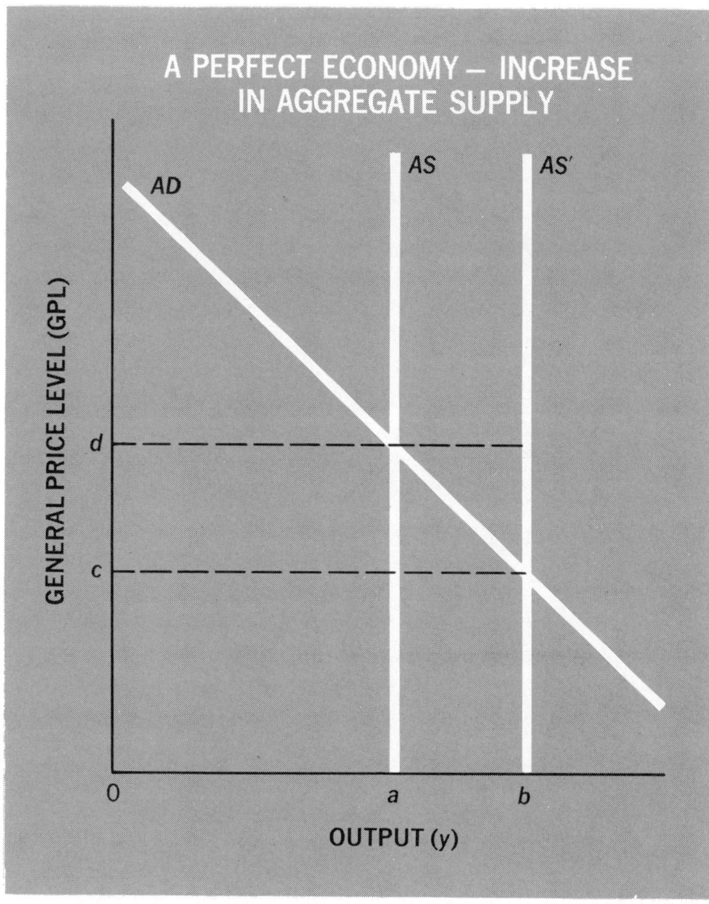

Figure 14-3

After the shift in supply from *AS* to *AS′*, output supplied exceeds output demanded at the *initial* level of prices, *0d*. Therefore, a surplus exists that forces suppliers to cut prices. As prices fall, the quantity demanded rises and the additional output is absorbed into the economy at the lower price level, *0c*.

The final possibility in our perfect model is for aggregate supply to decrease. Let us say that a war destroys a significant fraction of our plant capacity, and, as a result, supply shifts back from *AS* to *AS′* in Figure 14-4. Now, output supplied (*0a*) is less than output demanded (*0b*), and the resulting shortage leads to a rise in the GPL. As the prices rise, the output demanded falls, and we end up with a new General Price Level (*0d*), higher than the initial one.

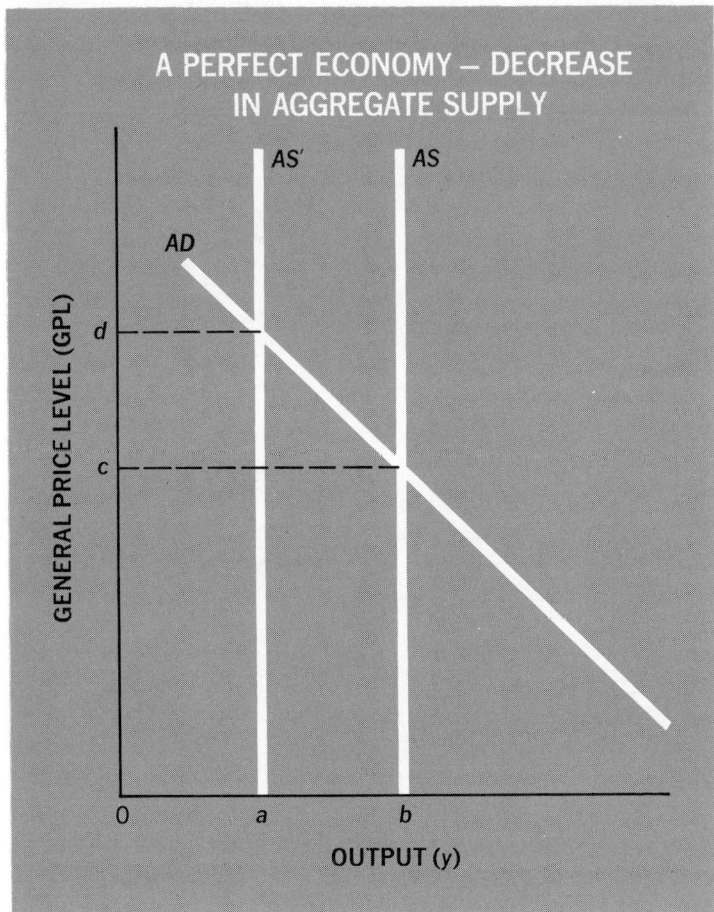

Figure 14-4

Notice that in all four examples, *aggregate supply* has been the determining factor for the level of output in the economy. Aggregate demand has only served to determine (along with aggregate supply) the General Price Level. Our assumption of flexible prices and wages leads to that result.

Now, look at just the opposite assumption as far as price and wage flexibility is concerned. We now adopt the proposition that businessmen respond to changes in the demand for their products (in the aggregate) by changing the level of output rather than changing wages and prices. They do this as long as they can, but, at some point (and it probably would be a

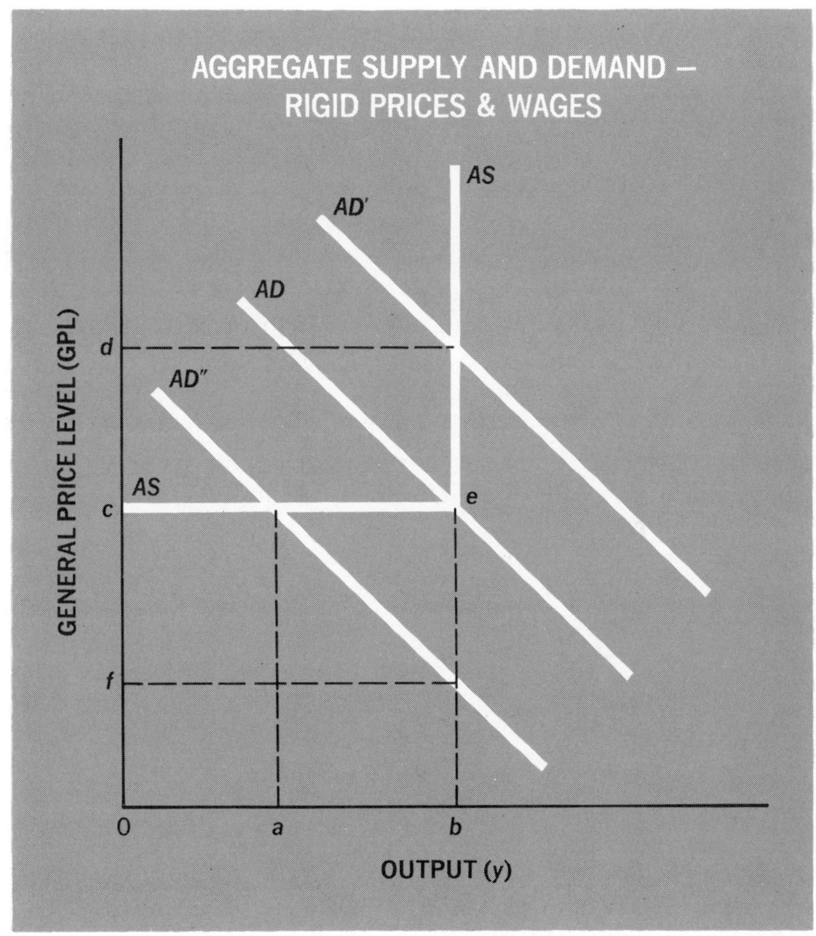

Figure 14-5

range rather than a point), the capacity of the economy is reached and, from there on, output can no longer increase so that the upward movement of prices is the only mechanism left. In Figure 14-5, this set of assumptions is illustrated by the L-shaped aggregate supply curve, *ASeAS*. With an initial level of aggregate demand at *AD*, we have an equilibrium level of output *0b*, and this level of output is at the capacity level for the economy. Should the demand increase at all, such as *AD'*, then the economy will adjust solely through a rise in the GPL. Output will remain the same (*0b*) and the price level will rise from *0c* to *0d* just as in the previous examples.

However, any decrease in aggregate demand works the other way. A shift from *AD* back to *AD″* is now taken up as a decrease in output from *0b* to *0a*, and the prices stay the same. The reduction in output, *ab*, represents not only a decrease in the output of goods and services but also factors of production that are now out of a job. Two things could happen to cure this gap between actual and potential output. If it persists long enough, prices and wages *will* go down. It may take a long time, but it is bound to happen sooner or later. When it does, the price level will fall toward point *f* and the lower prices will stimulate quantity demanded back up to the full employment level of output *0b*.

Someone has pointed out, however, that in the "long run" we are all dead. Politically, if not economically, it is unlikely that massive unemployment would be tolerated for any extended period of time. So, the alternative course of action is to stimulate aggregate demand in an attempt to get it back up to the full employment level of *0b* output demanded. As will be seen, this stimulation can come from conscious effort on the part of the government either to reduce leakages from the aggregate demand or to increase injections into that demand.

There are two additional ways of looking at this problem, using other tools we have developed. First, the *Keynesian Cross* illustrates the problem of less-than-capacity output under the assumptions of rigid prices and wages. In Figure 14-6, we assume that the full employment level of output (income) equals *0b*. This is the same level of output represented by *0b* in Figure 14-5, with initial demand level *AD*. Now, assume that one of the injections into the economy is reduced. For example, investment is reduced from *I* (equal to *S* in this simple example) to *I′*—a reduction of ΔI. Now, resources are being withdrawn from the circular flow by the amount equal to the continuing level of saving (*S* minus the now-reduced level of investment, *I′*). Goods are going unpurchased, which builds suppliers' inventories. The inventory buildup provides the incentive for suppliers to cut back production, which means an equal cutback in income. Income (output) falls back to the new equilibrium level of *0a* (same as *0a* in Figure 14-5). Notice that we have a multiplier here working in reverse. A cutback in investment of only ΔI produced a much larger cutback in output, ΔY. As before, the problem could be handled by an increase in the injections into the system by private investment, government spending, or export demand. Alternatively, leakages could be reduced by cutting taxes, reducing imports, or saving.

Finally, we can see this situation reflected in the money market. The point was made that the government controls the supply of money in the country, and so it is. But a reduction in aggregate demand caused by an increase in leakages is analytically equivalent to a cutback in the *circulating* money supply of the country. An increase in saving, imports, or taxes has the effect of shifting the supply of money back from $S_m S_m$ to

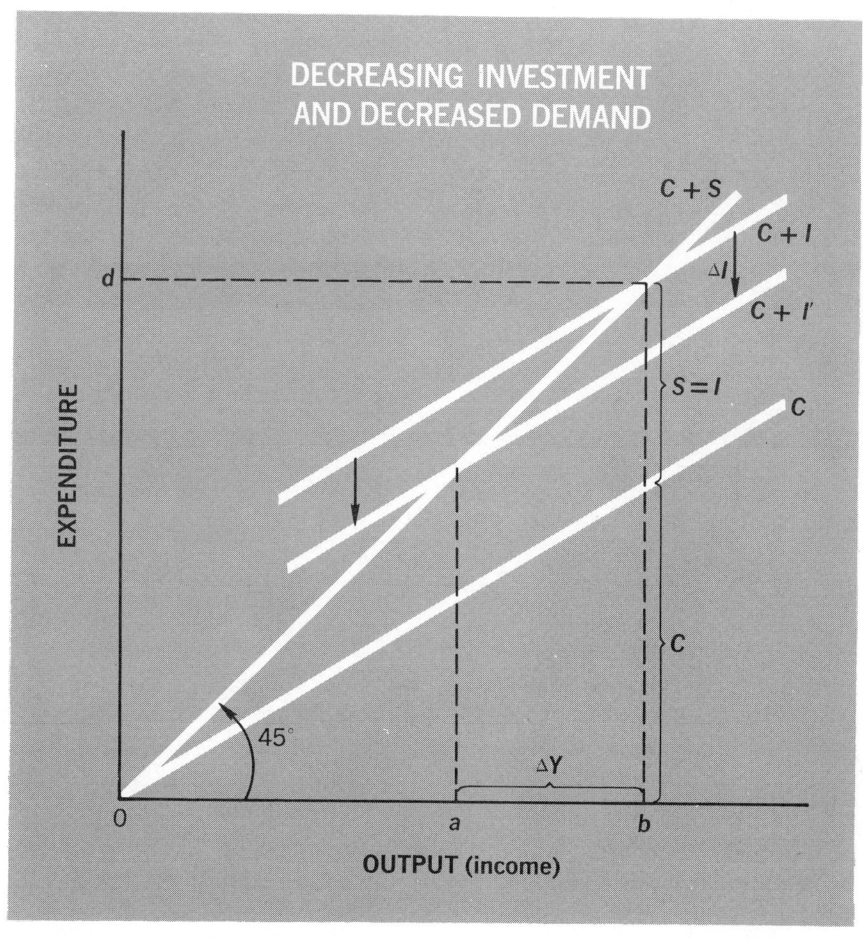

Figure 14-6

Sm′ Sm′ as shown in Figure 14-7. At the initial price of money (GPL equivalent to *0c* in Figure 14-5) the quantity demanded remains at *0p* but the effective quantity supplied has fallen to *0n*. We have a shortage of money (a shortage of purchasing power) equal to *np*. If prices and wages were flexible, the purchasing power of money would rise and the GPL fall to level *f* in Figure 14-7 and *0f* in Figure 14-5. But, because the prices are rigid and cannot fall, the shortage of money makes itself felt in the economy as a surplus of goods. Inventories build, suppliers cut back production, and we have the same situation as before.

In actual fact, our economy probably does not have the kind of rigidities suggested by the L-shaped supply curve just used. Nor does it

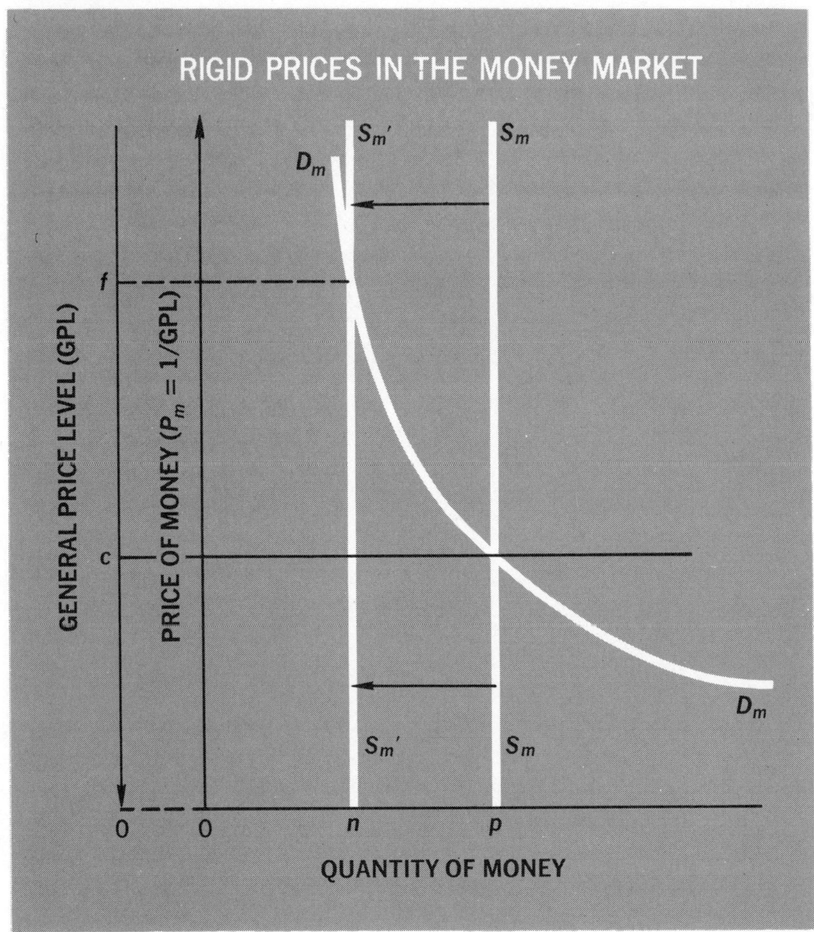

Figure 14-7

have the perfect flexibility suggested by a perfectly inelastic supply curve. In fact, it is probably almost perfectly inelastic in an upward direction and somewhat elastic for price level decreases, such as the example in Figure 14-8. In this case, a fall in aggregate demand will cause both a reduction in prices and a reduction in output as well. The "stickier" the downward movement of prices and wages, the flatter will be the tail, and the more flexible the prices and wages, the steeper will be the tail. In this figure, we can see the possible adjustment mechanisms to a reduction in aggregate demand. With a reduction in demand from *AD-AD* to *AD′-AD′*, the classical solution would have assumed flexible prices and wages. Such a solution would have had no

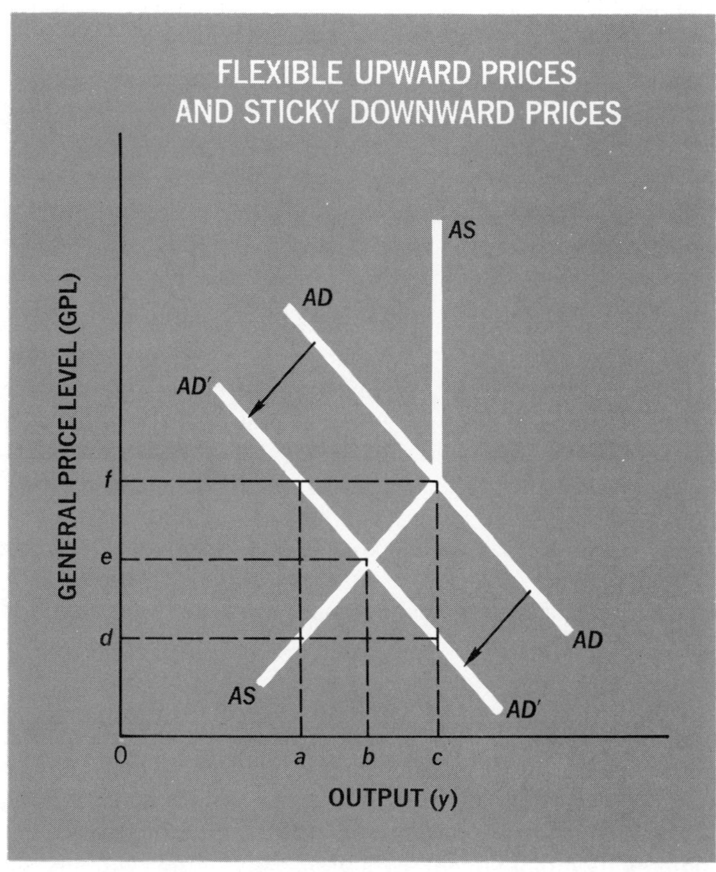

Figure 14-8

impact on output (*0c* would remain the same), and the price level would have absorbed all the impact by falling from *0f* to *0d*. The Keynesian solution calls for rigid prices and wages and, under this solution, the price level would not change (*0f* remains the same) and the output level would absorb the entire impact. Output would fall from *0c* to *0a*. Assuming "sticky," but not completely inflexible downward prices and wages, both output and price level share the impact of a decrease in aggregate demand. In the graph, output falls by *bc* and prices fall by *ef*. Any upward shift in demand from a position of full employment demand will cause just an upward movement in the price level and no significant increase in output. This is the model we will assume to exist for the policy discussions coming up in the next few pages.

One other note about the effectiveness of any injection-induced multiplier (investment, export, government spending). If any injection into the system results in *some* price increases, these price increases will tend to absorb part of the potential multiplied impact of the injection. The simple multiplier we looked at in Chapter 12 assumed absolutely rigid prices and wages.

FISCAL POLICY

Usually, potential government operations on the aggregate demand in the economy are separated into what are called *monetary policy* and *fiscal policy*. Supposedly, monetary policy deals with the government's management of the money supply and fiscal policy deals with government taxing and government expenditures. But, the two policies are bound to get mixed up in the process. When the government collects taxes and doesn't spend them, the *effective* money supply of the country is reduced. The opposite is true of government expenditures from previously held balances.

The purpose of government policy of any type is to attempt to maintain the economy at an equilibrium of full employment of resources without having excessive inflation. Throughout the history of this country, and most others as well, there has been a tendency for economic activity to run in cycles with periods in which excessive demand caused inflation in the economy where resources were already fully employed. Other periods have been characterized by reduced economic activity and unemployment.

Since 1946, the federal government has had the *official* charge of maintaining a full employment level of activity in the economy and there have been conscious efforts by the government to accomplish that goal. How successful the results have been is difficult to evaluate, but some of the attempts and problems they entail are fairly simple to grasp.

We already used the example of a decreasing level of private investment as one thing that could happen to reduce aggregate demand in the country. Suppose that this reduction in investment is accurately anticipated by the President's Council of Economic Advisors. As a result, they recommend, and Congress goes along with, a program of government expenditures at a level that will just offset the reduction of the private investment injection. In this way, the total level of activity should remain the same, and everything will roll along without problems. The most difficult task of a government planner is to anticipate the thinking of the tens of millions of people who are actually making the decisions that may need to be offset by a counter-policy of the government. Not only do the planners have to know what the expenditure patterns of the public are going to be, they must also have a good idea of the "when" of those expenditures.

Take a simple numerical example. Assume that the full employment equilibrium output level of our country is one trillion dollars. We expect that private investment is going to fall next year by $20 billion. Assume also an *effective* multiplier of five. This means that unless something happens to stop it, the GNP could fall by $100 billion, or a 10 percent decrease. In the first place, we assume that the planners really hit it right on the head. Every time a dollar of private investment was withdrawn, it was immediately replaced by one dollar of U.S. spending. It would seem that this should do the job and do it just right. Maybe.

If the monies withdrawn from private investment were put into hoards by investors—*if* they virtually sterilized these balances—and *if* the government made its expenditures from taxes that were currently being collected from *saving*, from the same sort of hoard accumulation, *then* everything could work fine. Of course, there is still the problem of the actual goods *not* being purchased by the private sector and the actual goods *being* purchased by the public sector. Again, if they are identical, no problem. But, if they are different goods, there may be some problems getting resources into the newly demanded industry and out of the previously demanded industry. But think of a few other possibilities. What if the government taxed people to pay for the countercyclical spending program, and all of the taxes came from monies that were being spent on consumption goods by the private sector? In this case, although aggregate demand is being stimulated by the government spending, the taxes to pay the increase in spending might be reducing aggregate demand by the same dollar amount. Again, however, just because the dollars offset, do not think that the goods necessarily will offset each other. An example cited earlier in the book is of interest.

When the aerospace industry was being whittled down by the reduction of federal spending on the space program and the supersonic transport, there was a good deal of pressure to take those funds and use them in such alternative programs as pollution control and poverty programs of one sort or another. As a matter of fact, spending in some of these other areas *did* go up, and yet, unemployment in the aerospace industry remained incredibly high. Engineers with PhD's and years of uniquely specialized knowledge were on food stamp lines and taking any job they could find, from ditchdigger on up. The *money* could be transferred from one alternative use to another, but that did not mean that the specialized resources needed in each endeavor would automatically appear. It certainly did not mean an automatic answer for the two-fold problem of unemployment in aerospace and factor shortages in the pollution-control area.

From a longer-range view, the reduction in demand in the one area will have a strong negative incentive on new talent entering the aerospace field. Wages are lower than before and unemployment is still a problem. The increased demand in pollution control has led to higher wages and more job opportunities. The positive incentives are there for development of new resources to enter this field. But, time for training and for other development processes is still needed. It does not happen overnight. This is just another example of the danger of aggregate numbers. *Always,* one has to get behind and beneath the averages and summaries to find out what really is going on in the world.

There is another problem of our friendly planner in Washington as he programs countercyclical spending. What happens if he misses the timing of these spending programs? It might not even be his fault. Perhaps, the spending patterns that the public *thought* it would exercise just did not come to pass. People changed their minds and left the planner high, dry, and doing more harm than good. If his spending programs happen to get *in phase* with the cycle of private spending rather than counterphase, then the cycles are made more pronounced rather than smoother. To the extent that a multiplier is actually working, a one-dollar addition to aggregate demand at a time when inflation is already going on can be magnified several times in its impact.

By law, our government has the responsibility for using its power to maintain a full employment economy, and, as time goes on, it is to be hoped that it will be able to exercise this charge with increasing skill and effectiveness.

There are a few government fiscal tools that have some degree of automatic operation. For example, the progressive income tax not only increases total taxes in times of high economic activity, it also increases the *percentage* of incomes paid in taxes during these times. Thus, it tends to brake inflationary portions of a cycle and, conversely, its impact goes down in bad times, thus reducing the leakages from demand and stimulating recovery. But, here again, differing time lags can even foul up the effectiveness of these stabilizers and make them *de*-stabilizers instead.

MONETARY POLICY

The purpose of monetary policy is the same as fiscal policy—to maintain a full employment economy with little or no inflation. Why do people get so upset about inflation? After all, inflation is merely the general increase of prices and wages, right? Only in the models. We have been careful to specify that increases in the General Price Level were, in fact, that kind of an increase. All prices and wages have been assumed to move together. In this case, inflation probably wouldn't hurt anything very much because the several markets that might be affected would be able to include expected rates of inflation in the prices involved. As we have already seen, expected inflation will raise interest rates so that the *decrease* in the buying power of any loan will be offset by an increased money-rate of interest. If inflation is expected to be 6 percent per year, and the real rate of interest is 4 percent, then the money rate will probably be close to 10 percent per year. But *unexpected* inflation is another thing. Here, inflation can make very painful transfers of purchasing power from one group to another. For example, a senior citizen who bought a fixed money value annuity twenty years ago with his full savings, now finds that wealth almost halved in terms of what the monthly check will buy. Debtors gain and creditors lose in the game of inflation. With this in mind, it is interesting to note that the biggest debtor in the system is the U.S. government and the largest creditor consists of the households of the country. Historically, certain categories of salaries have tended to lag well behind inflation rates and others have tended to lead the inflation. It might not be exactly true today, but in the past, the salaries of civil servants, teachers, and white-collar workers tended to lag behind any inflation and those of skilled labor tended to equal or exceed the inflation rates. There is recent evidence that even though the senior citizen in the example gets hurt by inflation, poverty groups in general tend to do better in times of rising prices than in other periods.

As far as putting the brakes on an inflation, either cutting back on the rate of increase in the money supply or actually decreasing the money supply has got to cut back on aggregate demand. But, there are substantial lags involved, as we all found out in the late 1960s and early 1970s. When a well-fueled inflation is underway, including the public's expectations for continuing inflation, getting it stopped can be extremely difficult and not without its costs. Because of some of the imperfections in flexible prices, wages, and factor mobility, there seems to be some relationship between very low or zero rates of inflation and increased rates of unemployment. This relationship is called a *Phillip's Curve* of inflation and unemployment, these two factors being inversely related.

Returning to the presentation earlier in this chapter of rigid prices in the money market (see Figure 14-7), when aggregate demand was reduced because of hoarded saving, the effective money supply was reduced. Countercyclical action on the part of the government could have been adding new money to the system to make up for that which was being hoarded. In the diagram, the reduced money supply $S_m'S_m'$ would have been shifted back to its original position S_mS_m by the action. This also would have shifted aggregate demand back out to its original position.

One criticism of this policy is that increases in the money supply will continue to be hoarded because of low interest rates (and, hence, opportunity costs of holding cash). This so-called liquidity trap is interesting theoretically but of doubtful validity in the real world.

As an historical note, it is interesting that during the worst of the

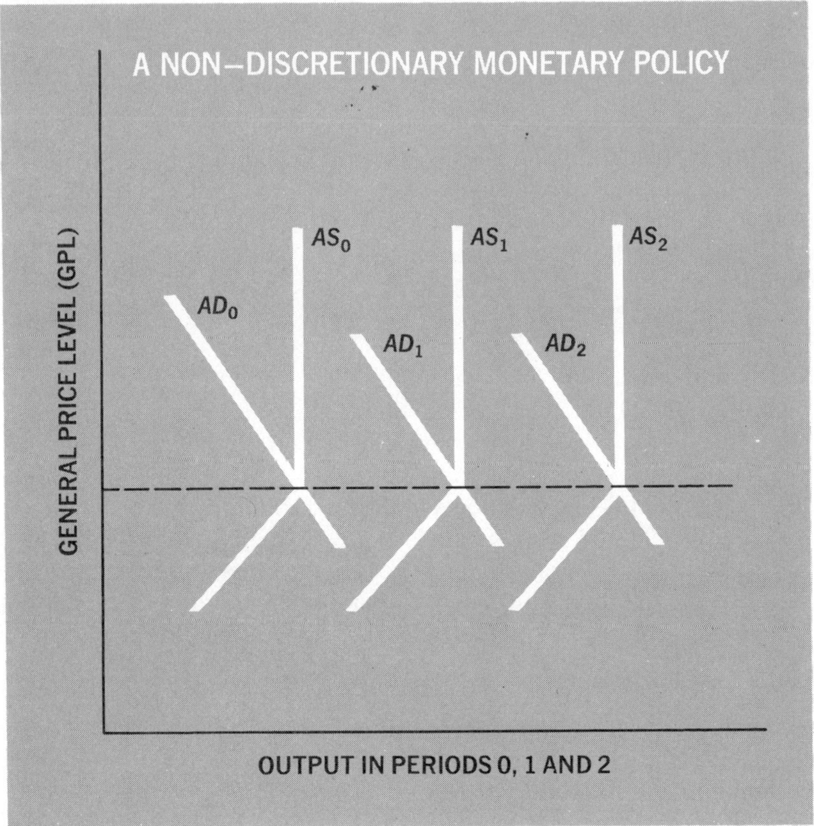

Figure 14-9

Great Depression, our monetary authorities actually *reduced* the money supply in the country at the same time that the supply was reaching new lows. Of course, this policy compounded the decreases in demand. Hopefully, our monetary authorities are a bit wiser about their powers today.

A noted economist, Milton Friedman, has put forth a proposal for the monetary policy of the country. Friedman suggests that the money supply of the country should be increased each year by a predetermined and announced constant rate. The increase would be enough to accommodate comfortably the increase in the demand for money generated by our economic growth, but not enough to cause much, if any, inflation. Graphically, the idea is illustrated in Figure 14-9. Aggregate supply keeps shifting outward as the productivity of the economy increases. If money stocks are not increased to keep pace, and we also have sticky downward prices, some unemployment could result. But, by increasing the money supply to keep pace, aggregate demand would also increase with perhaps a small increase in the General Price Level.

The main feature of Dr. Friedman's idea is to take the *discretionary* power away from the monetary authorities. By having this formula concept instead, a great deal of uncertainty about future price changes could be eliminated which in itself would help to create the price stability that most people would like very much to achieve and maintain.

DIRECT CONTROL

We have actually covered this possible government policy, at least as far as the theory is concerned. Direct controls refer to the imposition of price and wage controls in the economy. These controls are always for price movements in an upward direction. They invariably are meant to prevent inflationary movements. In Figure 14-10, the problem and attempted control is illustrated.

As usual, we start with an equilibrium position *AD-AD* and *AS-AS*. The GPL is *0c* and output, *0c*. Aggregate demand is on the increase as shown by the shift from *AD-AD* to *AD'-AD'*. At the new level of demand, output demanded has risen from *0a* to *0b* and output supplied remains at *0a*. The resulting economic shortage amounts to *ab*, but, in this case, prices are prevented from rising above the *0c* level. The shortage becomes chronic and the price system can not solve it anymore. There is one short-run effect that *could* be of significant value in this policy. If, by imposing the price ceilings, people in the economy *feel* that inflation will be stopped, then expectations of inflation may be reduced. As pointed out earlier, this could actually help stop a well-developed inflation and inflation psychology.

But beyond this possibility, wage and price ceilings have very little to recommend them. They are very expensive to enforce. In fact, they are impossible to enforce across the board. As a result, the economy usually ends up with a controlled sector and an uncontrolled sector. The controlled sectors will tend to be the large and well-organized areas of the economy, such as basic industry and the larger trade unions. Imposing controls in these areas means that prices and wages in those sectors will be fixed and prices and wages in the uncontrolled sector will rise. This will cause at least some factor movement and reduce output in the basic industries, which can compound the inflation problem by accentuating the shortages that already were responsible for the pressure on prices.

As a long-run solution, wage and price controls *must* end up producing the shortage predicted by our simple geometry. Of course, if they are not really enforced, and people can get the price and wage increases that

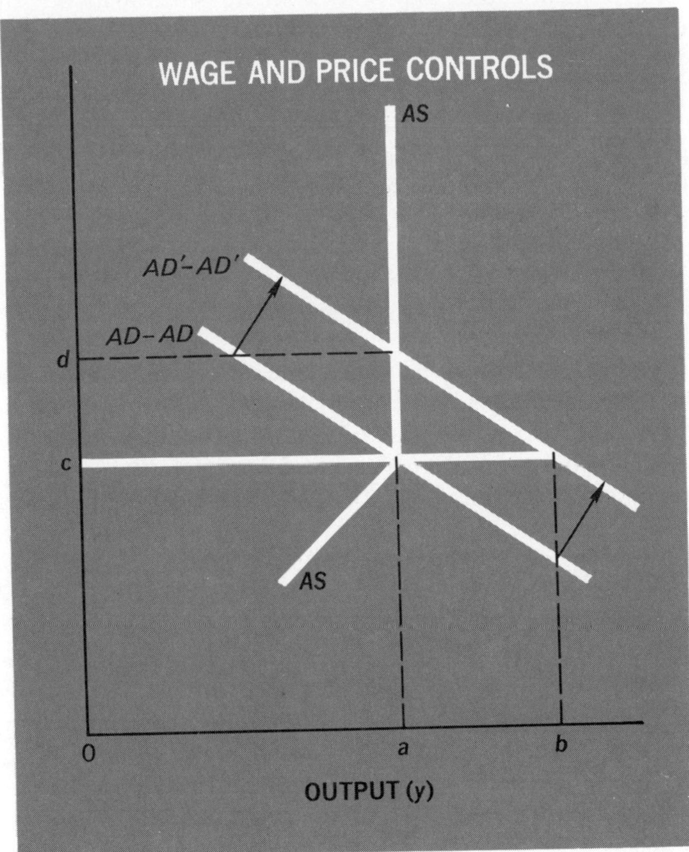

Figure 14-10

they push for, then the only real problem is the resources that are wasted on false enforcement. The *problem* is an excess of demand over supply. The *solution* to inflation must recognize that fact, and either increase the quantity supplied or reduce the quantity demanded. Keeping a figure on the indicator needle of the barometer when there is a storm approaching, can make the person feel much better. But this is not going to stop the storm. In fact, by jamming the indicating mechanism, he may not get the signals needed to take protective or corrective action. Prices are nothing more than indicating devices. They not only indicate problems like inflation, but also signal the entire complex of factor and product allocations needed by everyone in the economy. When they are fixed, those indicators do none of us any good and may unbalance the entire mechanism.

A SUMMARY OF POLICY

Between monetary and fiscal policy, the federal government has at its command all of the tools that are needed to adjust the basic direction of the economy. We have tried to cover enough examples to show how complex the whole thing can be. As to whether fiscal or monetary policy is best, there is no one answer or general response. Monetary policy will tend to hit more broadly across the economy than many fiscal policies. But certainly, "tight" or "easy" money, which is bound to be a part of any changing of the money supply, will hit markets in which credit is important. It will hit these markets (like housing and major consumer purchases) much harder than markets that do not depend so heavily on available credit.

But clearly, fiscal policy *can* be aimed at more specific areas within the economy. If you want to tax the rich, that can be done. If you want to hit the poor, that also can be done. As has been pointed out, however, beware of the simple initial impact of any partial policy. Like the pebble in the water, the reverberations reach far and wide, sometimes unpredictably.

If we are serious about keeping the market system, some other policies might be in order, such as trying to improve the operation of the markets themselves by reducing or eliminating some of the rigidities that make government intervention look like the only solution. More is said about this in the Postscript.

The other important point that must be kept in mind, no matter what kind of policy one is considering, is the tremendous importance of timing and the perils of things going wrong if the timing is mistaken. Much of the timing problem ties into the business of the public's expectations. We do not understand much about the things that make people expect certain events or about the ways those expectations are changed. This makes a planner's life very difficult.

QUESTIONS

1. With perfectly flexible wages and prices, changes in aggregate demand only change prices, but changes in aggregate supply change both prices and output. Explain.
2. Discuss the problems involved in the timing of government efforts to stimulate or cool down aggregate demand.
3. It is sometimes said that increasing output (aggregate supply) is the best solution to virtually all economic problems of the total economy. Discuss the pros and cons of this idea.

4. What things could be done, and by whom, that would increase the mobility of factors in the economy. Would such increased mobility help solve any problems?
5. Discuss the differences in the government's use of monetary policy versus fiscal policy in fighting unemployment. Explain how these two types of policies overlap.
6. Explain what increasing the money supply and increasing government spending have in common in an economy suffering from unemployment of resources. Explain the differences.

15

Poverty and Development

OBJECTIVES

Poverty is not a simple condition in life that can be defined and/or described for all people at all times. It is in large measure a relative concept. In order to attack effectively the problem of poverty or under-development, it is essential to examine the anatomy of the problem and get at the root causes of different categories of poverty. No single policy, no matter how well intentioned, can possibly resolve the problems for all people. For those people who can work, income supplements can be used to improve purchasing power while maintaining at least some measure of incentive to perform productive work. For other groups, such as the very young and the very old, the problems can only be partially alleviated by subsidies or doles. Many problems of the poor go far beyond the problem of merely increasing purchasing power in the present.

INTRODUCTION

In this chapter, we touch briefly on the subject that occupies a major portion of economic issues being discussed today. The whole area of alternative economic systems is included again in this chapter. The reason is that much (although certainly not all) of the discussion about alternative systems has been generated by the apparent failure of traditional systems, Western and Eastern, to cope with the problems of the poor—be they poor people or poor countries. In some countries, this failure has been accompanied by a failure to develop a base for production of the material goods desired by most peoples of the world.

Usually, when one thinks of lack of economic development, pictures of Latin America, much of Asia, and of Africa come to mind. Most people would agree that, in some sense, many of the countries in these areas are "less-developed." If the speakers were pressed to define their terms, they would express this lack of development in terms like "low GNP," or better, "low real GNP," or better yet, "low real GNP per capita." Others might say that they are less-developed because large portions of the population are still engaged in agriculture. Still others would say that a lack of economic institutions (banking, credit, and so on) is *descriptive* of a less-developed area. If people are pinned down to giving a *definition* of lack of development, they refer to the ocean of statistical numbers that may or may not describe some economic condition believed to be below some magic norm. It is difficult to arrive at a definition that is broad enough to cover the problem and yet specific enough to be useful.

The trouble with descriptive definitions is that they often hide the problems. As discussed earlier in the book, if one uses real GNP per capita as a measure of development, then the most developed country in the world is the tiny sheikdom of Kuwait. Outward and visible signs, at least, would not support that claim. Similarly, using the norm of high agricultural populations, countries like Denmark and New Zealand would be in the category of "underdeveloped." Again, that would be an unusual listing.

This discussion will focus on *one* aspect of underdevelopment—the aspect of poverty. This word, too, defies definition and evokes different images from different people. We will be using it in a specific way that may be helpful in tackling some of the roots of this weed that afflicts humanity.

Mike Todd, an impresario who made and lost several fortunes during his lifetime, reputedly made the comment that he had been "broke" many times, but never "poor." As trite as that statement may sound, it points up a major problem in discussing the subject of poverty. How does one define or describe the term so that it will be similarly understood by persons of different societies with varied levels of material wealth? Clearly, the state of poverty implies more than a simple lack of command over goods. Other abstractions must be included, such as reduced hope of future improvement and lack of participation in determining the events governing one's life. This discussion, it should be noted, is by the author as an economist who readily admits the limitations of his discipline in solving the plight of a significant number of persons living in *this* country as well as others throughout the world.

Because economics is the study of choices made between scarce alternatives, it is appropriate that the subject of poverty should occupy a major position among interests of economists. The following is a working

definition of our subject that is potentially useful at this time. *Poverty is a condition of man in which the choices and expectations he faces are restricted relative to some large portion of the world he knows.*

Implicit in this definition is the idea that not all choice restrictions are necessarily in the field of material goods. Nevertheless, a large portion of the problem makes itself felt through *markets* in terms of low incomes and low levels of expectations for future incomes. This is true not only of economies in the so-called capitalist worlds, but of those in socialist countries, as well. It appears that raising these low incomes is a *necessary* but insufficient condition for the reduction of poverty. Incomes would have to be raised to reduce poverty, but this *by itself* will not necessarily do the job.

Over the years, a large part of economic thought has been directed toward maximizing the value of output, given scarce inputs. Particularly in the United States, the relatively free market has been relied upon to distribute the output of the economy between factors, and within each category of factor, according to that factor's contribution to total output. Given the *ethical* goal of distribution according to contribution, the system has worked and continues to work very well, indeed. In general, the productive, as defined by the markets, are rewarded, and those who are unproductive, as defined by the same markets, receive little or nothing from the unimpeded operation of the system. At the same time, total output and output per capita have reached levels beyond the wildest dreams of man even a few decades ago. Yet, poverty is still with us and it could be argued that, using the definition involving relative choice, the problem is more serious today than in the past. Great segments of the population have gained expanded choice sets of great magnitude but others remain at the same or even lower levels than previously.

Concurrently, the aggregate U.S. society has experienced a change in its goals as expressed through the market as well as through the political structure. To an increasing degree, poverty is yielding a *disutility*, not only to the poverty-stricken, but to the taxpaying public as well. Several reasons are advanced for this increased concern: humanitarian grounds, wasted human resources, fear of violent reaction, and increasing markets for goods. Regardless of motive, it is a fact that the citizens of this country are increasingly willing to *pay* for the reduction of poverty. Put another way, the economic goal of maximizing the value of production from scarce resources has been joined by another goal—the minimizing of poverty, *but subject to cost constraints*. We are willing and able to take a portion of our total output and apply it (as efficiently as possible) toward the increase of incomes and/or potential incomes of persons in our economic basement.

This can be accomplished in two basic ways. Part of the income of high-income groups can be redistributed to low-income groups without overtly attempting to improve the earning power of the recipients. Second, a portion of the income from the high-income groups can be invested in various programs that have as their goal the development of human capital, or, in other words, the improvement of the potential productivity of the recipients and their dependents. Programs having both goals have been established by all levels of government with varying degrees of success and potential success.

POVERTY GROUPS

Before going further, let us break down the poverty problem into the groups that comprise the aggregate. Without this breakdown, it is impossible to analyze the problem in a way that will permit any hope of solution. To begin, divide "the poor" into two groups—those with marketable skills sufficient to eliminate their poverty and those without such skills. Among the first group—those with marketable skills—there are at least three subgroups. Some of the persons will be restricted in their job opportunities by racial, religious, sexual, or other discrimination. Another group simply does not wish to work at the existing wages for their skills. That is to say, they prefer *leisure* to the level of income they could receive at the existing market wages for their services. We will discuss this group in more detail when we talk about the effects of a dole program. Finally, there are those whose productive abilities are not limited by skills or training but rather by physical handicaps or old age.

Let us now look at the group that lacks skills or training and divide this category into subgroups. To begin with, there are those who are too young to be productive, regardless of the training program in which they might be enrolled. This group will be particularly large in populations with high birthrates, and, unfortunately, most poverty groups exhibit comparatively high birthrates. Long-run increases in national productivity depend *critically* on the implementation of training programs for the oncoming generations and breaking the poverty cycles also depends upon the training of this group. The *problem* in the training of the very young is the length of time that society will have to wait to recover such investments through increased productivity. For example, a person eighteen years old taking a six-month technical training course in basic machine shop operations might reasonably be expected to utilize his training within a few months of completing the course. Under the assumptions we are using, this increased productivity will not only be reflected in higher wages to the trainee, but also in increased value of product for society—the same society that has subsidized his training course. The training costs, or investment, will therefore, be recovered in a relatively short time. On the other hand, society's investment in providing first-year primary education will not begin to be recovered until the individual student enters the work force a number of years later. Again, it is most important *not* to interpret these remarks as meaning that investment in the very young is a "bad" policy. What the remarks do suggest is that short-run costs and benefits are very different for human capital investments made in different age groups. Another example can be found in comparing the expected returns to investment in vocational training between two persons, one eighteen-years old and the other fifty-years old. Assume that a given investment of resources will produce the same increase in productivity for both individuals. Even if this is true, it is probable that the working lifetime of the eighteen-year old will be at least four times that of the fifty-year old. Thus, from society's standpoint, the increased product will be many times larger over a thirty- to forty-year period through investment in the younger person. This discussion has, thus far, omitted the factor of compound interest, which must also be considered if society is faced with alternative choices. In other words, society could receive either explicit or imputed returns from a whole range of investment possibilities. These returns are themselves capable of further investment and, thus, should be considered as properly calculable in compound interest terms. This tends to accentuate the potential investment differences already enumerated.

To summarize, training for a productive skill is a viable policy from which fairly quick and substantial returns could reasonably be expected *under certain circumstances*. The magnitude and timing of these returns will depend critically on the age of the trainees; the degree of sophistication of the program, and, hence, the duration and cost of the training; and the pretraining ability and adaptability of the trainee.

This final point brings us to the last group in this breakdown—those who cannot be trained for skills of sufficient value to their community to raise them from their poverty. To say that any group is "untrainable" is a dangerous, if not completely inaccurate, statement. It is probably correct to say, however, that the cost to society of training certain groups of persons would never be recovered either by the people within the group, or by society as a whole. This probability is further increased by the fact that most systems used in choosing candidates for any training program tend to select trainees with the greatest talent for the program concerned. As these programs are increased in magnitude, the "untrained" become more and more "untrainable." That is, a given effort in terms of resource expenditure will become less and less effective, and, sooner or later, the point will be reached at which a residual of virtually untrainable persons remains.

One further limitation of training or retraining programs as a means of reducing poverty is that some portion of those who have successfully completed that training program will probably re-enter the poverty group

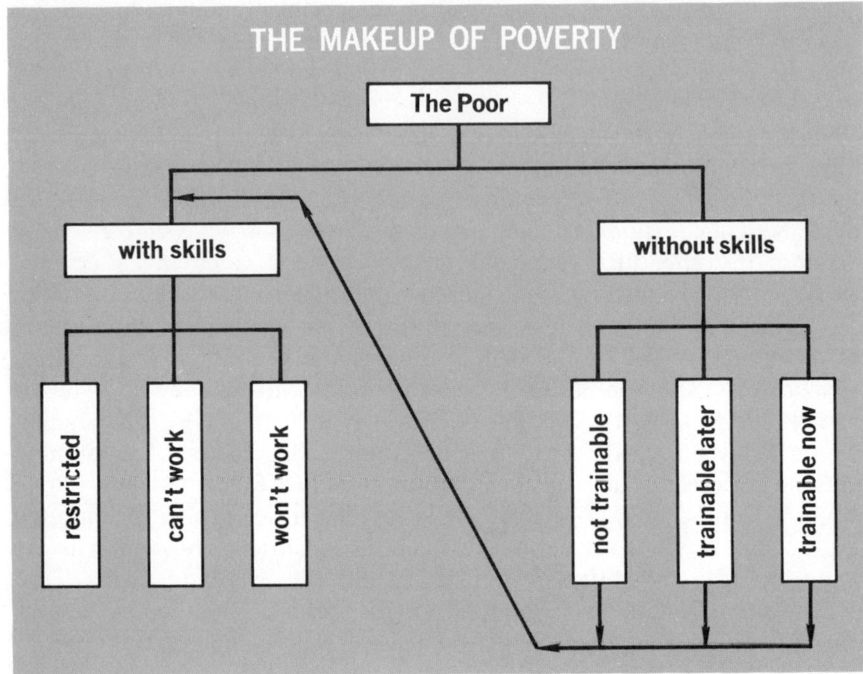

Figure 15-1

despite their newly acquired skills. They become part of the group with skills but against whom various restrictions are raised. Thus, mere completion of a training program does not by itself *insure* an effective reduction in a poverty condition.

We have taken an aggregate group that by some fairly arbitrary standards is called *impoverished*. In a market system, their poverty comes in large measure from relatively low income, which, in turn, is a reflection of low productivity. We have broken down the aggregate into subgroups, each of which requires a distinct policy if efforts to reduce poverty are to be successful. This breakdown is illustrated in Figure 15-1. Look in more detail, now, at the characteristics, problems, and potentials of these six groups. It is obvious that even this breakdown could be further divided into more specific categories; however, for our discussion, some degree of generality will be useful.

THE RESTRICTED GROUP

Among this group are those who suffer from true discrimination on the basis of race, religion, sex, or some other characteristic totally unrelated to their productive abilities. *True* discrimination because it is essential to make a strong distinction between this type of behavior on the part of a potential employer and the refusal by employers to hire minority groups because, *in fact*, their productivity, as a group, *is* lower. For many persons in minority groups, the latter situation is common. They may *not* have the same abilities as their cohorts because of poorer education and training, poorer nutritional standards, and inferior living conditions. The act of the employer preferring the more productive white over a less productive black, for example, *is not itself discriminatory*. The fact that there exists a difference in the productivity of some whites and some blacks may well be the result of *past discrimination* that resulted in productivity differentials. The difference between "true" and "resultant" discrimination is very important because they are *two* problems requiring *two different* solutions.

Short-run solutions, such as requiring employers to hire lower quality (less productive) employees from minority groups, may be an effective method of providing these people with on-the-job training that they would not otherwise obtain. This training, however, is not without cost. Using less productive labor will increase costs and reduce output from the levels possible if qualified personnel were used. The actual impact of these costs will depend upon the supply and demand elasticities of the products involved. Figure 15-2 shows what should now be a familiar example in which increased costs decrease the supply of the product. The quantity marketed goes down and the price of the product rises. The share of who pays what will depend on the elasticities involved. In the example in Figure 15-2, consumers pay increased prices for the product (Δp), both producers and consumers lose from the reduced quantity marketed (Δq), and factors of production in the industry lose from decreased employment—not the decrease caused by displacement by the minority group, but the decrease caused by the reduced levels of output. The trainees themselves may well end up paying more for this type of training than would otherwise be the case. Many times, on-the-job training is not the most efficient way to obtain skills. Interestingly enough, to the extent that customers buying the product concerned are themselves part of low-income groups, then the low-income group ends up paying the price of their own retraining. Perhaps this is the intent of some programs, but, generally, it is not.

Other restrictions may be faced by persons whose training should be sufficient to allow them to exceed poverty level incomes. These restrictions are imposed by the existence of monopolistic or monopsonistic influences operating in the labor and/or factor markets. Remember, monopolistic influences in the product market tend toward utilizing smaller quantities of factor inputs because of restricted levels of output. Thus, job potentials may be lost. Further, the existence of monopolistic profits may prevent persons from receiving the remuneration they would receive under conditions of perfect competition. One of the suggestions for solving this

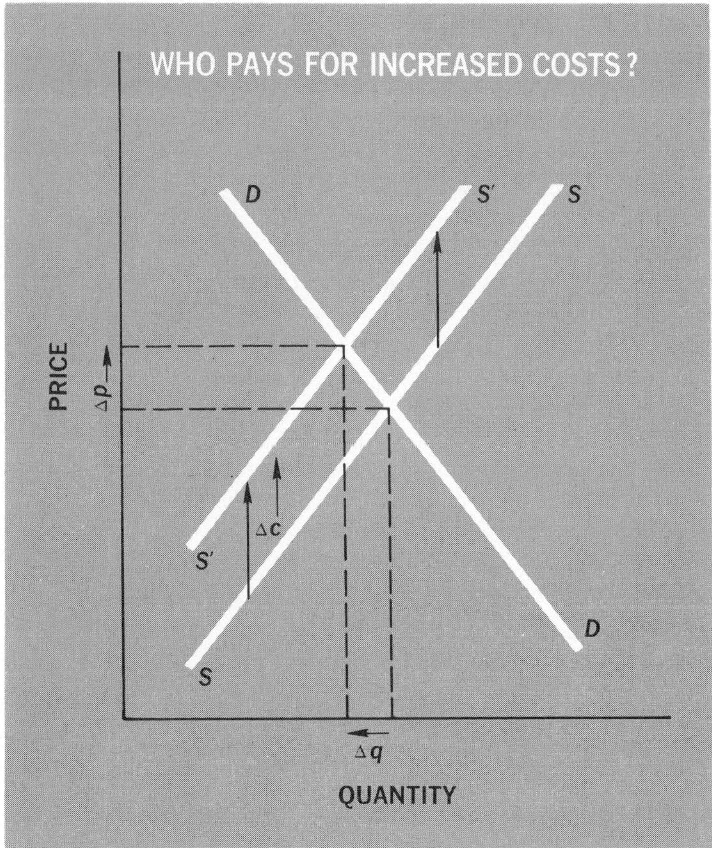

Figure 15-2

problem is to break up existing business and labor organizations to insure a more competitive, and, therefore, more efficient, economy. This policy, however, is also not without its attendant costs. There are *some* (although certainly not all) industries in which reduction of the sizes of the firms would make production costs higher, thus reducing output and increasing costs and product prices. In other words, some industries do have *economies of scale* that would be lost in a breakup program. Without some value judgments, one cannot say that the end result would be better or worse. One can only say that *costs* and benefits should be estimated before using such a policy—the costs of decreased and more expensive output versus the benefits of increased competition and higher employment.

THE GROUP THAT WILL NOT WORK

At almost any level of income, there are persons who, given the choice, will prefer leisure (not working) to working *at the existing wage for their skills*. The latter qualification, often forgotten, is of considerable importance. It suggests the possibility that higher wages might bring forth productive efforts from this group. These higher wages (over and above the wages that represent the value of their product in the market) could be provided by government subsidy, were the improvement of this group's income a goal of society. An alternative policy would be the *dole*, in which grants of either goods or money are provided with little or no requirement for any productive work. An often forgotten ramification of dole programs is that they tend to generate new candidates for the programs. In general, these new candidates will come from the group we are discussing—those who do not want to work at the going wage rate. The reason is simple enough. An individual's decision to work or not to work is based in large measure on the alternatives available. For example, if someone received fifty dollars per week from welfare payments with little or no effort on his part, he may choose this alternative instead of working forty hours a week for, say, eighty dollars. If the welfare benefits are increased *relative* to the working wage, additional persons are likely to accept the welfare program in lieu of productive work. By the same token, should the working wage be increased relative to the welfare payments, a larger number of persons are likely to choose the work alternative. Again, the welfare payments here are of the dole type requiring no work to receive them.

The implications of the above analysis are obvious. When estimating the cost of dole programs, current numbers of persons qualified must be adjusted to include *additional* persons who will accept the dole in lieu of work, given the opportunity. On the other hand, payments made in the form of a salary supplement or subsidy may actually encourage more productive effort and result in a smaller net welfare cost per person and in total. In addition, a larger *number* of people are more likely to choose the alternative of at least some productive work instead of leisure.

THE GROUP THAT CANNOT WORK

Analysis of this group is similar in many respects to the classification just discussed. Again, the description "cannot work" is an absolute concept seldom found in the real world. A more useful expression would state that there are handicapped or elderly workers unable to find employment in a competitive labor market that includes equally skilled and trained persons who are not similarly handicapped and who are in younger age groups. It can readily be seen that, again, the use of income supplements or subsidies will have a much less disruptive effect on incentives and resource allocation than would be the case with a dole. The elderly present a special situation in which basic goals may be modified to a considerable extent. In this case, it may be decided that productive activity is no longer going to be encouraged; rather, the individuals should be completely subsidized. If so, who is going to pay the costs, and in what manner? Is the family of the elderly person going to be required to meet the entire cost? If so, why should the government be involved at all? What about the accumulated savings of the older person? Are his benefits going to be reduced by the amount of this accumulation? By a portion of this accumulation? Or, should savings be left intact? These questions all bear heavily on the whole business of incentives, the impact of which could affect the saving decisions of upcoming generations and their saving/investment patterns. As with the "do not want to work" group, we are dealing with important incentive considerations that could change the entire shape and direction of the economy. Clearly, if society is going to pay the bill for support of the elderly, much of the purpose of saving among younger people will be reduced or eliminated. In turn, investment funds would have to come from somewhere else—some other sector of the economy—if levels of output are to be maintained or increased.

Another group that is difficult to classify as "cannot work" or "does not want to work" is that of mothers with young children. A large majority of the persons presently on welfare are in this group. Without adequate day-care facilities for the children, the potential skills of these women are lost to society and to themselves. Some mothers, of course, prefer to stay home and raise the children, especially, faced with the alternative of relatively low wages for women in this society. But, many would prefer to work, at least part-time, if day-care were available that they felt was taking good care of their children. Some economic questions that apply to this situation are: Where should the money for the day-care come from? Should the government provide funds and should the programs be set up by the parents involved? Could the firms that hire the mothers include day-care as part of the package of workers' benefits, like insurance and vacations? And, if this occurs, why should not the firms that hire the fathers also be responsible for day-care? If day-care becomes a reality, should mothers who prefer not to work receive a dole? All these questions contain value judgments about whether children are the responsibility of the parents, the mothers, or of society as a whole. Perhaps the reason that day-care has not been an issue until recently has been because of the social value judgment that mothers belong in the home with the children. We return to the original problem: alternatives must be weighed; choices must be made.

Let us summarize the major points and their implications in connection with the impoverished who have basic skills necessary for productive activity.

First, further education or training is not the simple answer that it might be for some of the unskilled population.

Second, lack of job opportunities resulting from discrimination may be the result of true economic discrimination now, or it may be the result of some past discrimination, such as poorer training opportunities that have resulted in relatively lower productivity in the present. True discrimination can probably be reduced by making its practice more expensive to employers through legal sanctions enforced by government action. Low productivity from poor past training will not be efficiently solved by such laws. Imposition of so-called equal-opportunity employment laws will impose hidden costs on producers, consumers, and the factors themselves, including, perhaps, the very groups for whom the benefits were intended.

Third, dole programs, that is, programs that merely transfer goods or buying power to the poor, can effectively raise the real income of the recipients. However, it is probable that some form of income supplement program will be as effective in raising incomes and will also have fewer adverse effects on incentives and the productivity of the recipients.

Fourth, old age assistance programs should be evaluated carefully in terms of their potential impact on the current savings decisions of the younger generation.

Fifth, the impact of day-care's allowing more women to work to supplement the family's income (from husband or welfare) should be considered.

THE GEOMETRY OF INCOME SUPPLEMENTS

We have talked about the differences between doles and income supplements several times. Before going further, it may be useful to introduce a simple geometric representation of this. In Figure 15-3, we illustrate the total number of hours available to any individual in a thirty-day month—720 hours. Next, let us *define* all activity of an individual as either *work* or *leisure*. For example, a person working a 40-hour week would have approximately 180 hours of work per month and 540 hours of leisure for a total of 720 hours. These hours are shown on the horizontal axis of the graph. Notice that a movement from left to right along the axis indicates an increase in work and a corresponding decrease in hours of leisure. Conversely, the right-hand corner of the graph indicates zero hours of leisure and 720 hours of work so that movements to the left decrease work hours and increase leisure hours. The vertical axes on both sides of the graph indicate income.

Now, we will make two simple assumptions: that most people prefer

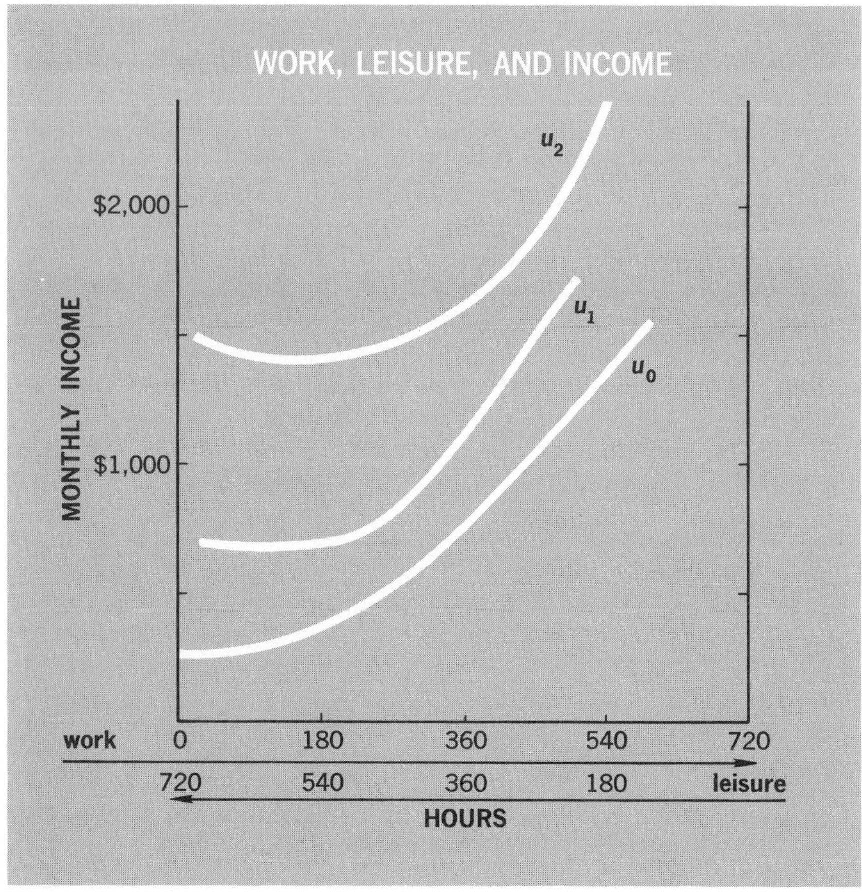

Figure 15-3

leisure to work at any given level of income, and that there is some degree of substitution between income and leisure. In other words, one would be prepared to work more (give up leisure) if one's income were increased at least within a reasonable range of hours. With these assumptions, it is possible to construct what the economist calls an *indifference map*. Actually, it is a contour map like those used to show topographical features of the land. In this case, however, points along the contour lines represent equal *utility* or *satisfaction* to the worker rather than elevations above some base. The fact that they slope upward to the right merely says that increased levels of income are necessary to maintain a given level of satisfaction if the work time in a given month is increased, and the leisure time is decreased accordingly. It also shows that, given any particular set of work/leisure hours, satisfaction will be increased with increases in income. There is nothing very complicated about this idea, and the assumptions seem quite reasonable as descriptions of the real world.

One other assumption is implicit in the shape of the *indifference curves*. The fact that they bow toward (are convex to) the horizontal axis says that as one approaches extremes of all work and no leisure, greater amounts of income are needed to *forego* additional hours of leisure. If a person works many hours per month, that person will lose much more utility in working another hour than would be the case if he were working comparatively few hours. Similarly, he would require a larger increase in income to perform an extra hour's work when working many hours than when working few hours. With this very modest graphical approach and the simple assumptions embodied in it, let us examine some expected behavior, given some type of program designed to increase people's incomes.

First of all, we can portray any wage *rate* by straight lines through the left-hand origin. Such lines represent total monthly income divided by total hours worked which *is* the wage rate per hour. Figure 15-4 illustrates the point. For example, along a \$2.00 per hour rate line, 180 hours will yield a total income of \$360 per month. 360 hours per month will yield an income of \$720 per month, and so on. A wage rate of \$3.00 per hour is represented by a steeper wage rate line, and a \$4.00 per hour rate by a still steeper line.

Now look at some point of equilibrium and see what it means. If our man in this example is capable of earning \$2.00 per hour and no more, he will, in this case, work 180 hours, have 540 hours of leisure, and attain a maximum level of utility shown here as u_0. How did he arrive at this point? Given the convex shape of the indifference curves themselves he is constrained from reaching any higher level of utility. He can reach higher levels of *income* by working more hours (this is without any consideration of possible higher wages for overtime), but, if he worked more than 180 hours, his own valuation of the leisure he would have to forego *exceeds* his valuation of the extra income received. Similarly, if he worked less than 180 hours per month, the value *to him* of the leisure gained would be less than that of the income lost by working fewer hours. In this example, were his wage *rate* increased to \$3.00 per hour, he would be prepared to work more hours (270) and would receive the corresponding monthly income of \$810. (Notice, we do not need any numbers of the curves themselves other than values indicating one is higher or lower than another. No one can actually *measure* levels of utility except on a comparative basis. Notice, in this example, his behavior is not dependent upon whether the increased wage rate comes from increased productivity or merely a *per hour* supplement of \$1.00. The source of the increase is very important to society, but not to the individual receiving the increase.

Contrast this reaction with the alternative of a lump-sum payment of

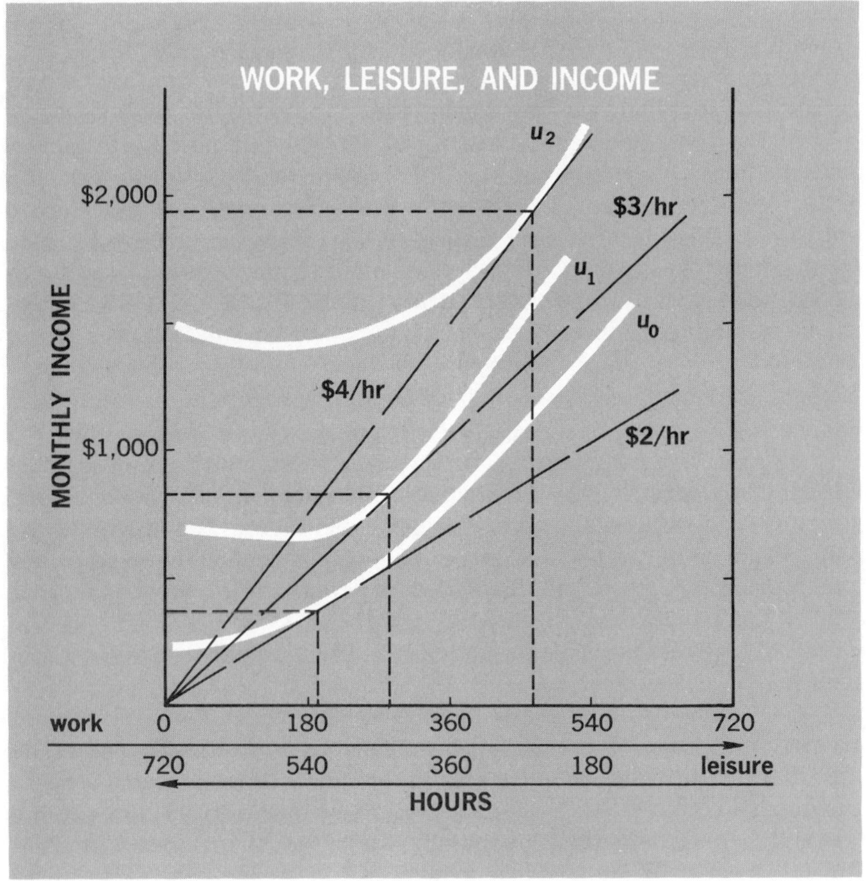

Figure 15-4

so much per month, say $360. In this case, the individual can work from zero to 180 hours and receive a guaranteed income of $360 per month. He can move to higher and higher levels of utility by *reducing* his work time to zero and by taking 720 hours per month in leisure—a full-time idler.

It is true that there are some persons to whom full-time idleness would actually yield a *dis*utility. They would even be prepared to *pay* some amount to work rather than not to work at all. Graphically, this could be shown by bending up the utility indifference curves as they approached the left-hand axis. Utility would be *increased* by working up to some comparatively low level of labor. The existence of these individuals would mitigate the situation of persons ceasing to work when given payments not related to their work. They would not cease to work even though their entire income was subsidy.

It is hoped that this example with its geometry helps explain the difference in the impact of doles and income supplements. The proposal for a negative income tax fits into this scheme. Under this scheme, recipients of welfare payments would *not* lose their entire subsidy if they worked. Some incentive for work would still exist.

Now, let us turn our attention to the other broad category of the impoverished—those without the basic training and skills needed to find productive employment. Again, the group has been divided into three subgroups to be discussed separately.

THE UNTRAINABLE

In many ways, this group is analytically similar to the "cannot work" group discussed previously. In an absolute sense, the untrainable are probably a very small group, but there are many for whom conventional training programs will not suffice in producing skills. There are also persons for whom training would require such high levels of resource expenditure that the practicality of the program would be questionable. For this group, little can be done except some form of direct subsidy, preferably an income supplement rather than a straight dole.

THE TRAINABLE-IN-THE-FUTURE

We already mentioned some of the significant costs involved in training the very young. The future of society very much depends, however, on how good a job is done in training those youngsters who are born into poverty environments. We already are living with second and third generation welfare recipients and the vicious circles causing this trend have not been broken as yet. Not only do they need to be trained, but *we* need to figure out new and better ways to train them. Unfortunately, the segments of society least able to afford massive investments in human capital development are the same segments with the greatest need.

THE CURRENTLY TRAINABLE

Our last category of the poor without skills is, unfortunately, the smallest portion of the total poverty population. It consists of those at or approaching the working age for whom training will bring comparatively fast returns both to themselves and the community. Compared to the others, this group seems to have the most potential in the shortest time, but problems remain. One, for example, is that in all likelihood, the human capital *base* on which training can be built is probably much lower than that embodied in the nonpoverty population of the same age group. Again, this will mean comparatively large resource requirements in programs designed to build potential productivity.

THE VICIOUS CIRCLES

Many are familiar with the concept of a vicious circle. It is a chain of events or circumstances that tend to perpetuate and increase a given problem. In the area of poverty, one can view many of these chain reactions; our analysis provides another example. Even if the programs of human capital development are successful, the persons who have gained the skills may merely change sides on the chart. They may become trained but then enter the impoverished group "with skills" without breaking the chain.

We have been discussing the use of education in its broadest sense as one method of increasing productivity and income among the poor. Implicit in our discussion is the fact that many of these programs will be carried out on a planned basis rather than having been spontaneously brought about by the operation of a free market. It is possible that the market system *could* have produced solutions, but, at least in our country, it has not yet done so. Planned programs should also be initiated and operated in such a way as to maximize *net* product to the individuals and to the society that is paying the bills. This is not to say that the *cheapest* program should be used any more than the use of the cheapest machine tool is necessarily the best way to produce some industrial product. It does say, however, that scarce resources are going to be used up, and, as a result of their being used up, something else is going to have to be given up—either now or later. In other words, there is a large economic component to this problem. Many of the poverty programs in the past have not used the tools available for both design and operation. It is in this area that many economists plead for careful analysis in future attempts to help the poor. We do not say that the "heart" should be ignored in dealing with problems of human misery. This is ridiculous and impossible. Neither do we say that programs should not be "political," because without practical political support, they are all bound to fail. The basic message at this time seems to be that *all* of us should use, to a greater degree, along with our hearts and political skills, the most valuable resource we own—our minds. Many wars can be won by emotions, and emotions play an important part in our wars on poverty, as well. But, most successful campaigns have also had a cool thinker behind the lines who planned and directed both strategy and tactics. The war to abolish poverty in the world must have no less.

POSTSCRIPT

A large portion of this course and book has been devoted to analyzing the basic economic problem of human choices when faced with scarcity. We have shown that, *given individual freedom of choice*, the people are able to solve the allocation problems through markets and the relative prices they generate. Many assumptions, some explicit and others implicit, have been made in the analysis. For example, we have assumed that markets are allowed to operate free of forces other than supply and demand. Some of the problems that occur when restrictions are placed on the market also have been discussed.

The most basic assumption is that individual free choice is the proper basis for economic decision-making. In our Charlie and Clyde economy, the two worked out the allocation problem by bartering with each other in their simple two-man, two-good world. Charlie did not really know what gave Clyde the greatest utility, nor did Clyde know what Charlie's utility function looked like. But each traded until a point was reached where they were as mutually satisfied as possible. They traded and haggled just as long as each one felt he was gaining as compared to the no-trade position. Then, the trading stopped. If Charlie had tried to "plan" Clyde's production and consumption, it is unlikely that Clyde would have been as happy as he was under the free-trade situation. If Charlie had been the planner and had held the power to carry out his plans, then probably Charlie would have made sure that he would be the one to come out ahead on the deal. Even if Charlie had been "benevolent," would it be likely that he could have analyzed Clyde's desires as perfectly as Clyde could have done himself? The problem really gets complicated when the two-good, two-man world expands to billions of people and billions of products. When any device other than a market system is used to allocate resources, those faced with making the allocation decisions find themselves with a monumental task, to say the least. Why not, then, allow complete freedom in the marketplace to accomplish the rationing of resources? There are many answers given by different people as to why uninhibited market action will not always produce the optimal results.

One of the most widely used excuses for interference is differential power among various persons or groups of persons. Assume Charlie was able to round up all the skunks and brontosauri in the area and claim them as his own. Clyde's choices have now changed. He no longer has access to the resource (in addition to his own labor) required to produce coats. Chances are that Charlie will still want some coats, and he may hire Clyde to make them. It is likely, however, that Clyde's wages will be considerably less than before, when both partners had access to the raw materials. At a more complex level, we saw how monopoly power can affect the operation of the market system. When monopoly conditions extend into a major portion of the economy, the optimality of the free-market solution is certainly questionable. Power concentrations, in almost any form, pose threats to the free-market system. This power may take the form of differential wealth or differential political power (the two are usually related).

What is the result of dropping the assumption that individual free choice is the proper basis for economic decision-making? This whole idea of individual freedom is a fairly recent notion, at least when applied to a large portion of the people in a society. A much more common practice was to have an elite group who made most of the critical decisions and left a comparatively small number of choices to the masses. This system worked well as long as the real choices available were not that many. The serf working under a feudal lord probably could not have done better on his own, and, alone, he certainly would have been in trouble trying to defend his existence when faced with aggressive neighbors who did not have respect for his rights. As levels of material prosperity and productivity increased, however, the story changed. As people began to see that a better life was possible, they began to want it for themselves. They also became more willing and able to *pay* for it, even if the payment included changing old structures in a very forceful way.

For many reasons, some countries managed to emerge in a comparatively bloodless way from an old feudal economic system into one in which *most* of the population has a great deal more to say about their own economic activities than has ever been the case in recorded history. They have been able to say a great deal more *about a great deal more*, because there has been such an increase in the material goods being produced. The free market system has *never* been completely free nor completely market-oriented. It has been, however, the basic model from which we have operated. Make no mistake! Nobody really planned or set up a free-market system. It developed with a minimum of conscious planning from the basic notions of individual freedom of choice. When problems have developed with its operations, the reaction has been to tinker with it a bit, but there has been little general sentiment in favor of throwing the whole thing away for something completely different.

This has not been the case in many other countries in the modern world. Because of differences in history, culture, and happenstance, these countries have dropped the assumption of individual sovereignty in favor of the idea that the state must come first and that individuals must sublimate their separate wishes to those of the state. Of course, in many instances, the assumption of individual freedom never existed in the first place, and, in these cases, a transition to this philosophy did not involve a big change. It was particularly easy if the new "state" that demanded the individual's allegiance actually *delivered* on promises of a better life for many of its inhabitants. Again, a better life did not have to be *very much* better in many instances. Combine this with new hope of future improvements (expectations, again) and you have a package that is not hard to sell. And sold it has, particularly in the "have-not" countries of the world in which the little wealth that existed was held by a few people who did not seem to care about solving the problems of the other 98 or 99 percent of the population. Unfortunately, many of the prerevolutionary regimes claimed to be operating with a free-market economy. Of course, they were *not*. They were using markets, true enough, but they were anything but free.

One of the problems that revolutionary governments faced when they took over was that they were dedicated to the proposition that anything the former regime had been doing must have been bad. Because markets were a part of this old way, markets were clearly *bad* and had to be replaced. The ideal interim solution (interim, because after a brief period of state control, the nature of man would change and he would become a "selfless" being who no longer required government of any kind) was to take the most dedicated revolutionaries who had proven their merit in combat and have this group plan the allocation problems of the economy so that social welfare would be maximized. Markets were not necessary because the people would accept what was best for them, and the state, by definition, knew what was best for them. It sounded good and many thought the world was truly on the road to Utopia.

Some problems developed. In many countries, it turned out that there was less than unanimous support for the state and its policies. As a result, a trend developed to eliminate opposition. After this was accomplished, the regimes found that they did have extensive, if not unanimous support, and they settled down to the building of a new economy. The planners soon found that the world had changed since the days of Charlie and Clyde. They faced *millions* of goods and millions of people. "From each according to his ability and to each according to his need" sounds fine, but putting this in terms of concrete allocation decisions takes some of the bloom off the rose.

Nevertheless, plan they did, and plan they do. As one might imagine, the planners' errors were legion. From Czechoslovakia comes the story about a problem that developed in Prague. In much of the new housing, ceilings began to cave in. The problem was traced to ceiling lighting fixtures. It seems that production quotas for ceiling fixtures had been established based on the weight of total production. Needless to say, the weight *per unit* of this commodity got *very* heavy *very* quickly.

Nevertheless, there is no question that astounding economic development has taken place in many of the economies that have taken this route. The best example is the Soviet Union, which has experienced very high growth rates, particularly since World War II. To say that a planned economy cannot develop is clearly an error. However, it must be remembered that, in most cases, this growth has been extracted at tremendous costs. The relevant question is whether or not this development would have taken place at smaller costs, both in physical resources and human beings.

The revolutionary movements have utilized a combination of incentives that we have mentioned before, but need to emphasize. There has certainly been a measure of production brought forth by the threat of imprisonment and/or loss of life. One can argue that this is a fairly strong incentive. In addition, memories of past problems combined with revolutionary fervor and expectations for the future can be counted as having helped in encouraging the citizens to produce as well as to forego current consumption in favor of capital accumulation for the future.

There is one final point that should be mentioned. In spite of hatred of the price system, no country has been able to eliminate it. Prices and markets have been downgraded by planners, but, in the final analysis, they have been forced to use them. A particularly interesting trend is taking place in the more advanced socialist countries today. As production *has* increased, and more goods *are* becoming available, the original incentives of the revolution seem to be losing their effectiveness. The price system is gaining a measure of respectability—including such exotic ideas as profit to encourage production and productivity of factors.

After reading this book, you must realize that we have some very strong value judgments. The impression might have been given that we believe that planning in an economy is not worthwhile. Not true. First of all, it does not make much difference what we think. What is *very* important is *whether you think*! Now, as throughout history, the world is full of peddlers trying to sell simplistic solutions to the complex problems of mankind. They do it with slogans, banners, and religious zeal. A great deal of what they are trying to sell has to do with economics. It will be up to each one, as citizens of the world, to weigh carefully the alternatives they propose.

Because the only thing certain today is that change will take place tomorrow, it would be folly to suggest that the economic system of this country or any other is the last word in the human struggle to solve the problems of scarcity and choice. We have come a long way since Charlie and Clyde. A market system such as ours has helped this struggle along. The next time you go into a supermarket, look around you. The strawberries in the fruit counter may have been flown in from Mexico. The corned beef on the shelf may have come from Chicago or Argentina. The lettuce could have spent last night in a field in California. No one planned it, yet the complex mix of events and resources necessary to put these goods in the store has come together. Reaction to prices all along the line did it, and whether you pick up those goods or not will influence their availability tomorrow. We are not saying or suggesting that the system is perfect or cannot be improved. We are saying that improvement is one thing and "throwing the baby out with the bath water" is something else.

Many people maintain that increasing material wealth is destroying whatever "good" people have within them. What a pessimistic view of human nature! As wealth increases, everyone's choices increase, your choices increase.

QUESTIONS

1. List some difficulties in constructing national income accounts. There are others besides those in the book. How would the problems of arriving at these numbers be more difficult in an underdeveloped country?
2. List some similarities and differences in the economic development problems of the inner city of a major U.S. urban area and the problems of an underdeveloped country.
3. Do you consider yourself poor? Why or why not.
4. What kinds of solutions can you come up with for solving the problems of senior citizens who lack purchasing power?
5. Can you describe a situation in which the market could be used to reduce discrimination?
6. Do you think the time will ever come when we can all get a "free lunch"?

Index

A

B

C

G

H

I

L

M